PERMANENT LONDONERS

An Illustrated Guide to the Cemeteries of London

Judi Culbertson
and
Tom Randall

Robson Books

First published in Great Britain in 1991 by Robson Books Ltd,
Bolsover House, 5-6 Clipstone Street, London W1P 7EB

Copyright © 1991 by Judi Culbertson and Tom Randall
Maps copyright © 1991 by Walter Vose Jeffries

British Library Cataloguing in Publication Data
Culbertson, Judi
    Permanent Londoners: an illustrated guide to the cemeteries of
London
    1. Cemeteries. London (England)
    I. Title. II. Randall, Tom
    914.21

ISBN 0 86051 735 7

Printed in the United States of America

CONTENTS

Preface   1

CENTRAL LONDON

1 · Westminster Abbey: Nave and North Side   5

2   Westminster Abbey: North and
    South Transepts   27

3   Westminster Abbey: Royal Tombs   45

    Chapel of St. John the Baptist   45

    Chapel of St. Paul   46

    Chapel of Henry VII   47

    Chapel of St. Nicholas   63

    Chapel of St. Edmund   64

    Chapel of Edward the Confessor   65

4   Westminster Abbey: Poets' Corner   71

5   The Tower of London   105

    St. Peter ad Vincula and Tower Green   105

    St. Mary-at-Lambeth   113

6   Bunhill Fields   117

    Wesley Chapel   128

    St. Giles Cripplegate   130

7   St. Paul's   135

8   Brompton   163

NORTH LONDON

9	Kensal Green	179
10	Highgate and St. Michael's	197
	West Cemetery	198
	East Cemetery	212
	St. Michael's Church	224
11	St. John-at-Hampstead	229
12	Hampstead	243
13	Golders Green and St. Marylebone	257
	Jewish Cemetery	268
	St. Marylebone	270

SOUTHWEST LONDON AND WINDSOR

14	Putney Vale and St. Mary Magdalene	279
	St. Mary Magdalene	287
15	St. Nicholas, Chiswick	293
16	Windsor Castle and Frogmore	301
	St. George's Chapel	301
	The Royal Mausoleum	313
	Sources	319
	Index	323

Acknowledgments

As with all the books in this series there have been many people who have made significant contributions. In their help with Permanent Londoners we would like to offer thanks to:

Paul Bahn for his enthusiasm and up-to-the-minute information; Mr. and Mrs. Usher at St. Paul's for their assistance and cordiality; Eva Lord for her hospitality in Edinburgh; and Mrs. Jean Pateman, chairman of the Friends of Highgate Cemetery, and the Friends for their efforts in restoring this historic cemetery.

Our son, Andrew, for his help and input; Elizabeth Randall for her knowledge and the use of her many books on British history; Nancy Mullen for her enthusiatic support; Professor Frank Mullen for his advice on matters scientific; Jim Morris and Michael Mendel for their help with photographic supplies and questions; and the Port Jefferson Library staff for their willing assistance in many areas of information gathering.

Julia Rowe for her talented cover work; Ann Aspell for the beautiful layout; Ruth Kreitzman for her editing; Howard Chesshire for his diligence at the computer; Walter Jeffries for the clarity of his maps; Cannon Labrie for his intelligence and insight on matters too numerous to mention, and Chris Holifield for her effective efforts as literary agent.

On the home front our cats thank Gordon and Jean Thomsen for their care and feeding while we were traveling, and we thank our friends and family for their forebearance during our work on the book.

And finally, as always, to Margo and Ian Baldwin, our publishers, for their support, dedication, and high standards.

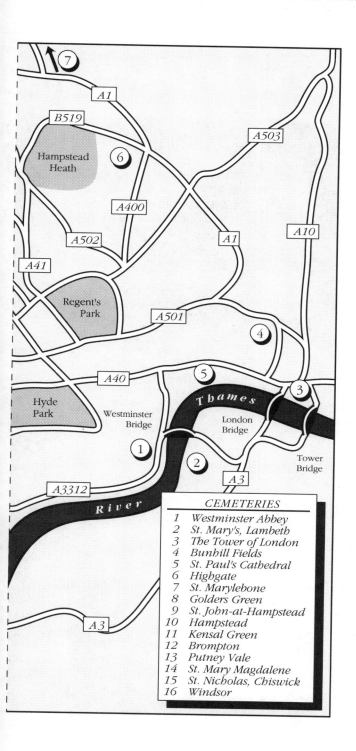

CEMETERIES

1	Westminster Abbey
2	St. Mary's, Lambeth
3	The Tower of London
4	Bunhill Fields
5	St. Paul's Cathedral
6	Highgate
7	St. Marylebone
8	Golders Green
9	St. John-at-Hampstead
10	Hampstead
11	Kensal Green
12	Brompton
13	Putney Vale
14	St. Mary Magdalene
15	St. Nicholas, Chiswick
16	Windsor

To Brian and Elaine
with love

Preface

LONDON IS A cemetery town. Proud of her dead kings, poets, and villains, she is quick to memorialize them in Westminster Abbey, Madame Tussaud's, and on Guy Fawkes Day. Eccentricity among her citizens has always been encouraged. It is this spirit of acceptance of the human heart which makes visiting burial sites in London so entertaining.

It also makes writing a guidebook more difficult. What can be left out? If you limit the contents to Central London, you will miss Richard Burton's stone tent at Mortlake, Thomas Tate rising from his deathbed at St. Marylebone, and the whole cast at Windsor: Henry VIII, George III, and Victoria and Albert. Confining the book to churchyards and cemeteries is also out of the question. To exclude Westminster Abbey would be to visit Dover and bypass the White Cliffs.

So we have included cathedrals, churchyards, cemeteries, and crematoria. Westminster Abbey has been given four different tours: one includes scientists such as Newton, Darwin, and Lord Rutherford; another includes a collection of musicians and a feud of politicians — Wilberforce, Peel, Pitt, and Gladstone. Elizabeth I and her rival, Mary Queen of Scots, lie under the same roof and are included in the tour of Royal Tombs. Finally, there is Poets' Corner in which, to paraphrase John Donne speaking about St. Paul's Cathedral, "Every grain of dust that flies here is a piece of writer."

St. Paul's Cathedral is also included, celebrated as the repository of Sir Joshua Reynolds, Alexander Fleming, and the twin warriors, Admiral Nelson and the Duke of Wellington. Other churches include St. Giles Cripplegate, where John Milton is interred, and St. Peter ad Vincula at the Tower — a sobering way to experience the last moments of Anne Boleyn, Sir Thomas More, Lady Jane Grey, and Lady Margaret Pole, a spry septuagenarian who made her executioner chase her around the scaffold.

Grave hunting in London is, however, more than just tracking down the famous and experiencing history. There are touching monuments and epitaphs which belong to

Londoners who are otherwise unknown. Everywhere there are verses such as:

> The call was so sudden, the shock severe.
> We never thought your end was so near.
> Only those who have lost you alone can tell
> The pain of parting without a farewell.

In Highgate one can see everything from Harry Thornton's carved piano and Karl Marx's carved head to the grave of Lizzie Siddal in which a remorseful Dante Gabriel Rossetti buried a collection of his poems then had them dug up by firelight seven years later. Kensal Green has writers such as William Makepeace Thackeray, Anthony Trollope, and Wilkie Collins, as well as tightrope walkers and patent-medicine salesmen.

Few cities we have written about cover such a broad swath of history — nearly a thousand years — or have such a range of colorful personalities. London by itself is a fascinating place to visit; London underground is irresistible.

Westminster Abbey, North Entrance

CENTRAL LONDON

Westminster Abbey

Nave and North Side

NO ONE WHO has ever seen Westminster Abbey can forget their first view of this English Valhalla. White marble statesmen jam the walls like worshippers at Easter. Above their unknowing heads, allegorical deathbed scenes are being played out again and again. Three thousand people are actually buried in the Abbey, and hundreds more—from Franklin D. Roosevelt to William Shakespeare—are commemorated by statues or plaques, though interred elsewhere. Because of space constraints, we will be limiting biographical material to those who are actually in residence.

The origins of Westminster Abbey are buried in legend. There is a pretty story that the original church was consecrated by a visit from St. Peter himself, giving rise to a once-a-year salmon banquet in which local fishermen brought their catch as "tithe." It is more likely, however, that the first church was established around the late seventh or eighth centuries. Sebert, king of the East Saxons, allegedly built the first structure and had it consecrated by Mellitus, the first Bishop of London, in 616 A.D. A church in "Thorney" (the area around Westminster Abbey, originally designated as the "Isle of Thorns") began to be referred to in writings around 700 A.D.

When Edward the Confessor created his version of Westminster Abbey he left nothing of the original building save several great columns which are now below the pavement. The Abbey was built in the Norman style of Romanesque and consecrated in January 1066. Since that time various chapels—most notably that of Henry VII—have been added or remodeled. The last major addition to Westminster

Westminster Abbey, from the Nave

Abbey was the front west towers, which were designed by Christopher Wren and completed by Nicholas Hawksmoor and John James in 1745.

As you enter Westminster Abbey through the West Door, you may be startled by its size. The vaulted ceiling leaps to 102 feet, and the entire structure is 513 feet long, reaching 200 feet at the transepts. Sixteen Waterford chandeliers, each containing 500 pieces of crystal, cast a constant, moneyed light. They were given by the Guinness family to commemorate the 900th anniversary of Westminster Abbey in 1965. Each fixture weighs approximately 280 pounds. Like St. George's Chapel in Windsor, the Abbey is a royal peculiar, meaning that it is not under the jurisdiction of the local diocese. It is therefore a church rather than a cathedral.

In one way, Westminster Abbey is a victim of its own success. Once an hour everything pauses while a prayer is read over the loudspeaker to remind the wash of visitors that they are in an active church and not some English Disneyland. On Sundays the royal chapels are closed to visitors, and tourists are discouraged from wandering around the Nave during services. Although taking photographs in the Abbey is not allowed, on Wednesday evenings from 6:00 to 7:45 P.M. that rule is suspended and admission is free. When the barrier is removed, the east end lights up like a match struck in the dark.

To start your tour, come through the West Door and walk straight ahead, past the green marble stone with the words "Remember Winston Churchill" (the statesman is buried in St. Martin's Churchyard, Bladon) to the Grave of the Unknown Warrior. Carved from black Belgian marble, it is surrounded by red poppies and has the explanation in brass that

> Thus are commemorated the many
> multitudes who during the Great
> War of 1914–1918 gave the most that
> man can give life itself.
> For God
> For King and Country
> For Loved Ones Home and Empire
> For the Sacred Cause of Justice and
> The Freedom of the World.

The inspiration for this remembrance is said to have come from David Railton, an army chaplain who saw a rough wooden cross in a backyard at Armentières, France, with the pencilled inscription, "An Unknown British Soldier." Four years later, in August 1920, he wrote to the dean of Westminster Abbey suggesting it as a memorial for the more than one million British soldiers who died during World War I.

To make certain that the soldier selected was truly unknown, the remains of three soldiers from three different battlefields in France were brought to the Abbey and placed in a chapel. In the dead of night someone else came in and chose one coffin. The burial casket was oak, decorated with brass from bullet casings. On a nearby pillar hangs the U.S. Congressional Medal of Honor, presented on October 17, 1921, by General John J. Pershing.

Turn back toward the West Door by which you entered. Above it you will see a memorial to **William Pitt the Younger** (1759–1806), prime minister of England between 1783 and 1801 and again from 1804 until his death. Pitt had to contend with unrest in the American colonies, rebellion in Ireland, war with France, and financial woes at home and died, exhausted, at 47. His monument, executed by Richard Westmacott, shows him orating as History takes down his words and Anarchy, in the form of a naked male in chains, crouches at his feet. Pitt is interred in the North Transept (see Chapter 2) with his father, **William Pitt**, First Earl of Chatham.

If you look to the right, you will see a memorial to **Jeremiah Horrocks** (1619–1641), Curate of Hoole in Lancashire. His epitaph reads, "Having in so short a life detected the long inequality in the mean motion of Jupiter and Saturn, discovered the orbit of the moon to be an ellipse, determined the motion of the lunar apse, suggested the physical cause of its own revolution and predicted from his own observations the transit of Venus which was seen by himself and his friend William Crabtree on Sunday the 24th of November, 1639. This tablet, facing the monument of Newton, was raised after the lapse of more than two centuries, December 9, 1874."

The young astronomer also gave the most correct estimate to that date of the distance of the sun from the earth. Above Horrocks' cement bier is a black cast-iron medal with his profile, showing him attended by two cherubs. He is buried in Liverpool in Toxteth Park.

On the other side of the door is a plaque to **Franklin Delano Roosevelt** (1882–1945), praising him as "A faithful friend of freedom and of Britain, four times president of the United States. Erected by the government of the United Kingdom." Roosevelt is buried at his family estate in Hyde Park, New York.

Close to the pillar on your left is the in-ground plaque to

Louis, First Earl **Mountbatten** (1900–1979), naval officer and Viceroy of India, and **Edwina**, Countess **Mountbatten** of Burma (1901–1960). They are facing each other in stylized brass, with a crown and coat of arms above them. Lord Mountbatten died when IRA terrorists blew up his yacht in Mullaghmore Harbour, County Sligo. Although a cousin of Queen Elizabeth and the uncle of Prince Philip, he had not been considered a terrorist target before an explosive was placed on board his fishing boat. His grandson Nicholas, 14, a family friend Paul Maxwell, 15, and his daughter's elderly mother-in-law also died in the explosion. The Earl of Mountbatten is buried in Romsey Abbey.

Around the corner to your left is the monument to the "Chief Scout of the World." The top of the marker reads, "Give thanks for **Robert Baden-Powell** (1857–1941) and **Olave Baden-Powell** (1889–1977) 'World Chief Guide.' " There are Boy Scout and Girl Guide flags and two very attractive small brass cameos of the couple. Baden-Powell wears his traditional scout cap; his wife is pictured in a helmet. The ashes of both are buried in Nyeri, Kenya.

If you are beginning to feel that no one is actually buried here, proceed to the bust of playwright **William Congreve** (1670–1729) sculpted by Francis Byrd. He rests below in a sarcophagus decorated with theatrical symbols. The author of one of the earliest suspense romances, *Incognita* (1692), Congreve turned to playwriting with *The Old Bachelor* (1693) and *The Mourning Bride* (1697), reaching his peak with *The Way of the World* (1700). The plots of Congreve's plays foreshadow eighteenth-century opera with their emphasis on mistaken identities, misplaced legal documents, and weddings in masquerade. He defended *The Old Bachelor* against charges of immorality by claiming that he had written it only to amuse himself while recovering from an illness — prompting his critic, the Reverend Jeremy Collier, to comment, "What his disease was I am not to inquire; but it must be a very ill one to be worse than the remedy."

Suffering from gout in his later years, Congreve was injured in a carriage accident and died from internal injuries. His mistress, Henrietta, the Second Duchess of Marlborough, used some of the £10,000 he left her to have this Westminster Abbey monument erected; the rest paid for an ivory statue of Congreve which moved by a clockwork motor and sat at the dinner table while she conversed with it.

Walk directly across the way to reach a small group of reformers and socialists. **Charles James Fox** (1749–1806), the political rival of William Pitt the Younger whom

Mʳ WILLIAM CONGREVE.

Dyed Jan ẏ 19ᵗʰ 1728 Aged 56. And was buried near this place.
To whose most Valueable Memory this MONUMENT is Sett up by
HENRIETTA Dutchess of MARLBOROUGH as a mark how dearly
She remembers the happiness and Honour She enjoyed in
the Sincere Friendshipp of so worthy and Honest a Man,
Whose Virtue Candour and Witt gained him the love and
Esteem of the present Age and whose Writings will be the
Admiration of the Future.

he outlived by only a few months, has a touching memorial which reflects his liberal interests. A marble likeness of Fox is supported on his deathbed by Liberty; another woman, representing Peace, hovers unhappily in the background while near his feet an African kneels to show his gratitude for Fox's work to abolish the slave trade. The sculpture by Richard Westmacott captures well the worried pouchiness of Fox's face in later years.

Charles Fox was a brilliant, charming, and passionate

child who at five was attending plays and devouring literature. He took charge of his education, dictating which schools he should attend, and finished at Eton in 1757. On vacation with his family in Paris, he learned to gamble and never stopped believing that victory was in the next roll of the dice. He joined Parliament at 19, but by 1774 had thoroughly alienated George III.

From that time on, Fox was primarily in the opposition party, rarely holding office, but continuing as a political force. Perhaps recalling his own need for autonomy as a child, he favored American independence, making a famous and passionate speech for it in Parliament on February 2, 1775. His libertarianism extended to the French Revolution, Catholic rights in England and Ireland, and the abolition of slavery. It extended to his own life as well, to allow him happiness (and poverty) in gambling halls and in the company of prostitutes. In later years Fox shocked England by making his mistress, a Mrs. Armistead, his legal wife and insisting it be kept secret.

His campaign against slavery was waged at the end of his life when he was struggling against dropsy, an accumulation of water that can signal serious heart, liver, or kidney disease. Fox saw his bill for the abolition of the African slave trade pass the House of Lords on June 10, 1806, shortly before he died.

Another social reformer, **Clement Attlee** (1883–1967), has a stone on the floor near where he is buried. A lawyer by profession, Attlee worked as a social worker, taught at the London School of Economics, and entered Parliament in 1922, finally becoming prime minister in 1945. Attlee nationalized the energy industries and helped grant independence to India, Pakistan, Burma, Palestine, and Ceylon. His secret dream of becoming a poet was tempered to produce books such as his autobiography, *As It Happened* (1954), and his memoirs, *Twilight of Empire* (1962). An advocate of the United Nations who told Congress in 1945 that "We cannot make a heaven of our own country and have a hell outside," Attlee's epitaph reads simply, "For twenty years leader of the Labour Party."

Sidney James Webb (1859–1947) and **Beatrice Potter Webb** (1858–1943) are close by. The Webbs, who married in 1892, were united by their firm commitment to socialism. Before marriage, Beatrice, a social economist, had studied working life in London, and had written *The Cooperative Movement in Great Britain* (1891). Beatrice, one of nine talented daughters of Richard Potter, maintained a close friendship with her parents' friend, Herbert Spencer.

He arranged for her first essay to be published, and requested that she be made his literary executor.

In the melancholy year that her father died, Beatrice met "the little figure with a big head who was to become my man of destiny, the source of unhoped-for happiness." Soon after meeting they became secretly engaged and began research for their first book, *The History of Trade Unionism* (1894). The Webbs were instrumental in developing the Fabian Society and the London School of Economics, and founded the *New Statesman* in 1913. They also authored four other books. After Sidney entered Parliament via the Labour party in 1922, he headed the Board of Trade and was given a baronage, Lord Passfield, a title his wife refused to share except for formal occasions.

Although they are buried elsewhere, stones in the floor commemorate **James Ramsey MacDonald** (1886–1937), "First Labour Prime Minister of Great Britain and three times Prime Minister" and **David Lloyd George** (1863–1945), Liberal leader and twice prime minister.

Most of David Livingstone is actually buried in the center of the sanctuary in a huge floor crypt. "Brought by faithful hands over land and sea here rests David Livingstone, missionary, traveler, philanthropist. Born March 19, 1813, at Blantyre, Lanarkshire, Died May 1, 1873, at Chitambo's Village, Ulala. For thirty years his life was spent in an unwearied effort to evangelize the native races, to explore the undiscovered secrets, to abolish the desolating slave trade of Central Africa where with his last words he wrote, 'All I can add in my solitude, is, may heaven's rich blessing come down on everyone, Americans, English, or Turk, who will help to heal the open sore of the world.' "

DAVID LIVINGSTONE *b. March 19, 1813, Blantyre, Scotland; d. May 1, 1873, Chitambo, Africa.* The myths about Dr. Livingstone are as many as the Africans he wanted to convert: how, in the heart of the jungle, he dressed in formal wear every night for dinner; how it took Henry Stanley years to track him down, only to greet him with the understatement, "Dr. Livingstone, I presume?" And how, finally, he failed at everything he hoped to achieve. Except for the black tie story, those myths contain some truth. But to accept them at face value would simplify a very complicated man.

When Livingstone sailed for Africa in 1840, he was a very rough diamond. Sullen, homely, impatient with people less driven than he was, his sense of humor was yet to develop. His boyhood had been spent in the cotton mills outside Glasgow, working from 6:00 A.M. to 8:00 P.M. daily, then attending school and studying until midnight. Often he crawled the equivalent of 20 miles a day through the machinery—a feat that he was to replicate in fighting his way through the African bush.

Becoming a medical missionary gave Livingstone the chance to combine the evangelistic Christianity of his father with his own covert interest in science, as well as escape from a factory career. He worked his way through medical school in Glasgow and London, then embarked for the mission field. He was disillusioned quickly, writing home that he had been misled by the "fundraising propaganda" of the Missionary Society which promised easy converts. The reality was that most African missionaries toiled for years without making any converts at all.

Yet he loved Africa, loved her like the mysterious women who came to the repressed missionary only in dreams. He was fascinated by the terrain and the wildlife, and he understood African tribal culture, although all his life he would vacillate between what he believed he should feel and what he saw to be true. At times he wrote about Africans as living in paradise, unhindered by the conflicts and greed of civilization; at other times he described them as depraved, their only hope being "contact with superior races."

After laboring for years in Bechuanaland (Botswana), Livingstone made his first and only convert in 1848, a chief who quickly reverted back to polygamy. But Livingstone had already rejected the idea of spending his life in obscurity on one mission station. He was beginning to see his role as that of opening up Africa for commerce and new missions. He now had a wife and four children under six years old from a marriage of convenience to Mary Moffat, the daughter of another missionary. Livingstone described his bride in letters home as amiable and matter of fact with "a stout stumpy body."

Mary Moffat Livingstone was not destined for happiness. After their fifth child, an infant, died from the harsh conditions of their life, she and the family were dispatched back to England in 1852. Unable to cope with four children, too little money, and her straitlaced Scottish in-laws, Mary soon went from "stout and stumpy" to obese and dipsomaniacal. Her husband, meanwhile, was enthusiastically exploring the Zambesi River and discovering Lake Ngami and Victoria Falls. His later explorations would be less dramatic—finding that a series of rapids precluded the Zambesi from becoming an inland waterway, and mistakenly proclaiming that he had discovered the source of the Nile—but he returned to London in 1856 to great adulation. His book, *Missionary Travels and Researches in South Africa*, became a bestseller.

Although he broke with the London Missionary Society in 1857 to accept a government post, Livingstone still could not admit that he was, at heart, an explorer. His reason for returning to Africa became to expose the Arabian slave trade. He also wanted to prove that the missionary-bashing Richard Burton was wrong about the source of the Nile, thus striking a blow for Christianity and British commerce. Mary, still drinking, returned to Africa with him in 1862 but it was too late. She lasted only three months before dying of malaria at 41.

Livingstone himself, by then, was a walking Merck's Manual of diseases: repeated bouts with malaria and dysentery had left him with pneumonia in one lung and constant anal bleeding. His feet were ulcerous, a condition exacerbated by slogging through leech-filled mud and pouring rain for weeks at a time. With no new discoveries or mission colonies established, he was out of favor at home.

When *New York Herald* reporter Henry Stanley finally found Livingstone it was not in the jungle but in an Arabian village where he had collapsed, exhausted, awaiting grudgingly promised supplies. Stanley did indeed utter his famous question which he had thought out carefully; he could never see the humor in it, and despised being approached in later years by, "Mr. Stanley, I presume?"

But the meeting was rapturous. David Livingstone was amazed and grateful for the provisions the reporter had brought him, and Stanley's dispatches spiked *Herald* circulation. The men parted with tearful affection and the fear that they would never meet again. Their fear was realistic. A year later Livingstone's ill-treated body shut down for good. His internal organs were buried in a tin box under a tree, his body salted, then dried in the sun 14 days to preserve it. Because of local superstitions about corpses, Livingstone's African followers disguised him as a bale of calico. Nine months later, they reached the coast and—with no idea how well he had succeeded in opening up Africa to colonization and commerce—Dr. Livingstone was sent home.

Toward the front of the Nave are gates where you must pay if you want to see more. The tariff will take you first into the science area where the most impressive memorial is to Isaac Newton. Sculpted by John Michael Rysbrack in 1731, the base shows cherubs playing with scientific equip-

Sir Isaac Newton

ment — telescopes and measuring instruments. Newton reclines above them on a stack of his books — *Chronology, Divinity, Opticks,* and *Philosophiae Naturalis Principia Mathematica* — while two putti display a scroll with a diagram beside his left hand. Above him is a globe showing the constellations, the signs of the zodiac, and the comet of December 24, 1680, whose path he predicted. The monument is topped by a woman resting gracefully on a book, one leg hanging over the earth.

15

On the floor in front of the sculpture is the black slab under which the remains of this gifted man actually lie.

ISAAC NEWTON *b. December 25, 1642, Woolsthorpe; d. March 20, 1727, London.* Being born on Christmas Day did not lend to Sir Isaac Newton a festive spirit. He was the kind of man one would want as neither a best friend nor a worst enemy. Thin and shy to the point of reclusiveness as a young man, Newton ripened into a plump-faced, acidic old man. He pursued positions of authority with an arrogant and despotic hand. He lacked social graces, was gifted with genius, and pursued his work with the rarest kind of concentration and persistence. His ego, while humble in private thought, was arrogant and contentious in public. Most of all he was the determining figure of his age, and science, after him, became the propelling force in the advancement of civilization.

Newton's origins were hardly auspicious. His mother, semiliterate and just widowed, gave birth prematurely and the pint-sized infant seemed likely to perish. Newton survived, only to be farmed out at age two to his grandmother when his mother remarried. As a youth he was lonely, quick-tempered, agile with his hands, obviously intelligent, and unreliable because he was so often lost in thought. On one occasion he reached home with only the horse's lead, the horse having somewhere slipped his harness on the way and Isaac too wrapped in thought to notice.

Newton attended Cambridge where his education in mathematics was largely self-taught. His facility as an autodidact was to soon pay huge dividends. After graduating Newton went on for an advanced degree, but Cambridge, fearing the spread of the plague which was decimating London, closed in 1665–66. Newton returned to Woolsthorpe to live with his again-widowed mother. There, in little over a year, he produced his theory of light, developed the mathematics of fluxions (what we now call calculus), and developed his theories of gravity and centripetal force. Only Einstein's creative outburst in 1905 can match Newton's in its scope and revolutionary impact.

Because his was an age dominated by the military and commercial importance of sail power, many scientists were tuned to the skies in an effort to improve methods of navigation. Newton's theory of light sprung from his efforts at grinding lenses for his new reflecting telescope. In his efforts to understand bothersome colored fringe effects he performed experiments which proved that light, when refracted through a prism, was physically separated rather than being modified as was commonly held. He also demonstrated that white light is composed of all colors and propounded the idea that light was made up of "corpuscles" or particles.

At the same time he developed calculus. It was to be invaluable in proving his next theories regarding gravity and centripetal force. And here, once again, the apple enters human affairs. First it was the instrument of humanity's fall from grace; now it became an aid in the ascension from ignorance. It is an oft-told tale, but it may well be true, that the fall of an apple in his mother's orchard inspired in Newton a state of intense concentration regarding the cause. In constructing a mathematical proof using the inverse-square law, Newton realized that gravitational force did not operate on the apple at a distance of 10 feet but rather at a distance of 4,000 miles — that is, from the center of the earth. From there Newton enlarged his scale to include the moon. If not exact, his figures were close enough to show that earth's gravity influenced the moon in the same way as it did the apple.

Newton gained recognition with the publication of his *Opticks*. Strangely, however, he kept his thoughts on calculus and gravity a secret. Perhaps he was tired of arguing with his contemporaries as he had had to with his experiments on light, but undoubtedly the depths of the scientific waters into which he had plunged perplexed him and he may have laid the whole problem aside. The cause may have lain also in the inexactness of his figures due to existing errors in estimating the size of the earth. In the meantime he taught mathematics at Cambridge and continued to develop his scientific and mathematical ideas. By 1671 his reflecting telescope was delivered to the Royal Society, and quickly became the most popular type of telescope.

It took the young Edmund Halley to draw Newton back to public view. In an effort to show that the inverse-square law led to observed planetary motion, he sought the advice of Newton in 1684. To his great delight Newton not only agreed but advised Halley that he had mathematical proof. But Newton couldn't locate his proof. As Charles Gillispie notes, "While others were looking for the law of gravity, Newton had lost it." Only three years later in 1687, with the encouragement and financial support of Halley, Newton's monumental treatise, *Principia*, was published. *Principia* marked the beginning of modern physics and dealt with Newton's three laws of motion, with fluids, and with the "System of the World" in which planetary orbits and gravity were discussed.

The effects were profoundly felt in the areas of science,

religion, and philosophy. The idea of universal laws (that the world may be decipherable after all), and the advent of Deism with its notion of God as a great watchmaker who, having designed the world, set it in motion to run on its own, were spawned by Newton's work. Because his Unitarian beliefs denied him further advancement he left Cambridge. He served a silent term in Parliament (his only speech being to ask if a window might be closed), suffered a breakdown in 1693 due either to nerves or the ingestion of mercury used in his alchemical pursuits, and became director of the mint, a position that he used to enthusiastically grill accused counterfeiters, sending many to the gallows.

His later years were marred by his increasing arrogance and meanness. His chief victim was the great philosopher and mathematician, Gottfried Leibniz, who also claimed to have invented calculus. Newton was first but published late. Leibniz made the mistake of appealing to the Royal Society to impartially decide the issue. The results, because of Newton's corrupt influence and direct fraud, were utterly predictable. Newton clung to his tainted victory and gloated, upon hearing of Leibniz's death, of how he had broken his heart.

Newton took the raw material of an idea and hammered at it unyieldingly until he had forged an answer. His concentration drove him for days at a time without sleep. More than once he breakfasted on his congealed dinner from the night before. He was known to blindly resume his work while his guests sat in his living room. The solitary life seemed to suit him. Intimacy was not his way and he was never known to have a passionate relationship. He was more comfortable with the intricacies of theory and mathematics, with the question of "Why?" It was a question that inspired him, drove him, and ultimately humbled him. As an old man he confessed, "I seem to have been only like a boy, playing on the sea-shore, and diverting myself, in now and then finding a smoother pebble or prettier shell than ordinary, whilst the great ocean of truth lay all undiscovered before me."

Around Newton are clustered some of his spiritual descendants. **William Thomson** (1824–1907), First Baron Kelvin, was born in Belfast. Thomson was admitted to the University of Glasgow when he was ten years old and was a professor of natural philosophy there at age 22. Expert not only in the areas of mathematics and physics, he excelled at invention, navigation, and music. By eccentricity and force of personality Thomson developed into the grand old man of British science, a man one would not want to cross.

Among his most distinguished contributions were the development of the Kelvin scale of absolute temperature using $-273.15°C$ (absolute zero) as its base. From here he went on to demonstrate that heat is wasted, although not annihilated, in its transformation into work. In elaborating the principle of the dissipation of energy Thomson stated that heat falls from a higher to a lower temperature and in so doing equalizes the amount of energy available for work. In short Thomson predicted, based on then-current knowledge, that the earth could be only five hundred million years old. This put him in direct conflict with Darwin although his qualifier "current knowledge" hung around his neck like a reputational lifesaver. Darwin proved to be correct but could not have known that nuclear energy was the reason.

Thomson was also much involved with the laying of the transatlantic telegraph wire, and invented electronic measuring instruments which helped to systematize physics. In 1892 Thomson was made Lord Kelvin. His career, great as it was, might have been greater yet had his habits been less desultory. For 30 years he failed to finish reading any book and was not receptive to the ideas of others. His lectures, opening with prayer, were marked by sudden inspiration and then digression, during which he required his assistants to provide all forms of data including multiplication tables.

Nearby is **Ernest**, First Baron **Rutherford** (1871–1937) who carried on much of Kelvin's work. Great scientists are men of great vision and Rutherford's vision extended further than most. In response to Arthur Eddington's musings as to whether electrons would be known as anything but mental concepts Rutherford exclaimed, "Not exist? Not exist! Why, I can see the little buggers as plain as I can see that spoon in front of me!" Rutherford was an experimental physicist with the ability to visualize the atomic world and to demonstrate that vision through his research. His talent in research lay in his uncanny choice of direction and experiment. Rarely did he find himself in a blind alley.

Sporting an enthusiastic-looking moustache most of his adult life, Rutherford was a large, energetic man who was born and raised in New Zealand. His parents were farmers, his beginnings were humble, and he showed his potential early on in school. He won scholarships, attended Canterbury College in Christchurch, and then came to Cambridge to work under J. J. Thomson. At the Cavendish Laboratory he initiated his work on radioactivity. From there he moved to McGill University in Montreal in 1898 where he continued his research.

Working with Frederick Soddy, Rutherford developed the theory of atomic disintegration which rested on the observation that radioactive atoms emit alpha particles with such energy that heat is generated. Radium, for instance, produces enough energy to heat its weight in water from freezing to boiling every hour and to continue to do so for at least a thousand years. From here Rutherford discovered that this energy was generated by the spontaneous decay of atoms. The result was a rocketing particle and transformation into a new kind of atom. These findings garnered him the 1908 Nobel Prize in chemistry.

The fallout of this work was great for not only did it challenge the notion of the stability of the elements, but it also provided support for Darwin's proposed lengthened time scale so necessary for evolution, in that it demonstrated that the earth remains warm due to the radioactive energy which is being emitted from its core. By determining the half-life of various elements Rutherford also provided the impetus for radiometric dating of materials. More ominously such work also laid the groundwork for the splitting of the atom and hence the atomic bomb, although Rutherford did not envision such a device.

In 1907 he accepted an offer from the University of Manchester and settled down to work with Hans Geiger. It was at home in 1910, shortly before Christmas and a Sunday dinner that another inspiration came to Rutherford. This time he had imagined what the atom looked like: a tiny positively charged nucleus of great mass with negative electrons orbiting around it as in a tiny solar system. Once again Rutherford backed up his theory with clarifying experiments.

Another aspect of Rutherford's talent lay in his ability to attract students of the highest order. In Manchester that meant Harry Moseley, who died an early death at Gallipoli, and the great Niels Bohr. It was the latter who refined Rutherford's theory with his own insights into quantum physics. What a laboratory that must have been! Genius surrounded by genius, all being led and inspired by Rutherford's booming and sometimes intimidating enthusiasm. There is an amusing photo showing Rutherford gesticulating under a "Talk Softly Please" sign.

Rutherford was the type of scientist who belies the notion of the scientist as recluse. He enjoyed friends, talk, dinners, golf, and play. His usual golf group was made up of disparate athletic talents. In order to compensate for the difference, one of the standing rules was that a lesser talent received a surprise handicap (he could shout "Boo!" a given number of times per match as the better player was about to strike the ball). Rutherford was a man with a sense of preservation as well. In announcing his theory of atomic disintegration he spoke before a large and distinguished assemblage which included Lord Kelvin. Knowing that his views on the age of the earth contradicted Kelvin's, he was apprehensive of the older man's response. "Then sudden inspiration came, and I said Lord Kelvin had limited the age of the earth, provided no new source [of energy] was discovered. That prophetic utterance refers to what we are now considering tonight, radium! Behold! The old boy beamed upon me."

Genius takes many forms.

The third of the trio buried here is Sir **Joseph John Thomson** (1856–1940). Thomson's star rose quickly. By the age of 27 he had succeeded Lord Rayleigh as the director of the Cavendish Laboratory. Though his youth rankled some people there is no question that the appointment was a wise choice. Under his guidance the Cavendish Lab became a focal point for atomic research. Its policy of granting scholarships attracted many of the best available students from around the world such as Rutherford, Townsend, Langevin, and Zeleny, any of whom might otherwise have gone to the previously more prestigious European schools. It was a budget renaissance, however, for Cavendish's slim funding earned it the nickname of the "string and sealing wax" laboratory.

Thomson was better with his mind than his hands. Everett, his assistant, had to frequently place the fragile glass apparatus which Thomson himself had designed out of Thomson's easy reach lest experiments come to a premature end. His contributions far outweighed these minor failings and included the discovery of the electron (or corpuscle as Thomson called it for years) in 1897, and the discovery that gases charged with x rays were capable of conducting electricity. It was for this latter work that he won the 1906 Nobel Prize in physics. His work with positive ion rays also led the way for atoms and molecules to be assigned atomic weights.

There is a metal plate in the floor given by the Institution of Civil Engineers to commemorate **Michael Faraday** (1791–1867). (See Chapter 10 on Highgate for the biography of Michael Faraday.)

Although Charles Darwin's plain white slab, with just his dates, is on the floor near Newton, if you circle around into the North Choir Aisle you will see his head in bronze—a measure of the tolerance of the English at a time when most God-fearing Americans would have liked to have his head in some other way.

CHARLES ROBERT DARWIN *b. February 12, 1809, Shrewsbury, Shropshire; d. April, 19, 1882, Downe, Kent.* For a man who wrote the most important book in the nineteenth century, Darwin was an unlikely genius and a reluctant hero. Adjectives like shy, kindly, good-humored, and hypochondriacal seem to be more appropriate to this evolutionary figure. Reclusive and apologetic, he plodded his way into greatness.

In childhood Darwin left no traces of real precocity. His endless collecting (everything from pebbles to newts and beetles) and his enthusiasm for snipe shooting drove his well-meaning but domineering father to frustration. One intemperate outburst by the good doctor predicted that Charles would bring nothing but disgrace to the family. But collecting and classifying were in his blood. His grandfather, Erasmus Darwin, had produced the 1400-page *Zoonomia, or the Laws of Organic Life* (1794–1796). While his father would have preferred medicine for his son's occupation, Charles' exaggerated sensitivities would have none of the operating room.

After attending Cambridge Charles was referred to a job as naturalist for the H.M.S. *Beagle*, a small brig which had orders to survey the coast of South America. It was to be a five-year trip and perhaps offered Charles as much in the way of escape as it did in the pursuit of his field. His most vital possession was Charles Lyell's recently published *Principles of Geology*, in which the author outlined the geologic evolution of the earth. On this now-famous voyage Charles observed, collected, and classified innumerable species of all sorts. Of prime importance was a stop in the Galapagos Islands. Here Charles noted differentiation within a species. Tortoises, for instance, varied from island to island in the shape of their shell. Where an island was more arid and the ground vegetation sparse, the tortoises had a peak on the front of their shells and longer necks, both of which allowed them to reach more easily tree leaves or cactus branches. Where ground vegetation was readily accessible the tortoises had shorter necks and gently curved shells.

Darwin was able to combine such observations with Lyell's thesis that the earth evolved over a great span of time. He was then able to reason that not all offspring of a species were identical. In any clutch of newborn there might be differences. On the arid islands those young that were born with longer necks stood a better chance of survival and, having done so, came to dominate the species in that locale. It was the idea of natural selection, but it did not come to Darwin all at once. Like Newton he developed an idea and kept it secret for almost a quarter of a century. Darwin found a theory for his observations when, for entertainment, he read Malthus' *Essay on Population*. In the economic doctrine of competition lay the struggle for survival.

Before settling down to his arduous labors Darwin set about finalizing his one decisive prescription: "Marry, marry, marry. Q.E.D." His choice was Emma Wedgwood; not surprising since the Darwins and Wedgwoods seemed always to be marrying one another. It was a case where "the perfect nurse had married the perfect patient," for Darwin was frequently ill. With age his complaints grew worse and he spent more time in illness and convalescence. It has never been clear whether Darwin's illness was more or less hypochondriasis. Certainly he loved the attention of his doting Emma as did their many children who were also not loath to be sick.

Darwin's children grew up true Darwinians. They could hardly not, for the house smelled for eight years of the barnacles Charles was busy noting and dissecting, causing one of the young children to inquire about a neighbor, "Then where does he do his barnacles?" Darwin amassed information year after year, put off from publishing by his own timidity and by fear of hurting Emma's feelings, for she was a firm believer in revelation. In 1855 Darwin saw a paper by Alfred Russell Wallace which bore ideas remarkably similar to his own. More alarming yet was the force of Wallace's prose which far outstripped Darwin's pedestrian efforts. It was this threat of preemption that spurred Darwin to publish. Wallace was gracious in the extreme. A joint paper was given in 1858 and Wallace, based on Darwin's mountainous research, deferred his claim. In 1859 *On the Origin of Species* was published.

The outraged criticism was predictable, but backing was forthcoming as well. The prime pillar of support was Thomas Huxley, a brilliant scientist and a persuasive and sharp-tongued speaker. It was Huxley who demolished Bishop Wilberforce in their 1860 debate. Rising to speak after the Bishop had pondered aloud as to which side of his family did Huxley claim simian descent, Huxley won the applause and the day when he declared, "I would rather be the offspring of two apes than be a man and afraid to face the truth."

Darwin continued his quiet life while the controversy stormed about him. Sheltered in his cottage he took up the study of orchids. They were to be a delight and a solace for his declining years. Acceptance grew and with it fame. He published additional books and elaborated more theories, but it is *Origin* which contains the most profound impact. Darwin's theory has been adjusted and amended over the years but its foundation remains firm.

Like Richard Burton's, Darwin's deathbed conversion was manufactured. In Darwin's case the evangelist Lady Hope claimed to be the instrument of his conversion and, better yet, his recantation of evolutionary theories. With the help of Dwight Moody this canard was perpetuated for over half a century. Darwin needed no conversion. Bewildered by the spectacle of creation he had studied all his life he saw its design as the best argument for a God, but he was unable to reconcile this with the vast suffering on the planet. He was an agnostic. For the ultimate collector of facts, the fact of death seemed not to faze him. It existed as if it had its own order, its own genus. The day before he died he turned to his beloved wife and said, "I am not the least afraid of death."

In front of the Nave on the south side, the monument opposite Isaac Newton's belongs to **James Stanhope** (1673–1721). Also sculpted by John Michael Rysbrack, the memorial shows the Earl of Stanhope with a baton in one hand, a scroll in the other, looking into the distance. This general only rates one cherub and the figure of Minerva, who sits alertly on the military tent which houses Stanhope. During the War of the Spanish Succession, Stanhope helped to capture Barcelona and Minorca, but lost his army to the French. As secretary of state under George I, he strengthened England's diplomatic position with other European countries.

Turning to your right, you can see against the wall the monument of Major **John André** (1750–1780). The bas-relief on his sarcophagus shows scenes from his capture and his plea to George Washington, which went unanswered, that he be shot as a soldier rather than hung as a spy. A melancholy maiden, her head resting on her arm, and a doleful lion representing Britannia sit atop the white marble tomb designed by Robert Adam and carved by Peter Van Gelder.

The monument is "sacred to the memory of Major John André who raised by his merit at an early period of his life to the rank of adjutant general of the British forces in America and employed in an important but hazardous enterprise fell a sacrifice to his zeal for his king and country on the second of October 1780, age 29. Universally beloved and esteemed by the army in which he served and lamented even by his foes. His gracious sovereign King George III has caused this monument to be erected."

By all accounts, John André was a handsome and charismatic officer, given to dashing feats and admired by American friends for his artistic gifts. He was also, perhaps, operating under the belief that he could never die. André met with Benedict Arnold at West Point to plot the takeover of that fort by the British. Returning to New York, he was halted and searched by several American soldiers who had heard rumors of his quest. The plans of the fortress were found hidden in his stockings, and André was taken to Washington's headquarters at Tappan, New York, where, despite many protests, he was tried and hung.

At England's request, his remains were removed from Tappan 40 years later, given a funeral, and reinterred here.

In the two alcoves to the right of André are military friends, **William Hargrave** (1672–1751), Governor of Gibraltar, and Major **James Fleming** (1682–1751), who was wounded at Blenheim in the War of the Spanish Succession and fought valiantly at Culloden and Falkirk during the Jacobite uprising in Scotland. Both have statues by Louis François Roubillac, the former notable for the public sentiment it provoked. There was outrage that a person of such an undistinguished life as General Hargrave should merit a huge marble memorial complete with allegorical representations of Time, Eternity, and Death. Hargrave himself is seen struggling to rise from his tomb in response to the Last Trumpet — causing one wag to write underneath: "Lie still if you're wise; you'll be damned if you rise."

THIS MONUMENT
IS ERECTED BY PARLIAMENT,
TO WILLIAM PITT,
SON OF WILLIAM, EARL OF CHATHAM,
IN TESTIMONY OF GRATITUDE
FOR THE EMINENT PUBLIC SERVICES,
AND OF REGRET FOR THE IRREPARABLE LOSS
OF THAT GREAT AND DISINTERESTED MINISTER.

DIED ON THE 23ᴰ OF JANUARY 1806, IN THE 47ᵀᴴ YEAR OF HIS AGE.

Westminster Abbey

North and South Transepts

THIS TOUR BEGINS at the choir area, which is charming enough to coax a hymn out of anyone. Each individual choir stall of carved wood has its own brass lamp, topped by a small red shade. Beneath the pavement, just inside and to your left, is Canon **Robinson Duckworth** (1834–1911) who rowed the boat while Lewis Carroll read *Alice in Wonderland* aloud to Alice Liddell, his story's inspiration.

Move to your right into the South Choir Aisle. Just to your right is the bas-relief of **Thomas Thynne**, "who was barbarously murdered on Sunday the twelveth of February 1682." The bas-relief shows him inside his carriage, wearing a long curly wig, and holding out his hand as he expires — perhaps to demonstrate that there is no weapon in it. Three horsemen surround the carriage, one of them holding the revolver that has just shot "Tom of Ten Thousand." Thynne, a favorite at the Court of Charles II, was married to the heiress, Lady Elizabeth Percy. A Swedish adventurer, Karl von Konigsmarck, hoped to marry her next and hired the three assassins to murder Thynne in Pall Mall.

Although the gunmen eventually confessed, Konigsmarck was acquitted and fled the country before he could be challenged to a duel. A cherub points at the scene of the crime, but a long inscription which told the story was either forbidden or later removed.

The figure next to the Thynne monument, clutching a script and wearing a painted square black hat, red robe, and black sash, reclines stoically on one elbow on a gilt-decorated red and green cushion. **Thomas Owen** (d. 1598) looks sober as befits a justice of the Court of Common Pleas.

William Pitt "the Younger"

Nearby is a tablet to **William Tyndale** (1490–1536) placed here in 1938 to commemorate the "translator of the Holy Scriptures into the language of the English people." Tyndale was executed in the Netherlands for heresy. There are also memorials in this section to **John Wesley**, and **Isaac Watts**. (See Chapter 6 on Bunhill Fields for biographies of Wesley and Watts.)

Across the way and up in the next section is a monument to the man who declared, "By God, I will not be buried in Westminster . . . they do bury fools there." Sir **Godfrey Kneller** (1648–1723), court portrait painter, got his wish and is buried in Twickenham. But he could not prevent his wife from campaigning for this memorial, or the epitaph by Alexander Pope which Pope later decried as the worst thing he had ever written. It ends with the extravagance:

> Living, great Nature feared He might outvye
> Her works; and dying, fears herself may dye.

The nearby monument of Admiral Sir **Clowdisley Shovell** (1650–1707) created a controversy of its own. It shows him reclining on a couch in formal dress, but with a portion of his ample stomach sticking out. Joseph Addison claimed that it "had often given him very great offence. Instead of the brave rough English Admiral, which was the distinguishing character of that plain gallant man, he is represented by the figure of a beau, dressed in a long periwig, and reposing himself on velvet cushions, under a canopy of state. The inscription is answerable to the monument, for, instead of celebrating the many remarkable actions he had performed in the service of his country, it acquaints us only with the manner of his death, in which it was impossible for him to reap any honour."

Admiral Shovell was indeed a brave man, distinguishing himself in combat against the Dutch, French, and Spanish. Unfortunately, returning home from victory in Barcelona, on sighting English land the crew of his flagship got drunk for joy and wrecked the ship on the rocks of the Scilly Isles. The admiral was washed up on the beach where a fisherwoman killed him for his emerald ring. His body was recovered and embalmed, then transported to Westminster Abbey for burial.

Continue your tour by crossing the Nave to reach the spot we have dubbed Musicians' Corner in the North Choir Aisle. As you enter you will see a memorial stone to Sir **Edward Elgar** (1857–1934) who is actually buried in St. Wulstan's Churchyard, Little Malvern. Other musicians who are commemorated here but buried elsewhere are **Michael Balfe** (1808–1870) (see Chapter 9 on Kensal

Thomas Owen

Green), **Benjamin Britten** (1913–1976) who lies in Alde-
burgh in Suffolk, and Sir **William Walton** who is buried in
Italy. There are also memorials here to non-musicians **Joseph Lister** (1827–1912) (see Chapter 12 on Hampstead),
and **James Watt** (1736–1819), developer of the steam engine, who is buried near Birmingham.

Directly behind Elgar's stone, and fittingly near the bust
of Darwin, his great uncle, is the stone to Ralph Vaughn
Williams, below which his ashes rest.

RALPH VAUGHN WILLIAMS *b. October 12, 1872, Down
Ampney; d. August 20, 1958, London.* Ralph Vaughn Williams was a big-boned man whose shy, genial features were
topped by a thatch of black hair which seemed to become
thicker and wilder as it whitened with age. His dress was
sloppy, and his handwriting and scoring begged for legibil-
ity. Indeed his rumpled, windblown appearance lent him a

cheerful, boyish look which seemed an accurate reflection of his life, for there is no hint of scandals, affairs, alcoholism, or the pettiness which dissolves friendships.

Vaughn Williams was born to parents of standing. His father came from a line of distinguished lawyers; his mother was both a Darwin and a Wedgwood. With the death of his father when he was two, his upbringing fell to his mother. His first piece, "The Robin's Nest," composed when he was six, impressed his Aunt Sophy who tutored him through his early childhood. At 18 he entered the Royal College of Music and studied there with Sir Hubert Parry and later with Sir Charles Stanford, both advocates of nationalist music. Parry broadened his scope and made him think. Stanford inspired him through his brilliance and loyalty if not his sympathy: "Damnably ugly, my boy, why do you write such things?"

Nevertheless, Vaughn Williams' greatest influence was his fellow student, Gustav Holst. Both had an abiding interest in folk music and, like Bartok and Kodaly in Hungary, they took to the field to notate songs directly from shepherds, farmers, and townsfolk. In doing so they, along with Cecil Sharp, preserved a musical form and heritage which was to figure prominently in Vaughn Williams' music. Their friendship was one of rare honesty. In college they met weekly for "field days" when they would analyze each other's music with tactful honesty and offer encouragement. Though the frequency of the meetings declined with time and geographic distance, they continued the practice for nearly 40 years until Holst's death in 1934. There were few compositions that either wrote without the benefit of the other's advice.

Despite his nationalist background Vaughn Williams studied for several months with Max Bruch in Germany shortly after his honeymoon and later studied orchestration with Ravel. From then on he was on his own. His compositions eschewed the formality of the Germanic tradition in favor of the modal forms of the Tudors and his native folk music. As he evolved a unique voice his stature grew, and he supplanted Elgar as England's leading composer. His *Pastoral Symphony* (1922) was both praised and derided. Phillip Hesseltine likened it to "a cow looking over a gate." His *Fourth Symphony* (1935) with its storm and anger seemed to puzzle Vaughn Williams himself. While conducting a rehearsal he stopped and said, "Well, gentlemen, if that's modern music, you can have it." On another occasion he stated, "I don't know if I like it, but that's what I meant." The *Fifth Symphony* (1942) written during the war is peaceful and elegiac while the *Sixth* (1948) seems despairing, its last movement written pianissimo throughout, comparable in its eerie mood only to the coda of Chopin's *Funeral March Sonata* although far longer.

Vaughn Williams was shy, modest, and genuinely humble. Although in no danger of being drafted, he enlisted in the Royal Army Medical Corps at age 42 during World War I and performed the most menial tasks without complaint. While a nationalist he was no chauvinist. He saw his work as a necessary duty, but he saw no glory in war. Indeed, he stood up for fellow composer Michael Tippett when the latter filed for conscientious-objector status in World War II, even though he disagreed with Tippett's stand. Vaughn Williams was a populist and viewed his fellow enlistees without regard to their social position.

After the war he resumed composing and teaching. His shy personality kept him from being a great teacher but, remembering Parry and Stanford, he was dedicated. If he thought a student would get more from another teacher he was glad to refer him. He had his foibles: a quick temper if an orchestra or choir was unresponsive, and little tolerance for either the "wrong note" school of Schoenberg or the "painfully correct" notes of Mahler's *Second Symphony*. Students were fair game, as with the "wrong note" student at Yale who, after playing his piece, was told, "Interesting. If a tune should ever occur to you, my boy, don't hesitate to write it down."

Tunes were important for Vaughn Williams. He invented them, but he also borrowed whenever they provided inspiration, and he labeled himself a "simple kleptomaniac" for this practice. His 65-year compositional career was one of the longest of any composer and like Verdi he composed into his eighties. His *Ninth Symphony* was completed just a few months prior to his death. He left a body of music that includes hymn tunes; folk settings like the *Folk Song Suite*; pastorally inspired music like *The Lark Ascending*; concertos for oboe, harmonica, and tuba; religious works; masques; operas; and, of course, the masterpiece, *Fantasia on a Theme of Thomas Tallis*.

There are those who think Vaughn Williams is the greatest symphonist of the twentieth century. For others his music is too objective. Certainly his vision and passion were singular. In America he seems to be more admired than performed, while his banner is still strong in England. After many decades his best music speaks with clarity and strength.

There is a full-sized burial slab in the floor to **Henry Purcell** (1658–1695) as well as a memorial plaque against a column. Topped by an old-fashioned oil lamp, it has the epitaph, "Here lyes Henry Purcell Esq. Who left this Life And is gone to that Blessed Place Where only his Harmony can be exceeded."

Purcell was a composer of rare gifts. He has been likened to Mozart, not only for the shortness of his life, but also for his ability to utilize foreign styles. His music is original, at times sounding strikingly modern, with direct and unaffected emotion. While clearly superior to his predecessors his influence all but ceased with the arrival of Handel.

A fine keyboard player, Purcell was organist at Westminster Abbey. He composed sparkling pieces for the keyboard, church music, part songs (some with bawdy lyrics), and opera. His moving miniature opera, *Dido and Aeneas*, is still performed, as is *The Fairy Queen*, *Come Ye Sons of Art*, and *Music for the Funeral of Queen Mary*, this last being played later the same year for Purcell's funeral service at Westminster.

Musical imagery slipped into a number of epitaphs here. That of **William Croft** (1678–1727), the most individual of Purcell's successors, can be translated from the Latin as, "He emigrated to a Heavenly Choir, into that concert of angels for which he was better fitted, adding his own Hallelujah." The sentiment for a long-forgotten Abbey organist, **John Parsons**, is even more graphic:

Death passing by and hearing Parsons play
Stood much amazed at his depth of skill,
And said, 'This artist must with me away,'
For death bereaves us of the better still;
But let the quire, while he keeps time, sing on,
For Parsons rests, his service being done.

Across the way near the window is an attractive monument with an open hymn book showing the doxology, "Glory be to the Father and to the Son and to the Holy Spirit." It is a canon of four parts in one by Dr. **John Blow** (1649–1708). On either side above are two cherubs looking at a tablet with his biographical information. "He was a scholar, music master to the children of the chapel, organist, and composer. He died in 1708 in the sixtieth year of his life." Blow is well at home here for he was the organist for Westminster Abbey. The composer of keyboard suites of occasional charm and some choral works as well, Blow's chief contribution lay in being the teacher of Henry Purcell and Jeremiah Clarke.

Below Blow on the floor is the plaque to **Adrian Cedric**

Boult (1889–1983). Musical conductors enjoy, on the whole, an active and enviable longevity. Sir Adrian was no exception, living till the age of 93. He was born to Unitarian parents in Liverpool, showed the usual early promise, and attended Oxford, in whose musical life he took an active role and where he rowed for his college. After Oxford he moved to Leipzig and studied under Nikisch. His career started to move forward in the 1918–19 season when he conducted the Royal Philharmonic Society. By 1923 he was conductor of the Birmingham Festival Chorus, and a year later permanent conductor of the City of Birmingham Orchestra. In 1927 he headed the London Bach Choir succeeding Vaughn Williams. There he championed the production of the complete *St. Matthew Passion*.

Sir Adrian's chief accomplishment was to come in 1930 when he became director of music for the BBC. In this capacity he built the orchestra to a level where it enjoyed international renown. He was an adventurous conductor who programmed works of such diverse composers as Bach, Schubert, Ravel, Busoni, Berg, and Havergal Brian. Boult was particularly known for championing the music of his native land, that of Elgar, Holst, and, especially, Vaughn Williams.

After the war Boult tried to rebuild his orchestra, but was unable to raise it to its former level by the time of his retirement in 1950. Enjoying a worldwide reputation he continued to record and served as guest conductor through his eighties. Boult's interpretations tended to be classical, almost puritan. His style, in the manner of his teacher Nikisch, was conservative and avoided the histrionics and prima donna antics that marked, and still mark, so many of his fellows.

William Wilberforce (1759–1833), among the musicians instead of statesmen, is shown in a very natural pose with his legs crossed, holding a book, head cocked in an engaging smirk. His monument gives a long list of his accomplishments. Wilberforce is buried in Statesmen's Aisle and described there.

In this same area is a fascinating book under glass, *The Roll of Honour of the Women's Voluntary Service 1939–1945*. It lists the casualties of World War II, and has their names written in beautiful calligraphy. **Sarah Jane Moss**, a housewife, died January 6, 1941, "killed on duty looking after an elderly blind woman and her deaf and dumb daughter. They were all buried when a parachute struck a house two doors away. Very soon after, in the bitter cold, snow began to fall heavily."

William Wilberforce

Above Sarah Jane Moss is listed **Jane Ruth Peacock**, who was in charge of the Methodist Rest Center, and the wife of a Methodist minister. "She was killed while changing a book at the public library," dying January 4, 1945.

On the way to the North Transept, notice the painted memorial to an attorney in the reign of Elizabeth I, **Thomas Hesketh** (d. 1605). He looks like Sir Walter Raleigh, with a ruff collar and red shirt decorated with buttons. Hesketh reclines on a mauve and gold cushion.

The North Transept gives a nice sense of English history. Staying to your left, you will see the memorial of Dr. **Hugh Boulter** (1671–1742), late Archbishop and Primate of all Ireland. He has, in retrospect, a wistful epitaph: "A poet so eminent for the accomplishments of his mind, the purity of his heart and the excellency of his life that it may be thought superfluous to specify his titles, recount his virtues, or even erect a monument to his fame." Fortunately there is a statue of this otherwise forgotten man.

Although he is buried elsewhere, we should give a nod to **Jonas Hanway** (1712–1786), the first person in England to carry an umbrella. Given the climate, one might wonder why it did not happen until the eighteenth century, but Hanway was also involved in another surprising first, that of donating the first training ship in the world to the Marine Society which he helped found. His monument shows Britannia handing out sailor suits to three young men.

It is interesting to notice the regionalism of some monuments, such as that of Lieutenant General Sir **Eyer Coote** (1726–1783), commander-in-chief in India, who died in Madras. The statue by Thomas Banks was financed by the East India Company, and shows a small elephant, Victory pinning a cameo of Coote to a palm tree, and a naked native of India with his head shaved, covering his face in mourning. An angel crowns General Coote under a death helmet which covers his face.

The joint monument to Captains **William Bayne** (ca. 1732–1782), **William Blair** (ca. 1741–1782), and Lord **Robert Manners** (1758–1782) around the corner from Coote is colossal and cost £4,000 in 1788. The naval bas-reliefs on either side of the base show scenes from the Second Battle of Dominica and Les Saintes in the Caribbean in which all three died. The statue on the base appears to be Neptune, resting on a horse that turns into a scaly sea creature, reaching up toward their three cameos. Britannia is regarding them from the other side, along with a very unhappy lion resting on a shield. Fame at the top and two hovering angels complete the tableau.

The sculptor of this mighty work is Joseph Nollekens, who, along with Francis Bird, Louis François Roubillac, Peter Scheemakers, and John Michael Rysbrack, executed most of the memorials in the Abbey. Despite their contribution these men were not invited to lie under the same roof with their work, and even during their lifetimes had to contend with ungrateful critics. Oliver Goldsmith complained that the monuments "conferred honour not on the great men but on little Roubillac." Roubillac himself, though he often stood before one of his own favorite works in the Abbey and wept because it was too high up to be appreciated, returned from Rome with the comment, "By God! My own works looked to me as meagre and starved as if they had been made of tobacco pipes."

The memorial of **William Pitt** (1708–1778), First Earl of Chatham, in the next alcove also depicts Britannia. She is holding a trident with Neptune below, his privates discreetly covered by a clever dolphin. On the other side is a woman representing Earth; underneath her arm is a globe from which all varieties of fruit and vegetables spill out, signaling prosperity. Above them appear to be two adolescent children, Prudence with a mirror and Fortitude holding a column. At the top is William Pitt himself, waving.

William Pitt collapsed in the House of Lords after making a special trip there to oppose American independence, and died soon after. By then he had already brought his country into war with Spain and France, and conducted a personal battle with King George II. Pitt believed that control of overseas trade was the secret of England's strength, and was always energized by the prospect of a war to safeguard commerce.

Known as the Great Commoner, Pitt entered Parliament in 1735 as one of the "boy patriots," opposing Robert Walpole who felt that commerce flourished better under conditions of peace. Despite the King's detestation of the younger statesman, he was forced to make Pitt secretary of state in 1756. But Pitt did not become Earl of Chatham until 1766 under the more favorable eye of George III.

A thin-faced man with a hawk's nose and scornful eyes, Pitt enlivened Parliament with his sarcasm. But he battled interior demons as well. Serious depression, euphemistically referred to as "gout in the head," periodically made him irrational, then catatonic in a way that would not let him eat, speak, or move.

Even when lucid, Pitt's attitude toward the colonies was complex. He opposed the Stamp Act in 1766, and applauded the independent spirit of the Americans. Yet he took the withdrawal of British troops from the colonies as a terrible act of surrender, unable to believe that Englishmen could want freedom from the mother country. He would as soon "swallow transubstantiation," he claimed, forgetting that communicants through the ages have done exactly that.

William Pitt "the Younger" (1759–1806) achieved prominence earlier than his father did, and died sooner as well. After briefly practicing law, Pitt entered Parliament in

1780. He had been schooled in oratory by his father, and placed a high price on his own abilities. But even he was surprised to find himself appointed prime minister at 24, by George III. Despite parliamentary resentment over the King's interference, a general election in 1784 confirmed the appointment.

Unlike his father, Pitt put Britain's financial house in order internally and opted for neutrality and peace. Drawn into war with France in 1793, the country's resources were also weakened by the Irish rebellion. Pitt proposed a settlement which included Irish emancipation, which was strenuously opposed by George III who blamed his subsequent attack of porphyria on his prime minister. Pitt resigned.

By then his health was shattered. Years of privately relieving his stress by drinking or by turning it inward had exacted its measure. He was affectionate with only a few close friends, and had never expressed a desire to marry. Capable in the context of his times, Pitt would perhaps be surprised that he is chiefly remembered today for his lifelong conflict with Charles James Fox and for his inadvertent colonizing of Australia by first transporting criminals to Botany Bay.

Just opposite the Pitts is the monument of **William Cavendish** (1592–1676), First Duke of Newcastle, and his second wife **Margaret Lucas** (ca. 1624–1674). The monument, which was created during the Duke's lifetime by Grinling Gibbons, shows them resting side by side with implements of their personal interests. Cavendish is in a suit of armour and holding a baton, commemorating the regiment he raised and led in the cause of Charles I. The Duchess, a prolific author, has a pencase, inkstand, and book on her tomb.

A fascinating woman in her own right, Lucas surrounded herself with young women who were ready, day or night, to jot down her inspirations, which she then published. Although Samuel Pepys reported that "her dress [was] so antick and her deportment so ordinary that I did not like her at all," his was a minority opinion. As the Duke wrote in her epitaph: "Her name was Margaret Lucas, youngest sister of Lord Lucas of Colchester — a noble family, for all the brothers were valiant and all the sisters virtuous. . . . She was a very wise, witty, and learned lady as her many books do testify."

Behind the Newcastles, in the small Chapel of St. Michael, is hidden one of the more extraordinary monuments of the Abbey. Executed by Louis François Roubillac, it is a memorial to Lady **Elizabeth Nightingale** (1704–1731) who died after a miscarriage. Lady Nightingale languishes while her horrified husband, Joseph Gascoigne Nightingale, supports her and tries to stave off Death's poisoned dart with his upraised hand. Death, attacking from beneath them, is a dramatic enshrouded skeleton. It is said, with perhaps more hope than truth, that a burglar who once broke into Westminster Abbey saw the scene and fled, terrified.

On the floor closer to the entrance is the burial place of:

WILLIAM WILBERFORCE *b. August 24, 1759, Hull, England; d. July 29, 1833, London.* William Wilberforce was five foot three, thin, and plain. He was plagued by poor eyesight that grew worse with age, and his nose, later hidden by portraitists in the plump visage of his middle age, was too long for his face. Yet he was bright, amusing, and altogether outgoing. Although not the most flamboyant speaker of his time, he was nevertheless one of the most riveting and influential. According to Boswell, who observed one of Wilberforce's orations, "[I] saw a little fellow on a table speaking — a perfect shrimp. But presently the shrimp swelled into a whale."

Proof of Wilberforce's effect lay in the fact that he was voted a seat in the House of Commons at the age of 21. Such an achievement must have pleasantly surprised his family, for their money and influence had lain in mercantile rather than political success. In truth Wilberforce was indolent and unfocused as a youth. Deferring his Cambridge degree for two years, he sojourned in London spending many of his days there in the gallery of the House of Commons with William Pitt. It was Pitt, with his firm political aspirations, who provided an impetus and direction for Wilberforce by urging him to run for the House of Commons.

As we know, politics and maturity are not inextricably linked, and Wilberforce was young. He sowed his wild oats; he gambled, drank, and enjoyed the usual nocturnal adventures of a young man of his class, but when he was 25 he underwent a religious crisis which provided more focus and sobriety to his life. His guiding influence here was the hero of his youth, John Newton, a man whose own youth reeked of sailor, lecher, and slaver, and whose middle age was purged through conversion, ordination, and hymn writing, e.g., "Glorious Things of Thee Are Spoken," and "Amazing Grace." Under Newton's direction Wilberforce was able to reconcile the withdrawal of most evangelicals from public life with his own urge to serve in politics, and to push on with his career.

Elizabeth Nightingale

Around the same time Wilberforce became acquainted with the other great influences on his life, Captain Sir Charles and Lady Middleton, and James Ramsay. Already known as a young reformer, Wilberforce was approached by the Middletons in their effort to gather support for the abolition of the slave trade. They introduced him to Ramsay, both the man and his writings. The descriptions of the barbarous treatment of slaves and of the conditions on the slave ships were profound. The issue became Wilberforce's lifelong cause and passion.

Year after year Wilberforce introduced legislation to abolish the slave trade and year after year he suffered defeat. If his political opponents didn't offer enough resistance it seemed that fate would oblige. He once lost in the House of Commons because several of his allies were at the opera when the vote was taken. When not occupied with these efforts Wilberforce was busy generously donating money to charitable causes, starting a rural school, helping to engineer the settlement of Sierra Leone for freed slaves, and reforming child labor laws and penal conditions. To his enemies he was the bleeding-hearted liberal of his day.

On March 25, 1807, Wilberforce saw his Bill for the Abolition of the Slave Trade become law. But the fight dragged on, first in the realm of enforcing the law and trying to influence other nations to follow suit, and second in lobbying for the emancipation of the slaves. Encountering not only the old opposition to emancipation, Wilberforce also met resistance from reformer William Cobbett, who saw so well the horrible working and living conditions of Britain's white laborers, but who perceived the blacks only as "fat and lazy and laughing and singing and dancing," already, in fact, too well treated.

In their youth Dean Milner had told Wilberforce, "If you carry this point [abolition] in your whole life, that life will be far better spent than in being Prime Minister many years." Retired, in poor health, and all but blind, Wilberforce was living in London when he heard, on July 26, 1833, that the abolition of slavery had passed in Commons. Approval in the House of Lords was certain. Three days later he died. His point carried, he could rest in peace.

The statue of William E. Gladstone seems larger than life. He is clutching the lapel of his robe and looking out at the congregation imperiously. The sculpture was erected by Parliament. In the floor his plaque reads, "Here is buried William Ewart Gladstone (1809–1898) and Catherine his wife, the daughter of Sir Stephen Glynne, Eighth Baronet of Hawarden Castle." It is decorated only with a cross.

WILLIAM EWART GLADSTONE *b. December 29, 1809, Liverpool; d. May 19, 1898, Liverpool.* William Gladstone, who resembled a dour Old Testament prophet in his later years, felt called to the ministry as a young man. His wealthy Scottish father, a slaveowner in the West Indies, pressured him into politics instead, and Gladstone treated his political career as a holy mission — often alienating his fellow party members by suddenly changing his mind.

Gladstone's maiden speech in the House of Commons was a defense of slavery, in tribute to his father. He followed it up with a book, *The State in Its Relations with the*

Church (1839), which urged England to make Anglicanism the state religion and to ban Catholics and non-Church of England members from public employment. Not surprisingly, the book was ridiculed. Fortunately for his career, Gladstone was diverted into finance. Beginning in 1853, he served successfully as Chancellor of the Exchequer. By fostering free enterprise and removing trade restrictions, he helped create a new age of national prosperity.

By 1859 Gladstone was supporting the right of the individual conscience over an official state religion, and moved to the Liberal party under Lord Palmerston. His new moral cause became the elevation of the masses as the embodiment of pure Christian ethic; he alarmed Queen Victoria and his colleagues by advocating the vote for all men, and stumped the country with his wife, Catherine, meeting the working classes personally. The masses were flattered, not realizing that, far from offering them a bureaucratic hand up, Gladstone was opposed to such government intervention. An early believer in trickle-down economics, he felt that public need should be met by private charity. To that end he discouraged welfare and gave away much of his own fortune.

Gladstone also instituted a number of valuable reforms beneficial to the whole country. These included the secret ballot, competitive admission to civil service positions, outlawing of the sale of army commissions, and educational reforms. Though a Liberal party leader, Gladstone continued to support his own causes, advocating the independence of Ireland from the state-imposed Anglican religion in 1868, and becoming prime minister on that issue. In 1876 he denounced Turkish rule in Serbia and Bulgaria in a pamphlet, *Bulgarian Horrors and the Questions of the East*, and summoned Russia to invade those countries to set things right. It earned him the continuing fury of Queen Victoria, since the British government was adamantly pro-Turkish. It was bad enough that he lacked the charm of her beloved Disraeli. Worse, during his four stints as prime minister, he tried to bypass her as much as possible.

In what Freud might have labeled reaction-formation, Gladstone was obsessed all his life with "rescuing" prostitutes. He spent many hours in nightwalking activities; the urge came upon him to save streetwalkers most strongly when his wife was out of town or otherwise unavailable for sexual release. Though political enemies speculated about what Gladstone was actually doing in the company of fallen women, nothing was ever proven. He and Catherine Glynne remained married for nearly 60 years.

Queen Victoria's enmity didn't disappear after Gladstone's painful death from cancer of the jaw and cheekbone. She refused to mention his death in the Court Circular, and was furious when Bertie, the Prince of Wales, announced that he wanted to be a pallbearer. For once he defied her, with the country solidly on his side. The *New York Tribune* announced, "The world has lost its greatest citizen," but Gladstone might have considered his most fitting epitaph the words from a speech he gave to a group of schoolboys: "Be inspired with the belief that life is a great and noble calling; not a mean and grovelling thing that we are to shuffle through as we can, but an elevated and lofty destiny."

Next to Gladstone, **Robert Peel** has the face of a wise and compassionate man. Sculpted by John Gibson, he

William Gladstone   *Robert Peel*

stands holding a scroll in both hands and wearing classical dress. Among his other accomplishments, Peel began the first city police force, giving rise to their nickname of "bobbies." Peel, who entered Parliament in 1809 as a Tory, moved from opposing Irish demands for Catholic emancipation to sponsoring a bill to allow Roman Catholics to sit in the House of Commons, and to supporting Irish land reform. He introduced an income tax, abandoned custom duties, and repealed the Corn Laws which had subsidized agriculture and kept prices high at the expense of consumers, laborers, and manufacturing.

His support of the Corn Laws' repeal and relentless attacks by Disraeli led to Peel's political downfall. Even on his deathbed, succumbing to injuries suffered in a fall from his horse three days earlier, Peel was mourned by his countrymen, but was still considered by the Protectionists a traitor to his class.

Benjamin Disraeli (1804–1881), sculpted by Joseph Edgar Boehm, has a calm expression as he gazes out over the congregations that gather here. One hand is in the center of his chest, the other at his side. A sense of mischief guided the person responsible for placing his statue so close to Robert Peel's.

Disraeli could never understand why the older statesman took such an immediate dislike to him, but after repeated snubs and insults, began to retaliate. He did so with such enthusiasm, hounding Peel out of Parliament, that it was commented afterward that with Peel gone "Disraeli was like an anatomist without a body on which to operate." It is a pity Disraeli chose to be buried in the Hughenden Churchyard instead of Westminster Abbey, for his life is a fascinating study in wit and determination that cannot be described here. But the prime minister, who once described heading his Protectionist party as "dragging an omnibus full of country gentlemen uphill," may be just as happy to be free of his load and out in the fresh air.

...T NON ... MORTVA EST

PRECIOSÆ MEMORIÆ SACRVM ELIZABETHÆ
...VIT ANNA SOROR MOEREN...

Westminster Abbey

Royal Tombs

THE VARIOUS CHAPELS that ring Westminster Abbey behind the Nave are filled with royal history. They are not in chronological order, unfortunately, and not everyone you might expect to find is here. Edward, the Black Prince, rests at Canterbury, Henry VIII is in St. George's Chapel in Windsor, and Victoria built her own mausoleum at Frogmore. Anne Boleyn and others who came under the axe never escaped from the Tower. But that still leaves Elizabeth I, Mary Queen of Scots, Edward the Confessor, and the Little Princes in the Tower, who are included in this tour.

Most of the predominantly Tudor and Stuart effigies in the chapels are lying on their backs, stylized hands clasped in prayer, with their family symbols — dog, castle, or porcupine — under their feet. Two pillows are under most of the heads, one for the physical body and one for the soul. A number of the effigies also have smaller figures kneeling mournfully around them. These "weepers" represent family members; those clasping skulls are no longer living themselves; a few wear crowns to indicate royalty.

Except for that of Edward the Confessor, the chapels are little more than small rooms. We will describe a few highlights to look for in each, circling around from St. John the Baptist to the South Ambulatory.

CHAPEL OF ST. JOHN THE BAPTIST

This chapel is dominated by the monument of **Henry Carey** (1525–1596), Baron Hunsdon. At 36 feet it is the tallest in Westminster Abbey, but one of the less attractive. Two obelisks decorated with painted suits of armour and

Elizabeth Russell

gold swords flank a checkerboard-topped double sarcophagus. Above is a huge coat of arms surrounded by more marble columns, gilt and painted decoration.

It is suggested that Baron Hunsdon's son erected so grand a memorial to compensate for the capriciousness of the Baron's first cousin, Elizabeth I. Three times she signed the document to make him an earl and three times changed her mind. When she finally brought the robes and papers to his deathbed he refused to accept, commenting, "Seeing you counted me not worthy of this honour whilst I was living, I count myself unworthy of it now I am dying."

Along another wall is a plain, draped plaque with the coat of arms of **Thomas Ruthall** (d. 1523), Bishop of Durham. It was said that he signed his own death warrant by sending Henry VIII an inventory of Ruthall's own wealth instead of the volume of state papers he thought he was dispatching. Thomas Wolsey, no friend of Ruthall's, passed the book on to the King with the comment that if he ever needed a loan he knew where to look for one.

In the aisle outside this chapel is the touching **Crewe** family monument. Jane Crewe died in 1639, apparently in childbirth; the baby she has just delivered lies in a small coffin below her. Her husband, Sir Clipesby Crewe, and three other children sit mournfully by.

CHAPEL OF ST. PAUL

What may first catch your eye in this chapel is the colorfully painted effigy of Lady **Frances Sidney** (1531–1589), Countess of Sussex. She rests on two pillows in a red gown and robes with a white ruff around her neck. At her feet is a charming blue and gold porcupine, representing the Sidneys. Lady Frances was the founder of the Sidney Sussex College at Cambridge.

The effigy of lawyer **Thomas Bromley** (1530–1587) wears an elaborately carved robe, representing his position as Lord Keeper. The four kneeling ladies and the four small-scale gentlemen are his eight children. His was a bloody job, beginning with the conviction and Tower execution of the Duke of Norfolk in 1572 for plotting to put Mary Queen of Scots on the throne, and ending with his presiding over the trial of Mary herself in 1586. Exhausted, he died two months after affixing the Great Seal to her death warrant.

The memorial to Sir **John Puckering** (1544–1596) also has eight weepers. The two other figures are those of a purse-bearer and a mace-bearer. The carving is brightly painted, showing Lady Puckering in a white cowl and blue gown, and her husband in black. Both are wearing red shoes. At the foot of his effigy is a gilt deer; at the foot of hers a piece of armour. Puckering, twice speaker for the House of Commons, also took part in the trial of Mary Queen of Scots.

CHAPEL OF HENRY VII

This impressive chapel to the Virgin Mary was begun in 1503 and built by Henry VII in thankfulness for his reign. True, he had stepped over a few bodies to reach the throne, but Richard III, whom he killed in the Battle of Bosworth Field, was himself suspected of dispatching the Little Princes in the Tower. Once Henry VII was securely seated, his thoughts turned to the afterlife, to the construction of a magnificent chapel where his soul could be prayed for and his descendants could be buried. He wanted to reach back into history and bring the remains of his uncle, Henry VI, from Windsor to have him declared a saint; but the price of canonization set by Rome was too high, and Uncle Henry was never enshrined here.

After you enter through the bronze-over-wood gates which display various family emblems, move to your left. At your feet is a marble stone in memory of **Joseph Addison** (1672–1719) with the sentiment:

> Near to these chambers where the mighty rest,
> Since their foundation came a nobler guest.
> Nor e'er was to the bowers of bliss conveyed
> A fairer spirit or more welcome shade.
> Welcome forever, take this long adieu
> And sleep in peace next thy loved Montague.

When visiting Westminster Abbey, Nathaniel Hawthorne commented, "It was in Henry VII's Chapel that I found my foot treading on a flat stone in the pavement with Addison's name upon it, and Tickell's stately verse in honor of him. No other English author sleeps amid such royal and noble companions; nor does he owe it to his literature, but to his official position as Secretary of State, and, partly no doubt, to his connection with the Warwick family. There is a monument to him in Poets' Corner; and he would have found better bedfellows there."

It is difficult to know whether Addison would have really been happy amid such competition. He had difficulty with the idea that any writer was greater than himself, and he preferred to be the benefactor of other, younger artists rather than trapped in anyone's debt. The watchword of his life was caution. As a student and then a fellow at Oxford, he looked for a non-controversial career. Even becoming a clergyman appeared too dangerous. Translating ancient Latin verse anonymously seemed safer; and Addison was savvy enough to dedicate a volume to Charles Montague, Chancellor of the Exchequer.

It resulted in a four-year stipend for travel abroad for the 27-year-old Addison. On his return he secured the first of a series of political posts with his poem, *The Campaign* (1705), written to celebrate the Duke of Marlborough's victory at Blenheim during the War of the Spanish Succession. Beginning in 1708, Addison held a seat in Parliament in the Whig party until his death; true to his principles of caution, he never stood up and spoke. Indeed, he tried once, but got no further than, "I conceive—" repeated it twice more, then sat back down—having, as some wit later commented, "conceived three times and brought forth nothing."

But Addison's true ambition was to write. The production of an opera, *Rosamund* (1707), was bungled, but nearly three hundred years later his lyrics seem witty. When his *Cato* was produced in 1713, he insured its success by insisting that a Tory, Alexander Pope, write the prologue, and a Whig, Dr. Garth, write the epilogue. Another friend "packed" the house, and Addison turned all his profits back to the actors and production company to encourage their greatest efforts. Not surprisingly, the play was judged a "triumph."

Yet in the cooler light of history, Addison's greatest contribution seems to be the anonymous essays he wrote for the daily papers, and for the *Tatler* and the *Spectator*. These were, by and large, expressions of public opinion that already existed rather than a presentation of innovative ideas; but they were superbly crafted, and written with a wit and grace that make them interesting today.

Despite his attempts to shun controversy, Addison's relationships were often tempestuous. His friendships with Alexander Pope and Jonathan Swift ran hot and cold, and when repayment of a debt for the security for a house he had lent Richard Steele was not forthcoming, Addison had his own lawyer enter a judgment and sell the house and furniture from under his friend. Steele, the future editor of the *Spectator*, the *Tatler*, and several other journals, generously forgave Addison.

Because of his aloofness and characterizations of the "fair sex" as childish and given to tiresome social mistakes, London was surprised when, at 44, Addison married an old acquaintance, Charlotte, Dowager Countess of Warwick. There were rumors that the marriage was unhappy, but the Addisons hardly had a chance to find out. Three years later the essayist, who had been asthmatic and in poor health for several years, took to his bed and died.

Next to Addison is a triangle with a black metal coat of arms under which **Charles Montague** (1661–1715), First Earl of Halifax, is buried. Although he made his mark as a politician, Montague first attracted attention with his witty poems and epigrams, and burlesques of Dryden and others. Quick with his mouth as well, he moved from parliamentary speaker to a commissioner of the treasury where he created the National Debt in 1692 and the Bank of England in 1694. He also recalled a currency that was vulnerable to counterfeiting and reissued all new coins with milled edges. Montague himself was vulnerable to charges of financial irregularity, but though impeached twice was never convicted.

Also in the vault is **Edward Montagu** (1625–1672), First Earl of Sandwich, the admiral whose descendant first put a piece of meat between two slices of bread. Sandwich, an able strategist, lost his command after plundering the treasures of several Dutch East India Company ships during the Battle of Lowestoft in 1665. Later he became ambassador to Madrid, and during the Third Dutch War he returned to command the *Royal James*, though he had a premonition of his own death. Indeed, the ship was blown up and the body of Sandwich, sans bread, was nibbled by porpoises and washed up on the Suffolk coast.

George Saville (1633–1695), Marquis of Halifax, has an elaborate monument with a gilt effigy of his wife and himself, their hands clasped in the air. There are four children above, and at the end a classical figure blowing a broken-off trumpet. At each end are pillars supported by four bronze skulls. Lord Keeper of the Privy Seal, Saville was given an informal epitaph by a contemporary who did not appreciate his stance of political moderation: "A man of very great and ready wit, full of life, very pleasant, much turned to satire, but with relation to the public he went backward and forward so many times, changed sides so many times that in conclusion no one trusted him."

The focal point of this chapel is, of course, the tomb of Elizabeth I and her half sister, Mary Tudor. Elizabeth is shown in marble except for a gilt and red crown on her head, and an elaborate piece of jewelry around her neck. The pendant, collar, and crown are actually replacements made since 1975 of similar pieces stolen before 1723.

Around the edge of the monument are elaborate roses and fleurs-de-lis in a continuing alternate pattern. The monument, the joint work of Maximilian Colt and Jean de Critz, was completed in 1607 and is a realistic portrait of the Queen. The Latin inscription translates as, "Partners both in throne and grave, here rest we two sisters, Elizabeth and Mary, in the hope of one resurrection."

The monument accurately depicts the position of both queens in English history. Jointly fathered by a man who hoped to deny the throne to both of them, Elizabeth ruled magnificently, Mary less so.

Mary (1516–1558), the first child of Henry VIII, was sacrificed when the King lost interest in her mother, Queen Katharine. Henry attempted to pronounce Mary illegitimate. When he finally sent for her to come to the palace, it was to help care for her stepsister, baby Elizabeth. She was further betrayed by her younger half brother, Edward VI, who tried to divert the throne to Lady Jane Grey on his deathbed.

When she came to power anyway, at 37, she was tight-lipped and wary, clinging to her religious beliefs as the only constant in her life. But even her faith could not give her the child she so desperately wanted, or make her husband, Philip II of Spain, love her. She had two false pregnancies, later diagnosed as dropsy. Convinced that her problems were due to the heresies of Protestantism in England, Mary followed the example of the Spanish Inquisition and began burning Protestants at the stake. Though she gave them every opportunity to recant, her crusade earned her the epitaph Bloody Mary. In her five years of rule, she also managed to lose Calais, the last English possession in France. It was with some relief that the country turned to her sister:

ELIZABETH I *b. September 7, 1533, Greenwich; d. March 24, 1603, London.* Elizabeth Tudor was born, appropriately, under the sign of Virgo the Virgin. Tall and white-faced with a rooster's crest of hair, she inherited her father's small dark eyes and royal nose. In the spirit of the times she indulged in giant neck ruffs, sleeves resembling beehives, embroidered hoop skirts, and the coy sidecurls which signified maidenhood. She remained a maiden always, but in later years the make-up grew heavy, and luxuriant wigs covered her thinning gray hair. Undeniably vain, the illusion was fostered by the young men who swarmed her Court, eager to obtain land, titles, and gifts for their protestations of undying love.

At eight she declared, "I will never marry," a promise she kept despite pressure from her councilors and her own heart. But marriage and childbed may have held small allure for young Elizabeth. She had already experienced the deaths, at her father's command, of her mother, Anne Boleyn, and her stepmother, Catherine Howard. She had watched another stepmother, Jane Seymour, die from the complications of childbirth, and would lose the last, Catherine Parr, in the same way.

Elizabeth loved her father, Henry VIII, who changed her status from princess to bastard, depending on the political weather. Even as a four-year-old she was aware of fortune's reversals, demanding, "How haps it, Governor, yesterday my Lady Princess, and today but my Lady Elizabeth?" She loved her half-brother, Edward, who rewarded her devotion by bypassing her in the succession in favor of Lady Jane Grey. And she loved her half-sister, Mary Tudor, who had her locked up in the Tower for "treason" and for being Protestant.

It is small wonder that the watchword of her reign was caution. On controversial issues the Queen would not allow herself to be pinned down; even when forced into a decision, as with Mary Queen of Scots who had been shown to be plotting her overthrow, Elizabeth issued an order then retreated from its execution. After Mary was beheaded, Elizabeth complained furiously that she had never meant to have the warrant carried out. She had her

Elizabeth I

councilor, William Davison, tried for having "abused the Queen's confidence." He was heavily fined and kept imprisoned in the Tower for a year but, though never reinstated, drew his salary for the rest of his life.

This same equivocation was instrumental in forging a compromise religion, the Church of England. Initiated by Henry VIII, it did not completely please anyone. The Protestant reform groups felt Elizabeth had let them down by allowing Catholics to continue to say Mass and by refusing to make weekly attendance at church mandatory. Worse, she detested sermons, and would often interrupt the minister or send up notes telling him to cut it short. Roman Catholics were also unhappy; recusant priests were always plotting Elizabeth's overthrow, and she dealt with them severely. During her reign 183 Catholics were executed. Yet despite that, her compromise brought bloodshed to a close.

In foreign policy the Queen took a conservative line. She was slow to take the part of the Netherlands against the Spanish invasion because she feared alienating France and Spain at the same time. It was not until the Spanish Armada seized British ships and attacked England that Elizabeth struck back, routing the invaders with "the Protestant wind." She visited her troops in Tilbury and delivered her famous line, "I know I have the body of a weak and feeble woman, but I have the heart and stomach of a king, and of a king of England too."

Despite this, Elizabeth was judged as a woman. Her romances were public knowledge, and after the wife of Robert Dudley, her probable lover, fell down a flight of stairs and broke her neck, Elizabeth could not consider marrying him. She offered him to Mary Queen of Scots who chose Lord Darnley instead. But when Dudley secretly married Elizabeth's cousin, Lettice, the Queen demanded that both of them be thrown in the Tower. After being told that it would not be legal to imprison her fickle lover, Elizabeth retaliated by initiating a complex courtship dance with the French Duke of Alençon, who was 25 to her 45 years. A Puritan lawyer, John Stubbs, wrote a passionate pamphlet against the idea of her marriage to a foreigner and a Catholic. The Queen had the right hands of Stubbs and his publisher cut off; with his left hand he lifted his hat, cried, "God save Queen Elizabeth," then fainted away.

Such acts did not make Elizabeth popular, but she reigned successfully for another 24 years. She loved dancing, and there was always music at her Court, as well as much "courtly love" and flattery. All the arts flourished. At

69 she let a throat abscess go untreated. For four days she sat on a cushion in her room, refusing to respond to anyone. Finally weakened, she was put to bed where she died several days later. The Virgin Queen had ruled successfully, her honor mostly intact.

At the foot of the tomb is a memorial stone to the casualties of the religious wars which reads, "Near the tomb of Mary and Elizabeth remember before God all those who, divided at the Reformation by different convictions, laid down their lives for Christ and conscience sake."

Westminster Abbey has thoughtfully placed a mirror above the tomb of Princess **Sophia** (d. 1606) so that you can see her childish effigy inside. She rests in a gilt-decorated cradle, a white sheet pulled up to her babyish chin. Only the outer blanket, an ominous black, and her not completely closed eyes, indicate death at three days old.

Next to her is another of James I's daughters, the small painted effigy of Princess **Mary** (1605–1607). She lies facing into the room, her left arm resting on an ornate pillow, her feet against an anguished gold lion. Dressed in a black gown and white cap, she looks older than her two years. Maximilian Colt, who sculpted Elizabeth I, also did the effigies of both girls.

In a small sarcophagus between them rest the final inhabitants of Innocents' Corner. The bones inside it are believed to be those of **Edward V** (1470–1483), Prince of Wales, and his brother **Richard** (1472–1483), Duke of York, the Little Princes said to have been murdered by their uncle, Richard III. When the bones were discovered at the foot of a Tower staircase during some tile repair work, Charles II had them reburied here in 1674.

There is no conclusive proof that Richard III eliminated the young princes who barred his way to the throne, but he is the likeliest suspect. He abducted Edward V, after the death of his own brother, Edward IV, and had him placed in the Tower for safekeeping; he then blackmailed his sister-in-law Elizabeth into surrendering the younger boy. Although he obtained the throne in 1483 by declaring his nephews illegitimate on the grounds that their father had been engaged to someone else before marrying Elizabeth, no more was seen of them.

From here retrace your steps to the main part of the chapel in which a large number of royal personages are interred.

The first monuments in the center of the room before the altar are the black marble sarcophagus to **George II** (1683–1760) and his queen, **Caroline** (1683–1737), inscribed with their names and scepters. George was a small, red-faced man who kicked his wig around the room in fits of temper when not recounting his military exploits at Oudenarde. Intelligent, bawdy, and chastely flirtatious, Caroline made most of the political decisions. To do so she humored George by allowing his mistresses to live in the palace. The 280-pound Robert Walpole, statesman and financial wizard, was not blind to her power and enjoyed her confidence, once ironically remarking that "I have the right sow by the ear." Caroline recognized and encouraged the talent of Leibniz, Handel, and Newton.

The Queen was not blindly maternal, however, commenting after her son **Frederick Louis** (1707–1751) had been turned out of the palace, "My dear firstborn is the greatest ass, and the greatest liar . . . and the greatest beast in the whole world and I heartily wish he were out of it." King George was also unhappy with a son who, at 30, was still breaking windows for excitement and writing satires of his parents. When Frederick Louis died after a blow from a tennis ball resulted in a burst abscess, he was buried here "without anthem or organ."

Queen Caroline's death was a different story. Handel wrote her funeral anthem, and a grief-stricken George II refused her deathbed urgings to marry again. A daughter had to remove the queens from decks of cards so that he would not be ambushed by sorrow and break down. He arranged for their coffins to have a removable side so that their remains could be mingled, a wish that was carried out. The years after her death, which brought political unrest, skirmishes with William Pitt, and war with Germany, were not satisfying ones for the King.

George enjoyed one final triumph when, reliving past glories, he became the last British monarch to lead his troops into battle at the victorious Battle of Dettingen. His death was far less noble. Sitting on a throne of a different kind he died of a heart attack brought on by his prodigious exertions toward ending his constipation.

In the monument just behind George and Caroline is **Edward VI** (1537–1553), the son of Jane Seymour and Henry VIII, who succeeded to the throne briefly, at nine, after his father's death. A precocious child, Edward fended off interfering uncles and helped compose the *Book of Common Prayer*. The year before he died at 15 he contracted either smallpox or measles which weakened his constitution, leaving him open to consumption. Edward was the first sovereign to be interred using the burial service from his prayer book.

Back behind the altar are the effigies of **Henry VII** (1457–1509), builder of the chapel, and his queen, **Elizabeth of York** (1465–1503). They rest behind an ornately designed metal enclosure with locked gates. Around their joint coffin are cameos showing scenes of great piety and learning. Four gilt cherubs decorate the end, flanking a crown and the family's coat of arms. The bronze gilt effigies, the work of the great sculptor, Pietro Torrigiano, have their hands upraised in prayer.

In creating the chapel Henry had no idea that his 38-year-old wife would be its first burial. Elizabeth of York, sister of the Little Princes of the Tower, actually had a better claim to the throne than her husband, but their marriage made that academic. She was content to bear his children; greatly upset at the death of their firstborn, Arthur, at 15, she died the following year on her thirty-eighth birthday, in childbirth.

Henry VII, once settled on the throne, was a prudent and economic man, good at collecting taxes and cutting corners to lift his country out of debt. He also conserved funds by staying out of war with France in 1492, and making the French king pay him for his abstinence. What came to nothing, fortunately, was his scheme to marry Europe's richest woman, Jane of Castile. He abandoned it reluctantly when he learned that "Crazy Jane" brought the embalmed body of her first husband, Philip, everywhere she went.

At the foot of the tomb there was originally a small altar which held the tibia of St. George and a piece of the true cross.

Also in the vault with Henry and Elizabeth is **James I** (1566–1625). The King who commissioned the monuments of his cousin, Elizabeth I, his mother, Mary Queen of Scots, and his baby daughters, has none to be remembered by. But James was not valued in his own time. The English saw this transplanted Scottish king as unappealing, attracted to other men, and a spendthrift. He inspired the Gunpowder Plot in 1605, an attempt by embittered Catholics to get rid of him, still celebrated in England as Guy Fawkes Day. The activities for which future generations were grateful — his introduction of the game of golf to England from Scotland, his championing of Inigo Jones, and the King James Version of the Bible — were not appreciated.

One of James I's favorite males is buried in the alcove to the left of the altar. **George Villiers** (1592–1628), First Duke of Buckingham, was the first person of non-royal descent to be buried in the Henry VII Chapel. Although the service was performed quietly for fear of public outcry, his widow, the Duchess, subsequently erected an impressive monument with their effigies sculpted by Hubert Le Sueur. Perhaps to justify the company they are in, both are wearing crowns. Villiers was assassinated at 36 by a disgruntled soldier who explained that he felt he "should do God good service if he killed the Duke." Shortly before his death Villiers' father's ghost was said to have appeared to an old servant, telling him to warn his son that if he did not do something to abate the antagonism of the populace his days would be numbered.

In the next chapel are **John Sheffield**(1648–1721), Duke of Buckingham, shown wearing Roman armour, and his widow **Catherine** (d. 1743), dressed in more conventional robes. Time is shown spiriting three of their four children away. Catherine, the illegitimate daughter of James II, always insisted on being treated as royalty.

The Duke, who composed poetry as well as engaging in warfare and politics, preferred the excitement of London to his country estate. But when the Great Plague broke out, he fled to Yorkshire and endeared himself to his tenants—

so much so that a large group of them accompanied him on the first lap of his return journey. Because it was in their best interests to have him present on the estate, there were many cries of, "At what time may we hope for the happiness of seeing Your Lordship again?" Finally, unable to evade the question any longer, he replied, "My worthy friends, I shall make a point of being with you again, at the next plague."

Buckingham's epitaph, translated from the Latin, shows a more mature thoughtfulness. "I lived doubting but not dissolute; I died unresolved, not unresigned. Ignorance and error are part of human nature; I trust in an all-powerful and benevolent God. Oh, thou Being of Beings, have mercy on me."

Next door in the Royal Air Force Chapel is an impressive stained glass window created by Hugh Easton, and sculptures of St. George and King Arthur. The chapel commemorates 1,495 airmen killed in the Battle of Britain in September 1940.

In the next alcove is Dean **Arthur Penrhyn Stanley**

William Thynne

(1815–1881) whom all aficionados of Westminster Abbey know as the author of *Historical Memorials of Westminster Abbey*.

In the final chapel is a large monument to **Ludovic Stuart** (1574–1624), Duke of Richmond and Lenox. The impressive bronze figures which hold up the canopy represent Faith, Hope, Charity, and Truth and were sculpted by Hubert Le Sueur. The artist also created the Duke of Buckingham's monument across the way.

After leaving this large area, enter the smaller chapel on the right. As you come in you will see a plaque and worn cameo to **Cecil Rhodes** (1853–1902), founder of the Rhodes scholarships. Rhodes is buried in the Matoppo Hills in South Africa, the country in which he made a fortune in diamond mining.

The first tomb in the center of the chapel is that of **Margaret Douglas** (1515–1578), Countess of Lennox and the grandmother of James I. Margaret, reputedly more beautiful than her alabaster effigy, fell in and out of favor. She was committed to the Tower for becoming involved with the wrong man, then later for supporting her sons in treason against the Crown.

Mary Queen of Scots, hands clasped in prayer, has a marble effigy sculpted by Cornelius and William Cure under a very elaborate black and gold canopy. Around her are the smaller painted family members. At the end of her coffin a fierce lion, sitting upright with a crown and scepter and representing Scotland, lets you know whom you are viewing.

MARY STUART *b. December 8, 1542, Linlithgow, Scotland; d. February 8, 1587, London.* When the battle-fatigued James V lay dying, his last hope was for a son to continue his rule. Instead, word came of the birth of a daughter, Mary. The Scottish king turned his face to the wall to die, cursing his dynasty. "The Devil take it. It came with a lass and it will go with a lass." It was not an accurate prediction — his grandson was to rule England as James I — but the sense of doom he felt was visited on Mary in ways he could not have foreseen.

The young Queen of Scotland was universally described as beautiful, enchanting, and kind. Her charm was further enhanced when from the age of five she was raised in the the French Court as the betrothed of the young dauphin, Francis. They were married when she was 16 and he was a year younger. But Francis was a sickly boy whose internal organs had never developed properly; he was terrified of his mother, Catherine de Medici, who favored his younger brother. After the unexpected death of his father, Francis and Mary ruled briefly before he died of an abscess in his ear. It was probably malignant, but there were the usual rumors of poisoning that the de Medicis inspired. Catherine seized power, and Mary was forced to return to Scotland. Before leaving her beloved France she was proclaimed Queen of England as well.

Scotland, in her absence, had become largely Protestant, ruled during her minority by her illegitimate half brother, the Earl of Moray. The Catholic Mary had to contend with Protestant reformer John Knox howling outside the palace and pronouncing her one of the "Regiment of Monstrous Women," along with her mother and Elizabeth I. But with the help of her advisers she kept a religious balance, and steadied diplomatic ties with England and Europe.

If she had remained single and dedicated, as her cousin Elizabeth did, Mary's reign might have been as long. But she was not interested in sacrifing her passions—dancing, riding, and pageantry—to rule a damp, barbaric country. She also wanted to marry again. Her first cousin, Henry Darnley, four years younger, seemed a good choice. Next in succession to the English throne, he was tall and attractive.

The marriage, in 1565, was a mistake. Mary soon fell out of love with him. The bejeweled and effeminate Darnley retaliated by drinking in the streets and escorting prostitutes around Edinburgh. He also abetted in the murder of court musician David Rizzio, to whom Mary had turned for emotional comfort. Rizzio, rumored to be a papal spy and her lover, was widely resented for his influence over the Queen.

Mary, who was pregnant, never forgave her husband for the terrible scene in her apartments in which the shrieking Rizzio, clinging to her skirts, was butchered. She next turned to James Bothwell, Earl of Hepburn. Bothwell, a loyal supporter of the Queen but an ambitious and brutal womanizer, was rumored to have raped her. Mary, infatuated, had written him love letters and continued the affair.

What happened next has been hotly debated for four hundred years. In 1567 the house in which Darnley was recovering from either smallpox or syphilis blew up. When the smoke cleared, his body was found in the garden—not burned or blown apart, but strangled. Mary's supporters blamed the Protestant lords who wanted Darnley (and perhaps Mary) eliminated. Her detractors fingered Bothwell, with Mary cooperating. But Bothwell was acquitted of the crime in a sham trial. He immediately divorced his wife and, as an amazed world watched, he and Mary were wed three months after the murder.

The marriage lasted another month. After a losing battle with the Protestant lords, Mary was dragged through the streets of Edinburgh to cries of, "Burn the whore!" and "Drown her!" Imprisoned in Loch Liven Castle where she miscarried twins, the Queen was forced to abdicate in favor of her infant son. The Earl of Moray would rule in his stead. Bothwell escaped, but was to end up in solitary confinement in a prison in Denmark, chained so that he could neither completely sit down nor stand up.

Mary Queen of Scots

Imprisoned on an island with the Douglas family as caretakers, Mary's extraordinary charm almost saved her. Two of the Douglas boys plotted her escape and joined with an army of five thousand to place her back on the throne. But the army was defeated by the new rulers. Believing it to be her only option, Mary fled to England and threw herself on the mercy of Elizabeth.

One might call down the ages to try and stop her. Elizabeth did not immediately condemn her. But Mary was tried in absentia for her crimes in Scotland, found guilty, and kept imprisoned. For 18 years she was kept in dark and drafty confinement, caring for her pets, and writing secret letters, while developing crippling rheumatism.

But she was not forgotten. Plots were constantly being fomented in Mary's name to restore her to power, and a letter in which she appeared to welcome a scheme for Elizabeth's assassination was seized. Whether the letter was real or a forgery hardly mattered. As long as Mary was alive, Elizabeth's throne was not secure. Convicted of treason on February 1, 1587, she was executed a week later, her lovely head chopped off at Fotheringhay.

The gilt effigy of Lady **Margaret Beaufort** (1443–1509) does not try to hide her age. Her wrinkled hands are raised in prayer, her face is solemn and heavily lined. She is wearing a severe wimple with widow's robes and at her feet is a sensitive, doglike creature known as a Beaufort Yale. Originally the head, hands, and head covering were painted. The monument was created in 1511 by Pietro Torrigiano, who also sculpted the effigies of her son, Henry VII, and Elizabeth of York. Widowed four times, Margaret turned to religion, establishing charities and ruling those around her with a formidable piety. She endowed two colleges at Cambridge, Christ's and St. John's, and founded professorships of divinity there and at Oxford.

Nearby, the extremely large marble statue memorializing **Catherine Walpole** (d. 1737) looks down disdainfully on her audience; the sculpture is a copy of a Roman figure depicting Modesty. Catherine was the mother of Horace Walpole, whose letters and reminiscences give a graphic picture of Georgian England.

In the niche to the left is the monument to the Dukes of Albemarle, **George Monck** (1608–1670) and his son **Christopher** (1653–1688). It shows an elaborate mast with anchors and has two figures and a cameo of General Monck. Although the nautical emblems appear to refer to Monck's flagship, the *Royal Charles*, his most important act was the restoration to the throne of Charles II and the banishment of Cromwell. Not surprisingly, Charles was his chief mourner.

In front of this chapel is a plain altar, covered with a blue cloth and a tapestry. An oriental rug is on the floor and a tapestry showing the descent from the cross hangs from the wall. Above the altar are five stylized angels and statues on either side. The center statue is missing. In the floor in front are several small inlaid stones.

The first is in memory of the "Merry Monarch," **Charles II** (1630–1685), one of England's most entertaining kings.

His beginnings were harrowing—at 19 he saw his father die at the hands of Oliver Cromwell and spent the next 11 years as a fugitive himself—but once he returned to the throne, anecdotes abounded. Charles kept a cheerful collection of mistresses, from Barbara Villiers to Elinor Gwynn, and begged his friends from his deathbed, "Don't let poor Nelly starve." He commented that England had worse weather but a better climate than any country, and reassured his younger brother James II about his lax security precautions. "Don't worry, Jamie, they'll never kill me to make you king."

The main role of Charles II was to re-establish the English monarchy; he avoided conflict and the stirring up of wars. On his deathbed, before dying of a stroke, he proclaimed himself a Catholic. He was buried at Westminster Abbey at night with little ceremony.

James II ruled only three years after his older brother's death before abdicating. **Mary II** (1662–1694) and her husband **William III** (1650–1702) of Holland had been invited by Whig and Tory leaders to rule in place of the unpopular, strongly Roman Catholic James, and accepted; James fled for his life to France. William and Mary are buried under this paving. Mary, who wept through her wedding, fell in love with William afterwards and insisted that he rule England with her. Always self-effacing, she preferred to echo his political policies rather than make decisions of her own. She was lonely, estranged from her parents and sister, Anne, and without children or her husband's love when she died of smallpox at 32.

The Protestant William, no more sentimental about England than about his English wife, seized the country's assets to carry on his war against France and Catholicism. At the same time, Parliament was busy strengthening its power through the Bill of Rights which, beside ascendancy, gave that body control of the army and finances. Both bodies worked to good ends: England was put in a position of great military strength, and a balance between King and Parliament had been reached. William died after his horse stumbled into a mole hole and threw him, breaking his collarbone. After the accident his lung became fatally inflamed.

William and Mary's successor, **Anne** (1665–1714), who was Queen from 1702 to 1714, is here with her husband, **George of Denmark** (d. 1708). If Anne's likeness were here, it would have shown a woman over six feet tall with a melancholy face. As an adult she suffered from indigestion, bowel trouble, and gout, and often had to be conveyed from place to place by chair. Constant pregnancy also took its toll: in an effort to produce an heir she suffered endless miscarriages and gave birth to 16 children who died at birth. The seventeenth, though hydrocephalic, lived to the age of 11. Anne's agreeable partner, Prince George, had been nicknamed "little est-il possible" by her father, because he made non-committal responses to everything asked of him.

Although Anne maintained England as a Church of England bastion and allowed Parliament to assume its new powers, she fell under the spell of Sarah, the Duchess of Marlborough, and, by extension, her husband, John Churchill. The Duke of Marlborough was a military genius and helped set the foundations of the British Empire. But Anne, though slow-witted, finally had to admit that the contempt with which others thought Sarah treated her was real. The Marlboroughs were banished, but it made Anne no happier. She was ready for death at 49 when it came from complications of erysipelas.

Nearby on the wall is a bronze plaque which was presented to Westminster Abbey on its 900th anniversary by Trinity Church in New York. It mentions William and Mary who established Trinity Church in 1698 by land grants.

CHAPEL OF ST. NICHOLAS

William Cecil (1520–1598) and **Mildred Cooke Cecil** (d. 1589), Lord and Lady Burghley, have the most impressive monument in this chapel. The two reclining figures — Lady Burghley and her daughter **Anne** (d. 1588) are polychromed and red-robed, with four family members garbed in bright blues and purples kneeling around them. The three young women weepers are Burghley granddaughters, two of whom died in 1587. On the tier above is the kneeling figure of Lord Burghley wearing his royal robes and clasping a sword; above everything is the coat of arms. At the foot of Lady Burghley is a horse representing her family, the Cookes.

Mildred Cecil was a Greek scholar and one of the most intellectual women of her day. Lord Burghley, was Elizabeth I's secretary of state and Lord Treasurer and one of England's most able statesmen, although not a man of deep literary sensibilities. Elizabeth had ordered a payment of £100 to Edmund Spenser for some poems she had commissioned from him. But when Burghley took exception — "What, all this for a song?" — the Queen advised her treasurer to give Spenser "what was reason." When time passed and the poet received nothing, he presented to the Queen another poem:

> I was promised on a time
> To have reason for my rhyme.
> From that time, unto this season,
> I received neither rhyme nor reason.

Elizabeth, after a sharp reprimand to Lord Burghley, reinstituted the £100.

Perhaps Burghley's aversion to poetry had to do with the fact that his daughter Anne was unhappily married to an eccentric and hot-tempered poet, Edward de Vere. De Vere, who loudly questioned the paternity of his first child, emerged in the twentieth century as a contender for the authorship of Shakespeare's plays.

Anne Stanhope (d. 1587), Duchess of Somerset, has a painted effigy with a ruff and crown, lying on two pillows. The symbol at her feet is a small castle painted blue and the epitaph, "Many children bare this lady unto her lord of either sort, to wit: . . ." and then lists the names of three boys and six girls. She died on Easter Sunday at age 90.

Sir **George** and Lady **Elizabeth Fane** (d. 1619) have painted effigies kneeling upright and appearing to be in a box at a theater. His hand is resting on a skull on a podium.

CHAPEL OF ST. EDMUND

The Brocas monument is impressive, showing a gisant (a reclining figure) wearing his knightly helmet and a kind of armour. He has a thin drooping moustache. His feet rest on a lion. "Here lies buried Sir **Bernard Brocas**, third son of Sir John Brocas," the inscription above the tomb begins. It tells the story of his attempts to reinstate Richard II, explaining at the end that, "Sir Bernard's dispersing, he with many of his adherents, became an easy prey to the townsmen of Reading who executed several on the spot, but sent Sir Bernard to London where he was beheaded on Tower Hill in January, 1400."

Unfortunately, the inscription is mistaken. It is the father of Sir Bernard Brocas who died in 1396 who is actually buried here. The explanation of the presence of the crowned Moor's head on his crest as due to the notion that he once cut off the King of Morocco's head is also a later invention.

Legends abound in St. Edmund's Chapel. It is true enough that the statue of Lord John Russell's daughter, **Elizabeth Russell** (1575–1601), was the first effigy to be shown sitting up in Westminster Abbey. She is seated in a cane chair with the words in Latin, "Not dead but sleeping." But her finger pointing down toward the skull near her feet helped create the myth that she died after pricking her finger with a needle—a judgment on her for sewing on a Sunday. Elizabeth Russell, a godchild of Elizabeth I, actually died of consumption.

Lord **John Russell** (d. 1584) is a good-looking man with blond curly hair and moustache; he lies in repose in a polychromed red robe with white ermine trim. Two female family members hold his coat of arms above him. Interestingly, by his feet where an animal symbolizing the family usually goes is a small girl dressed in a blue robe, lying with her feet stretched out into the room.

Edward Bulwer-Lytton (1803–1873), the author of *The Last Days of Pompeii* (1834) and a series of domestic comedies beginning with *The Caxtons* (1849), is entombed in the floor. His own domestic life was not so entertaining. After the success of Wilkie Collins' novel, *The Woman in White* (1860), Lady Lytton wrote Collins to complain that his villain, Count Fosco, was a pallid creature compared to an example she could show him. "When next you want a character of that description I trust you will not disdain to come to me. I know a villain and have one in my eye at this moment that would far eclipse anything I have read in books."

Subsequently the Lyttons got a legal separation, and in 1839 she wrote her own novel, *Cheverly, or the Man of Honour*, to castigate Bulwer-Lytton. Declared insane in 1858, she lived on to 1882.

Jane Seymour (1541–1560) has a tablet set into the wall in rich gilt with her coat of arms above it. She is not to be confused with Jane Seymour (1509–1537), third wife of Henry VIII, who is buried in St. George's Chapel, Windsor.

One of the earliest burials here was **John of Eltham**, Earl of Cornwall, who died in 1336 at 19. His alabaster effigy by the entrance is interesting for his naturalistic face and the two small angels at his head ready to bear his soul away.

CHAPEL OF EDWARD THE CONFESSOR

This chapel has been saved for last because it can only be entered on the north side; traffic flows in a one-way direction and there are vergers in each area to answer questions. Considered the most sacred area of Westminster Abbey because of the presence of Edward the Confessor and such artifacts as the Coronation Chair and the Stone of Scone, it could easily fill a chapter itself.

In the past the Chapel's treasures were treated rather casually. In 1766 a schoolboy reached through a hole in the coffin of Richard II and extracted his jawbone. (Embarrassed descendants returned it in 1906.) Brass effigies and gilt weepers were often stolen, as were the silver head and scepter of Henry V. The mummified body of his queen, Catherine de Valois, was in an open coffin for two hundred years. No Sleeping Beauty, she stirred not when kissed on the mouth by Samuel Pepys in 1669.

Visits to this Chapel have been formalized since then. To get a sense of its history as you enter, look first to the center, to the tall shrine of **Edward the Confessor** (ca. 1004–1066). It rests on a colossal stone base and is made of green porphyry with gilt decoration. The sick knelt in the recessed areas, hoping for a miracle from Edward's remains. Edward himself has been moved at least five times, and has had his tomb redecorated through the centuries. The magnificent gold images of early saints and kings placed on the tomb by Henry III have long since disappeared. But Edward himself has not been forgotten.

Son of the piquantly named Ethelred the Unready, Edward was said to be of good size and an albino. He was raised in Normandy while the Danish invaders ruled, but acceded to the throne peacefully. Although his own wife, Edith, was Danish he did not trust his mother, Emma, who after his own father's death had married the Danish conqueror, Canute. He seized her property and kept her under surveillance.

Rumors of Edward's celibacy spread when in 1051, perhaps under the influence of a Norman faction at Court, he banished his father-in-law, Earl Godwin, and ordered Edith to a nunnery. The Godwins returned a year later with an army, and Edward gave up control of the kingdom to Earl Godwin while he pursued religion and rebuilt Westminster Abbey. In later years he was believed to be a healer and a dreamer of religious prophecies. His subjects flocked to touch "the Confessor" and be cured. The miracles continued after his death. In 1161 Pope Alexander III issued a Bull of Canonization, making Edward the Confessor a saint.

The monument to **Henry III** (1207–1272) is an oversized stone coffin with gilt and green marble insets. On top of it is a slightly smaller one with red porphyry insets from Egypt, quarried before the time of the Roman Empire; a gilt effigy rests above that. The effigy, executed by William Torel, has the smooth-flowing, idealized look of the French kings at St. Denis. Originally the entire tomb was covered with a fine gold mosaic.

It is not surprising that Henry's effigy has a French aspect. After his marriage to Eleanor of Provence her in-laws swarmed the countryside, devouring titles, offices, and lands. Henry introduced French art and architecture, and rebuilt Westminster Abbey as a Gothic cathedral. Generous beyond a fault, the King gave freely to charity as well as family members. His military skills were non-existent, however. He nearly lost his throne to his ambitious brother-in-law, Simon de Montfort, before being rescued by his own son, Edward I.

Eleanor of Castile (1245–1290), the wife of Edward I, is interred in an oversized stone coffin with a design of shields on the side. Her gilt effigy, like that of her father-in-law, was sculpted by William Torel and bears a resemblance to it. Eleanor's wavy hair and smooth curved cheek belie her 45 years and the fact that she traveled everywhere with her husband, giving birth to 17 children along the way.

The will of **Henry V** (1387–1422) directed that a high chantry chapel be placed over his tomb in Westminster Abbey, and this has been done. Delicate spiral staircases lead to an upper story, and the whole area is a mass of statues, canopies, turrets, and bas-reliefs. These show scenes from his coronation and military campaigns. Henry's effigy was once covered in silver with a solid silver head. Now the oak beneath is all that you can see. He is holding the remains of a papyrus and lies on top of a carved bier with the crown on his head (his head is a replacement made of polyester resin) brighter than the rest of the monument.

In life Henry was a tall, pious man with an iron will and no self-doubt. He passed into legend with his victory against the French at Agincourt, in which he used an army a fraction of the size of his opponents'. Henry had little time for a personal life; on his deathbed with dysentery at 35 he was busy making arrangements for his nine-month-old son, Henry VI's, future rule.

Edward III (1312–1377) is carved in dark gilt with stylized hair and beard, although his face and nose are more realistic. He is wearing his coronation robes. On the sides of his marble tomb are spaces for bronze effigies of 12 of his 14 children. Only six remain.

Edward came to the throne at 14 after his father, Edward II, was murdered by his mother, Queen Isabella, and her lover, Roger Mortimer. Four years later Edward III achieved autonomy by having Mortimer executed. His mother was sent to live in luxury in a remote castle in Norfolk. Tall, handsome, and congenial, he was a brilliant warrior, best remembered for the Battle of Crecy. Yet his successes were undermined by the Black Death which swept back and forth over London, and the death of his heir, Edward the Black Prince, in 1376. Escaping into senility and the influence of a greedy mistress, he died in ignominy, stripped of even the rings on his fingers.

Philippa (1314–1369) has her own monument of black marble, and a more realistic effigy. Originally the tomb had 70 figures, mostly angels and weepers, but these were stolen over time. Only the Duchess of Lancaster, holding a monkey, now remains, protected from theft by a grille. Philippa married Edward III when she was 13, occasionally accompanying him on military campaigns. Queen's College, Oxford, was founded in her honor.

On the other side of Edward III are the effigies of his grandson, **Richard II** (1367–1400), and Richard's wife, **Anne of Bohemia** (1366–1394). They lie, hand in hand, under chapel-like headdresses, their clothing stamped with the White Hart, the Lion of Bohemia, and several other family insignia. The tomb, built for Anne, whom Richard loved passionately, was originally decorated with precious stones. When she died at the Palace of Sheen, the grief-stricken king cursed the building and had it razed.

Richard II, son of Edward the Black Prince, came to power at age ten. He successfully handled the Peasants' Revolt four years later, though he emerged from it with the attitude that God had given him the power of absolute rule. He bided his time while five Lords Appellant governed during his minority, looking on as they sentenced several members of his Court to death. Then in 1397 he had the Lords strangled or exiled.

During his later rule Henry rebuilt parts of Westminster Abbey, sponsored Chaucer and other writers, and invented the handkerchief. He also imposed astronomical taxes, and seized estates. In 1399 he was overtaken by his enraged cousin, Lord Bolingbroke (Henry IV), who forced him to abdicate, kept him imprisoned in Pontefract Castle, and had him murdered there the following year.

Catherine de Valois (1401–1437) lies within the altar. The French princess was 19 when she married Henry V and had already given birth to Henry VI when her husband died two years later. By marrying a Welshman, Owen Tudor, she began the Tudor line. Her son Edmund Tudor fathered Henry VII. In front of the altar is an elaborately carved screen which shields an upstairs chapel. This chapel has about 20 seats but is not open to the public.

In the sanctuary is a small monument to **Anne of Cleves**

(1515–1557), sometime Queen of England. Whatever was on the monument in bas-relief cannot be distinguished any longer. Anne was procured by Thomas Cromwell for Henry VIII when his third wife, Jane Seymour, died after childbirth. She was pronounced unsatisfactory by the King, who compared her to a Flanders brood mare, and refused to consummate the marriage. Anne wisely agreed to an annulment, and lived unobtrusively in England until her death.

On the other side of the doorway through which you entered is **Edward I** (1239–1307). His chest tomb is of plain gray marble and has the inscription, "Edwardus Primus Scotorum Malleus" (The Hammer of the Scots) and "Pactum Serva" (Keep Faith). He wanted to be buried in a plain tomb until Scotland was wholly conquered, then moved to one of beauty. He never was.

Unlike his gentle and disorganized father, Edward I was lean and vengeful. Known as Longshanks because of his six-foot-two-inch frame, he was an effective warrior who had no qualms about capital punishment. Anyone caught pilfering from the Church had his skin nailed to the door, and Edward kept Scottish noblewoman Lady Buchan hanging in a crown-shaped cage outside Berwick Castle for four years for her role in crowning Robert the Bruce King of Scotland behind his back. When he was not out on a campaign, he helped formulate the English Constitution and develop the House of Commons.

Realizing he was dying within sight of the Scottish border on his last campaign, Edward demanded that his flesh be boiled away and the bones carried at the head of the army. Instead he was sent back to Westminster Abbey for a proper burial.

Out in the South Ambulatory is a plain niche in the wall with a black-painted bench and a stonework design above it. It says, "This tomb is by tradition that of **Sebert**, king of the East Saxons who according to medieval legend was the first founder of Westminster Abbey." There is little historical evidence to support that legend; in 1306 the tomb was plundered for relics and the preserved hand and forearm which were found were assumed to be his. Sebert, the first king to be converted and baptized, died in 616, the year that the Abbey was consecrated.

Westminster Abbey

Poets' Corner

WHEN NATHANIEL HAWTHORNE visited Poets' Corner in 1855, he felt an immediate kinship with those buried here. "It is a very delightful thing to find yourself at once among them," Hawthorne confided to his journal. "I never felt this kind of interest in any other tomb-stones, or in the presence of any other dead people; and one is pleased, too, at finding them all there together, however separated by distant generations, or by personal hostility or other circumstances, while they lived."

Although all the heroes of literature seem to be memorialized in this chapel, from Chaucer and Shakespeare to Dickens and T.S. Eliot, not all of them are buried here. Many have chosen to be interred in their native villages. We will be describing their memorials and epitaphs if interesting, but will give biographical information only for those physically in residence.

The first statue of note, on your right, is that of **David Garrick** (1717–1799). He is striking a dramatic pose, appearing to push back the theater curtain. Seated at his feet are two women, one with the mask of Comedy, the other holding the mask of Tragedy. About this memorial Charles Lamb (who is not here) commented severely, "I was struck with the affected attitude of . . . the celebrated Mr. Garrick. . . . I own I was not a little scandalized at the introduction of theatrical airs and gestures into a place set apart to remind us of the saddest realities."

The statue of David Garrick, with its sense of sudden appearance, is emblematic of the way he burst on the theater scene in 1741, inspiring a bad case of "Garrick fever." Alexander Pope raved, "That young man never had

Joseph Addison

his equal and never will have a rival." Others claimed that they had never known what acting was until they witnessed Garrick on stage. Short, with an elastic face, the actor combined high drama with a natural delivery.

David Garrick's family did not join the applause. They looked down on "players." Worse, Garrick had abandoned the wine business he shared with his brother, Peter. And soon he had a mistress, actress Peg Woffington. Despite many predictions he did not marry her, saving himself for Austrian dancer Eva Marie Viegel (Violette). It was an astoundingly happy marriage; childless, they could focus completely on one another.

Besides acting and writing plays such as *Miss in Her Teens* (1747) and *A Peep Behind the Curtain* (1767), Garrick was instrumental in reviving interest in Shakespeare. He was especially praised for his Richard III and King Lear. Warmhearted, vain, quick to quarrel and make up, the feisty little actor held London in thrall. It took a combination of gallstones, gout, and shingles to remove him at 72. His funeral was the social event of the year.

Nearby is a theatrical descendant of David Garrick, the most recent burial in Poets' Corner:

LAURENCE OLIVIER *b. Dorking, May 22, 1907; d. London, July 11, 1989.* Laurence Olivier believed in the effect of names upon destiny. If he had been born Laurence Oliver, he once claimed, he would have been a fumbling country parson, spouting inanities in the pulpit, and greeting parishioners at the door. His choice of a clergyman for his unfortunate near-namesake seems deliberate. His own father went from headmaster to minister in 1902, declaring that his true mission was "older souls to save, not young minds to develop." Gerard Olivier's career change caused an irrevocable rift between himself and his wife, Agnes, a sophisticated young woman from a family of freethinkers; their third child, Laurence, became the battlefield on which they fought.

Agnes Olivier overprotected her younger son badly, refusing to let him play sports and games because they were too dangerous—and, of course, because it would deprive Gerard of the athletic son he wanted. Gerard had fingered Laurence for the ministry and, when the boy was nine, sent him to All Saints, a strict boarding school for the sons of the clergy. Ironically, it was at All Saints that Olivier's acting ability was first recognized.

The struggle for his soul continued. When she was dying of a brain tumor when Laurence was 14, his mother whispered to him, "Darling Larry, no matter what your father says, be an actor. Be a great actor. For me." Predictably, his father banned him from participating in school plays. But Gerard came around gradually, and, at 17, young Olivier was headed for drama school.

The theatrical world was slow to recognize his genius. He had stage presence and a rich speaking voice. But he was considered strange-looking, with an undeveloped body and coal miner's face. He had a way of clowning and overacting on stage which alienated veteran actors. By 21 he had settled down slightly, and received glowing reviews as Alfred Lord Tennyson's Harold.

But unlike some actors who, on an upward course, continue to spiral, Olivier bounced between acclaim and censure. Part of the reason was the risk he took with roles; the rest was an inability to admit to his own limitations. When he and his first wife, Jill Esmond, went to Hollywood in 1931 as a British package deal, Olivier was found to have little screen personality. Unable to shift from the theatrical mannerisms and gestures of the stage, he found his services quickly terminated.

The actor returned, disgruntled, to England, and in an Old Vic production in 1935 put on a controversial Romeo, playing him as a virile young Italian of high animal spirits and low poetry. An athletic Hamlet followed, concentrating more on Douglas Fairbanks' acrobatics than melancholy. It was panned by the critics, but loved by the public. Olivier's more subdued portrayal of Henry V in 1937 pleased everyone.

He allowed his future wife, Vivien Leigh, to lure him back to Hollywood and did a creditable job in *Wuthering Heights* while she became Scarlett O'Hara in *Gone with the Wind*. Because they were both still married to other people and had young children, David O. Selznick would not star them together. In the end they were glad to return to London.

It was a wise move. Olivier came into his own with stage performances of Richard III and Oedipus which, according to one critic, "pulled lightning down from the sky." He also did well with film versions of *Henry V* (1944) and *Hamlet* (1948) which he directed as well as starred in. In 1947 he was knighted and, 23 years later, was awarded the Order of Merit which made him a lord. As Vivien Leigh's bouts with manic-depression worsened, the couple separated, and in 1961 Olivier married a third actress, Joan Plowright, whom he said reminded him of his mother.

A new career began when he became director of the Royal National Theater and played stage and TV roles in

British productions. And he had the last word in the Hollywood that had scorned his screen ability, triumphing in character roles. His genius remained strong; his body betrayed him with prostate cancer and a debilitating muscular disease, dermatomyositis.

Olivier would have enjoyed his memorial service in Westminster Abbey, a pageant which celebrated his life and triumphs. Derek Jacobi brought in the crown he wore in *Richard III*, and Michael Caine carried Olivier's Oscar which had been awarded in 1979 for lifetime achievement. Other mementos were laid on the altar, and speeches given. The man who wanted as an epitaph, "Here lies Laurence Olivier. He was funny," was given considerably more.

Joseph Addison is buried in Henry VII's Chapel, but his memorial is in Poets' Corner. It shows him in classical dress clasping a scroll with one hand and holding his robe shut with the other. The marble statue is larger-than-life and has several books, one with its pages curling carelessly. On the base are a cluster of unhappy Greek figures contemplating Addison's loss. (See Chapter 3 on the Royal Tombs for his biography.)

On the wall behind Addison is a bust of **Thomas Macaulay** (1800–1859). His stone is in the floor with the sentiment, "His body is buried in peace, but his name liveth forevermore."

Widely regarded as a prodigy, Macaulay had the kind of memory which enabled him to glance at a book once, then recite it accurately 40 years later. As an adult he divided his time between Parliament and political ventures such as establishing an educational system and legal code for India, and writing biographical essays and a brilliant five-volume narrative, *The History of England from the Accession of James the Second*. A contemporary commenting that Macaulay had become more agreeable since his return from India said, "His enemies might perhaps have said before (though I never did so) that he talked rather too much; but now he has occasional flashes of silence that make his conversation perfectly delightful."

The memorial of George Frideric Handel is a happy combination of an interesting monument and a great man. Best of all, he is actually here. Two stories above his stone in the floor, Handel is shown reclining against a drape-covered table. Behind him is an organ and a domed ceiling in front of which an angel plays the harp while seated on a cloud. A trumpet lies on the table to his left and a cello is seen peeking through the drape underneath the table. Handel is displaying the score of the larghetto "I Know

That My Redeemer Liveth" from *Messiah*. Curiously "Messiah" is spelled with just one "s" here.

GEORGE FRIDERIC HANDEL *b. February 23, 1685, Halle, Germany; d. April 14, 1759, London.* Handel was not a man who was without honor in his own time. His fame was known throughout the Western world and he was the first musician to be the subject of a biography. Not only a great composer, he was a virtuoso on the harpsichord and organ, and no slouch with the violin. He was outgoing, cosmopolitan, and philanthropic; large, lusty, and genial, although given to explosive outbursts of temper in which, in his coarse German accent, he frequently invoked the name of Beelzebub either to describe the ancestry of the object of his wrath or to show that, no matter how willful and spoiled, he could go them one better. Also a businessman, he produced his own operas, enjoying great success and enduring substantial failure.

As a public figure he cut a readily identifiable silhouette, and in many ways this is all we know of him. He had lovers, but only quietly and of short duration, and he never married. Of his inner thoughts and passions, of what lay at the bottom of his artistic drive, we know virtually nothing. How ironic that the biographical body of this lusty man provides such slim pickings.

Born and educated in Halle, Germany, Handel later moved to Hamburg where he studied composition. There he almost lost his life in a duel with his friend Johann Mattheson. Both young men were hotheads and an argument provoked a duel in which Mattheson's sword thrust was stopped by a metal button on Handel's coat. In 1707 Handel was in Italy where he learned the style of Italian opera and the easy flow of Italian melody. He was much influenced by Alessandro Scarlatti and was friendly with his son, Domenico, who was Handel's age.

In 1710 Handel was a court musician in Hanover for the Elector. Securing permission, he visited London where Italian operas were the rage. Knowing the style well by now he took advantage by composing *Rinaldo*, which proved to be a huge success. He returned to Hanover but, infatuated with London, applied for a return trip. The Elector consented, provided that he return within a reasonable time. Two years was not a reasonable time and Handel was still in London when Queen Anne died in 1714. Her successor was the Elector of Hanover, George I. Handel must have cast a worried eye eastward wondering how his new king would treat his defection.

Legend has it that it was Handel's *Water Music* (1717)

which brought about forgiveness, for the King ordered it replayed three times after first listening while he floated down the Thames in his royal barge. In all likelihood however, the King, whether forgiving by nature or charmed by Handel's music and personality, had already placed Handel back in his good graces.

Handel was now in England to stay. The immediate success of this corpulent Saxon did not go unnoticed. Addison, with a failed opera libretto under his belt, went after Handel in the *Spectator* with unrelenting venom. If Handel was concerned, he did not show it. Opera after opera flowed from his pen, all in the Italian style, featuring the great castrati singers whose vocal pyrotechnics, elaborate improvisations, and uncanny ability to sustain a tone held their audiences enraptured. Sometimes, that is. Opera audiences in those days would make today's nightclub habitués seem polite. They openly conversed, jeered, applauded, hissed, and reviled, with word or food. Plot and drama were all but nonexistent, and the singers were the stars.

Handel was hardly limited to opera. The *Te Deums*, suites, concerti grossi, sonatas, and solo harpsichord pieces provide music that is dramatic, ceremonial, pastoral, tender, or filled with sorrow. His is music of ineffable grace and lyricism. As a melodist Handel stands second to no one. At bottom his music always conveys the strength of his confidence and outlook for emotionally he was as healthy as any composer.

Italian opera eventually lost public interest and it was John Gay's *The Beggar's Opera* (the basis for *The Threepenny Opera*) in 1728 which greased the ropes of its burial. Handel lost money then and even more ten years later with the failure of his opera company. Quickly he turned to composing dramatic oratorios and was soon as successful as ever. Starting with *Saul* (1738) then *Israel in Egypt* (1739) he composed nearly twenty. *Messiah*, first heard on April 13, 1742, in Dublin, still is his crowning glory. Handel's inspiration was white hot. Part I took him six days, Part II nine days, and Part III six more. The orchestration and related matters took another three: 24 days in all. Even accounting for the fact that he borrowed some parts from his previous works (e.g., the chorus, "For Unto Us a Child Is Born," was originally a love duet) it is a stunning achievement.

Such borrowing, whether from one's own works or the works of others, was an accepted commonplace in Handel's time. Handel lifted liberally and in some cases blatantly, but his talent was such that frequently he dramatically improved the original. With age Handel began to lose his sight and by 1752 he was blind. Yet he still continued to compose and to play the organ. His sense of humor remained intact as well. When it was suggested that he conduct the blind organist, John Stanley, Handel roared with laughter and quoted the Bible passage about the blind leading the blind. But his health gradually deserted him. He made out his will and in his last codicil requested that he be buried in Westminster Abbey. No one had previously dared to be so presumptuous, but the request was only an honest acknowledgment of his achievement and an indication that by now Handel, accent and all, was thoroughly British.

Below Handel to your right is a bust of **William Makepeace Thackeray** (1811–1863) who is buried in Kensal Green.

You have to look rather unceremoniously among the folding chairs for some of the other in-floor plaques, including that of Charles Dickens, who has only his name in gold against black.

CHARLES DICKENS *b. February 7, 1812, Portsmouth; d. June 9, 1870, Chatham, Kent.* Charles Dickens was, at once, the most sociable and secretive of men. Blessed with high energy, he organized amateur theatricals, readings of his work, and vacations with friends while writing prodigiously and editing his magazine, *Household Words*. He walked several hours a day, and fathered ten children. Yet he kept the deep secrets of his own childhood stored away, using old angers to fuel what Ralph Waldo Emerson called the "fearful locomotive to which he is bound and can never be free from."

Part of Dickens' rage at his parents came from the shock of blighted expectations. John and Elizabeth Dickens encouraged Charles to sing, write and perform plays. He attended Giles School which emphasized academic and social aspirations. But though John was modestly employed as a clerk in the naval pay office, both parents had an exaggerated sense of entitlement and their own social superiority. When Charles was 12 his father was arrested for chronic debt and jailed at Marshalsea Prison for several months. To try to avoid that, Charles had been taken out of school and put to work in a factory pasting labels on pots of black shoe polish. His older sister, Fanny, continued to study singing at the Royal Academy of Music.

After John Dickens' release and the promise of an inheritance, the family (including three younger siblings) was reunited and restored to genteel status. Only Charles was still working at the factory. His release came when his father quarreled with the proprietor, who then fired Charles. Elizabeth Dickens went to Warren's Blacking to beg for her son's job back; John Dickens insisted that Charles return to school instead. It was a position Dickens never forgave his mother for taking. Her self-servingness and inability to nurture him showed up dramatically in the flock of motherless children — Pip, Little Nell, Oliver, David Copperfield, Florence Dombey, and others — who had to make their own way in the world.

Back in school Dickens had little idea of a vocation. He sat for the law, and worked as a court stenographer and journalist. In 1833 his first written sketch, signed Boz, appeared in the *Monthly Magazine*. Others followed, and with the *Posthumous Papers of the Pickwick Club* (1837) his reputation was made.

In 1836 he married Catherine Hogarth, an amiable, plump young woman from a literary family. He needed a nurturing and compliant wife, one who would create the family hearth that he felt he had been denied. Catherine's limited imagination would not trouble him for years. In return, he promised to be equally devoted and, unlike his father, a responsible provider.

Dickens then began his 30-year creation of classics: *Oliver Twist* (1838); *Nicholas Nickleby* (1839); *A Christmas Carol* (1843); *David Copperfield* (1850); *Bleak House* (1853); *A Tale of Two Cities* (1859); *Great Expectations* (1861); and *Our Mutual Friend* (1865). It is instructive to note that his triumphs were spread out over his lifetime. He did not burn out quickly nor take years to ignite, but glowed brightly with a steadfast flame.

The appeal of Dickens' books lies in their richness of language, humor, and astute characterization. Often the marvelous names say it all: Ebenezer Scrooge, Uriah Heep, Wackford Squeers, Peggotty. Part of his characters' psychological power, of course, came from their resemblance to people in his own life. Micawber and the bankrupt Dombey embodied aspects of John Dickens, while the vain and ineffectual Mrs. Nickleby was drawn from Dickens' mother.

Dickens wrote the psychological story of his childhood unhappiness again and again. He realized afterwards that the initials of David Copperfield were his own, reversed, but knew from the start that he was writing about himself. Pip, in *Great Expectations*, also played out his feelings of parental betrayal. Yet even his villains were capable of remorse and reform, and his sympathetic characters lived to triumph as the writer had himself.

For years Dickens seemed tireless, presenting elaborate theatricals for family birthdays and Twelfth Night, traveling on the Continent with his best friends, John Forster and Daniel Maclise, and engaging in social reform and philanthropic work. He recaptured his childhood love of performing by reading from his own works for large, spellbound audiences in England and America. Dressed in bright red vests and gold chains, the slight, graying man with the odd-shaped beard and high side curls soon disappeared into whatever character he was portraying.

Cheerful and gregarious in public, Dickens revealed very little of his true feelings. Society was shocked when, in 1858, he separated from his obese wife, Catherine, insisting that she leave the house. Except for their oldest son, Charley, he kept the children with him and his sister-in-law, Georgina Hogarth. The impelling factor for the separation was his love for an 18-year-old actress, Ellen Ternan. Unable to consider divorce, he maintained a clandestine relationship with her for the rest of his life. Dickens was also disappointed in his nine living children—"the largest family ever known with the smallest disposition to do anything for themselves"—and suffered from gout and chest pains.

The most popular author of his century was working on *The Mystery of Edwin Drood* when he collapsed and died of a brain hemorrhage at 58. As stipulated in his will, no announcement was made of the time and place of his burial. He was laid to rest here early in the morning with 12 people in attendance who had been instructed by his will to wear no black bow, long hat-band or other "revolting absurdity" of Victorian mourning.

Near Dickens on the floor is interred:

THOMAS HARDY III *b. June 2, 1840, Higher Bockhampton, Dorset; d. January 11, 1928, Max Gate, Dorset.* Thomas Hardy's birth cottage in Dorset lay in a wild, lonely spot. The grounds were comfortably inhabited by snakes, one even curling up to nap with baby Thomas as he slept inside. The village rested in the middle of the ancient countryside whose Druidic remains, white lime soil, and wild, capricious beauty was immortalized in Hardy's novels as Wessex. So keen was Hardy's identification with the area that fact and fiction are now intertwined and many local road maps bear both the real place names and those that Hardy gave to them.

Hardy's parents were married scarcely five months when he was born. While possibly premature, he was certainly not four months early; but he was so feeble at birth that the doctor passed him off as dead and only the ministrations of the watchful midwife saved his life. Apocryphal or not, the story survives, a testament to our love of irony.

Hardy was reading by age three, a result no doubt of his mother's avid literary interests. Likewise the fatalism that pervades his writings emanated from his mother, whose childhood poverty perpetually darkened her outlook, causing her dominant personality to successfully demand financial security from a husband who, given the chance, could lapse into indolence. If lacking the ultimate in entrepreneurial energy, Thomas' father did possess a love and skill for music which he passed on to his son. This included singing in the Stinsford choir, and playing the fiddle with his father at country dances after which he would not uncommonly pilot his unsteady father home.

As a child Hardy was the undisputed academic star of his town; when he was 16 his father accepted the offer of John Hicks, a local architect, to take Thomas on. Hardy studied and practiced architecture for 15 years, first with Hicks and later in London. In Dorchester he became influenced by Hicks' next door neighbor, William Barnes, known for his poems set in the Dorset dialect, and by Horace Moule, the well-educated, black-sheep son of a vicar, who helped to broaden and sharpen the boy's outlook.

Uncommonly bright, Hardy was equally shy, a condition which plagued him for life and was frequently mistaken for rudeness and snobbery. His disposition matched the solitude of the heath. Despite his shyness he was romantically attracted to pretty women, immortalizing some in verse and adapting others to the heroines of his novels.

When not working at architecture or dabbling with the idea of entering a seminary (a course which Darwin's *Origin of Species* did much to discourage), Hardy was writing novels. His first, *The Poor Man and the Lady*, was never published, but did earn him the constructive criticism of its reader at Chapman and Hall, George Meredith. *Desperate Remedies*, complete with a lesbian love scene, was published in 1871 to mixed reviews. While writing the book he met Emma Gifford, the daughter of an alcoholic solicitor, who took delight in racing her horse along the Cornish cliffs and whose enthusiasm counterbalanced Hardy's sedateness. When they married in 1874 Hardy quickly found such zeal to be overbearing. He retreated further, and the tension that was to mark their marriage began its growth.

Under the Greenwood Tree (1872) earned critical if not popular success. Hardy then turned to writing serials, a form which all his remaining novels would first take and came under the influence of Leslie Stephens, the stern, perfectionist, mountain-climbing editor of *Cornhill Magazine*. Hardy would later say that Stephens' approval was "disapproval minimized" but with Stephens' support he wrote *Far From the Madding Crowd* (1874), marking the appearance of the Wessex countryside and his popular success as a writer. Before finishing the book Hardy learned that his friend Horace Moule had committed suicide. This event served to reinforce the pessimism of Hardy's fatalism and the perverseness of his God, themes he dealt with in *The Return of the Native* (1878).

By 1885 the Hardys had moved into Max Gate, the house in Dorchester which Hardy designed. Plantings of Austrian pines secured privacy for Hardy while obliterating lovely views. Lost in this oasis his insularity grew, and the marriage continued its descent. His standing as a novelist shifted from popular to notorious with the publication of *Tess of the d'Urbervilles* (1891) and *Jude the Obscure* (1896). The bleak description of rural life, the questioning of conventional morality, and the openness of sexuality were all more than many could stand. Fame and venom were sent Hardy's way. Again he retreated, giving up novels to concentrate on poetry, but to Hardy's dismay, his poems never garnered the same critical or popular success as his novels.

At home the couple grew apart. Emma, still neglected, was now offended by Hardy's writings. She took refuge, with increasing solitude, in the tower of the house and died there in 1912. Hardy, always able to love at a distance, now felt keenly the loss of what he had shied away from in life. Neither poems nor trips to the sites where they had first loved could assuage his feelings. Marrying his secretary and housekeeper, Florence Dugdale, in 1914 helped, but it was more a matter of practicality than romance.

Hardy remained active well into old age. His solitude became less voluntary, but he did have regular visitors, including an impressed T.E. Lawrence who, in 1923, observed, "He is waiting so tranquilly for death." Five years later Hardy died peacefully in his bed. His heart was buried physically with Emma in St. Michael's Churchyard in Stinsford, at the church where Hardy had sung hymns 80 years earlier. His ashes were removed to Westminster Abbey.

Kipling's marker is a square stone in the floor with just his name and dates.

JOSEPH RUDYARD KIPLING *b. December 30, 1865, Bombay; d. January 11, 1936, London.* In 1907, when Sigmund Freud was asked to name his favorite writers, he chose Rudyard Kipling along with Emile Zola and Mark Twain. Because of their contrasts in outlook, it is startling to realize that the Viennese psychiatrist and the author of *The Jungle Book* and *Gunga Din* were contemporaries. Where Freud took pains to excavate and understand his untamed subconscious, Kipling was terrified of getting even an accidental glance. As the years marched by, the small, sepia-toned man with rimless glasses and military carriage clung more and more to the external virtues of patriotism, self-reliance, and bluff good cheer, hoisting onto his back what he designated as the "White Man's Burden."

Kipling's childhood would have given Freud some interesting material. Born and nurtured in the exotic bosom of India, the six-year-old Rudyard and his sister Trix, three, were brought back to England by their parents. Before the older Kiplings returned to Bombay for another six years, they brought the children to foster parents in Southsea and left without telling them it was to be their new home. Rudyard, a handsome, undisciplined child, was quickly subdued by the cold and pious Mrs. Holloway. To punish him she stitched a sign that read "LIAR" to his jacket, and forbade him his only consolation, reading fiction. Kipling's revenge came later in his memoir, *Ba Ba, Black Sheep*.

Boarding school with its bullies, thrashings, and crude practical jokes, seemed less traumatic. His school had the picturesque name Westward Ho! and there Kipling acquired a nickname, Gigger (short for "Giglamps," referring to his glasses). No longer anyone's victim, by 16 he was hirsute and smoked constantly. He was still a voracious reader, devouring Pushkin, Whitman, and Omar Khayyam, and picking up allusions he would later use in his own work.

As soon as he could, Kipling escaped back to India and became a journalist in Lahore. Snug in the Anglo-Indian society which included Trix and his parents, Kipling translated the spicy, sultry country into fiction, detailing its particular temptations to foreigners. He wrote verse and short stories, including those collected in *Soldiers Three* (1890). In India he codified his admiration of the military character, and became an apologist for British colonialism.

At 23 Kipling set forth into the wider world, achieving accolades in England, and traveling to Singapore, Hong Kong, and America. In 1892 he married Caroline Balestier, an American and sister of his close friend and publisher,

Poets' Corner

Wolcott Balestier. The Kiplings spent several years, from 1892 to 1896, in Vermont, but their experience was marred. A quarrel with another of Caroline's brothers, Beatty, led to Beatty's arrest and trial for threats and verbal assault on Rudyard, and served to highlight the Kiplings' local unpopularity. Although *Captains Courageous* (1897) glorified New England fishermen, Kipling's view of America was more critical. The family retreated to England; on a later trip to New York in 1899 the writer became critically ill with pneumonia, and his beloved daughter, Josephine, died from the same illness.

In 1907 Kipling was awarded the Nobel Prize in Literature. By then he had given the world *The Jungle Books* (1894, 1895), *Kim* (1901), *Just So Stories for Little Children* (1902), and *Puck of Pook's Hill* (1906). After that his work became more abstruse and less popular. He busied himself during World War I as a writer of jingoistic verse and speeches, and was an unofficial advisor to the government. From 1914 until his death 22 years later Kipling was constantly in pain from belatedly diagnosed duodenal ulcers which led to frequent hemorrhaging and vomiting.

Caroline, always a strong and possessive woman, exercised even more control over Kipling when his health was poor. He complained about this obliquely to friends, and his concerns showed up in stories such as "Unprofessional" and "A Madonna of the Trenches" which had themes of cancer and suicide. Yet when he came to die it was with his characteristic stoicism. When asked by his surgeon, "What's the matter, Rud?" he replied, "Something has come adrift inside." Kipling was cremated secretly at Golders Green and buried in Westminster Abbey.

Besides his best-known children's books, Rudyard Kipling left behind a wealth of expressions which have passed into general use: "little tin gods on wheels"; "an officer and a gentleman"; "hot and bothered"; "a rag, a bone, a hank of hair"; "the female of the species is more deadly than the male"; "East is East and West is West, and never the twain shall meet." There was also the part of Kipling which spoke to the heart of every Englishman:

> On the road to Mandalay,
> Where the flyin'-fishes play,
> An' the dawn comes up like thunder
> Outer China 'crost the Bay!
> Ship me somewhere east of Suez
> Where the best is like the worst
> Where there aren't no Ten Commandments
> An' a man can raise a thirst.

Above the door to the private St. Faith's Chapel is the cameo of **Oliver Goldsmith** (1730?–1774). It is adorned with ivy leaves, books, a mask of tragedy and drapery. Goldsmith was interred in the Temple Church, Fleet Street, until it was destroyed during an air raid in May 1941.

Of the cluster of luminaries on the back wall, the only one here is Samuel Johnson, buried under a plain black slab that gives his dates. He is honored by a bust sitting in a niche in the wall above his burial spot. Above him **Robert Southey** has a young man's bust even though his dates are 1774–1843. Southey is buried in Keswick, Cumbria.

SAMUEL JOHNSON *b. September 18, 1709, Lichfield, Staffordshire; d. December 13, 1784, London.* With one eye blind, the other impaired, and all but deaf in his left ear, Samuel Johnson both saw and heard the world dimly. Yet few men have observed it more clearly, for his inner vision was acute, his knowledge broad, and his memory prodigious. His verbal outpourings "were as correct as a second edition," and his wit cut sharply with cruelty or teased warmly with humor, though his quick temper often eliminated the middle ground between those two extremes.

If not for his intelligence and physical bulk Johnson would have suffered greatly as a child from cruel taunts, for the coarse, gross features of his face had been scarred by scrofula when he was an infant and later by smallpox. Advertising his appearance were numerous tics which kept his body in perpetual motion. When sitting his limbs flew about restlessly; when standing he rolled as if he were weathering a gale on board ship. Yet his wit and intellect endowed him with a charm which endeared him to those he favored with his company.

At the start, however, it was feared that his parents might have been saddled with an idiot. His speech and memory soon gave lie to that notion. In school Johnson was quickly recognized as an apt student, one who even looked forward to his weekly examinations. To appear less bookish, he hid what efforts his studies demanded. He read voraciously, retained much, but, with a mind as restless as his body, rarely finished any book. Johnson's father, whose outward trimmings of success disguised his ongoing financial ineptitude, provided him with little affection and was often away from home. His mother treated him unevenly, providing little understanding for her pleasure or wrath. His wit asserted itself early. When his mother in anger called him a puppy he asked if she knew what they called a puppy's mother.

Inspired by his older cousin, Christopher Ford, Johnson continued to expand his interests and readings, but finances dictated work at his father's bookshop rather than school. A small legacy and a generous friend allowed Johnson to attend Oxford for one year, but when those funds dried up he was forced to leave. Return to Lichfield found him in an extreme depression marked by hypochondria, impatience, and despair. He feared he was losing his mind. Long walks and eventual teaching jobs gave relief, but such moods affected him throughout his life.

In 1735 Johnson married a widow, Elizabeth "Tetty" Porter. Tetty was a lusty, full-bosomed woman 20 years his senior. It was, as Johnson described it, "a love marriage." David Garrick, one of Johnson's three resident students, spent more time at Johnson's bedroom keyhole than at his books, but the views were worth it. To amused guests Garrick would later recall Johnson "stumbling round the bed, calling 'I'm coming, my Tetsie! I'm coming!', falling upon his ample bride . . ." or the great man, mistaking the bed sheets for his shirt tails, stuffing them into his pants, and leaving bare his wife's pulchritude for Garrick's amused and eager eyes. The marriage soon ran out of fire and separation ensued. Even so, Johnson coped poorly with her death in 1752; her memory frequently conjured up feelings of remorse, self-pity, and sentimentality.

With Garrick as his companion, Johnson moved to London in 1737 and his love affair with that city began. Though he lived in poverty he was able to ignore the offensive odors and filth in favor of the exciting variety of the city. He survived by doing hack work for a variety of journals and by recreating, often far better than they had been delivered, the speeches of members of Parliament. The fact that publication of the proceedings was not allowed, that he had attended only once, and that he relied on the notes of others did not at all deter him.

Johnson toyed with the idea of a dictionary for some time before receiving financial backing for the idea in 1746. Confidently promising delivery in three years, Johnson, aided by six assistants, needed seven instead. The work was finally published to wide acclaim in 1755 and was far superior to previous efforts. It was not without fault, however, e.g., "*net:* anything reticulated or decussated at equal distances, with interstices between the intersections." Nor was he without venom, as in "*dedication:* a servile address to a patron" or "*patron:* commonly a wretch who supports with insolence and is paid with flattery."

Johnson worked on his own newspapers during this

time, most notably the *Rambler*, but his tone was too moral to appeal to the public in the way that Addison and Steele did. His daily schedule was marked by lethargy. Frequently he did not rise until the afternoon, then entertained company, went to the tavern for food and company, and did not return until the wee hours of the morning. Even then he sometimes stopped by the lodgings of his blind friend, Miss Anna Williams, for yet another cup of tea and some platonic conversation. Johnson was in need of such company, for he feared loneliness. When work was absolutely needed he would dash it off in a fit of inspiration. Occasionally he would try to organize his routine and his room but he never succeeded.

What Johnson enjoyed most was conversation. He helped found The Club at the Turk's Head tavern, an informal gathering which included Sir Joshua Reynolds, Edmund Burke, Oliver Goldsmith, and, of course, his famous biographer, companion, and sycophant, James Boswell. Among this auspicious group, Johnson was preeminent. His logic, wit, and vast fund of knowledge ruled. His joy was in victory of argument rather than consistency of position. As he argued he lubricated himself with enormous quantities of tea, a habit which did his sleep patterns no good.

Johnson received a pension in 1762 which freed him from having to write for his bread. It did not liberate him from his moods, however. Depression and the fear of losing his mind were never far away, and they hit hard and often. For years he was a frequent house guest of Henry and Hester Thrale. He formed a close relationship with Mrs. Thrale, even confessing and perhaps acting out his masochistic needs with her. He continued to write poetry, and also published his edition of Shakespeare's plays, eliminating many of the numerous corruptions and "improvements" made in various prior editions. His opening essay on the Bard is a masterpiece of criticism. In 1781 he published *Lives of the Poets*, with his essays introducing collections by various poets.

"Traveling over minds" was Johnson's joy and he avowed that no one had ever traveled over his. He was right. It was far too lush and fertile. He suffered a stroke in 1783 and his health further declined; his legs swelled painfully as did one testicle. Bedridden, he tried the night before he died to relieve the pain and pressure by slicing his leg open. He put at least his mind to rest. The next day he prayed intermittently, gradually fading into his final peace.

Although you can see his grave in Holy Trinity Church, Stratford-on-Avon, you can admire here the statue of William Shakespeare pointing to a list of his works. It is hanging from a podium that has three heads, said to be those of Elizabeth I, Richard III, and Henry V. Erected in 1740, it was sculpted by Peter Scheemakers, who also did the bust of John Dryden.

After Shakespeare's death there was talk of bringing him to Poets' Corner. But the epitaph on his grave in Stratford seems deliberately chosen to quell such a move:

> Good friend, for Jesus' sake forbeare
> To digg the dust enclosed heare;
> Bleste be the man that spares thes stones,
> And curst be he that moves my bones.

Behind Samuel Johnson's floor marker is one to **Richard Brinsley Sheridan** (1751–1816): "This marble is the tribute of his attached friend Peter More."

Richard Sheridan was a man who followed his heart. It led him down paths of extraordinary success, but also to debtor's prison toward the end of his life. But before that happened he wrote plays which are still being performed.

At 20 Sheridan tried to elope with a beautiful 16-year-old, Elizabeth Ann Linley, to help her escape the attentions of a married man. Their fathers retrieved them from Calais, but later on they married and set themselves up in grand style in London, a style built on faith rather than cash. Amazingly, Sheridan's first play, *The Rivals* (1775) was produced at Drury Lane Theater within the year and was a great success.

The next year he became part owner and manager of Drury Lane, and then outdid himself with *The School for Scandal* (ca. 1778) and *The Critic* (1781). His plays used stock situations which he updated for the Georgian age with wit and humor, giving them a warmth which had been lacking in Restoration comedies.

Sheridan's heart next directed him into politics in 1780. He entertained the House of Commons with soaring oratory; his speech promoting the impeachment of Warren Hastings was the first to be applauded by clapping. As a strong supporter of Charles James Fox, he opposed slavery. Americans especially felt that Sheridan's heart was in the right place. An ardent supporter of the American Revolution, he was voted a gift of £20,000 by Congress, which he refused.

In Sheridan's best years his income was £10,000 per annum. But after his beloved Elizabeth died at 36 of tuberculosis, and the new Drury Lane Theater into which he had invested all his capital burned down, Sheridan felt defeated. Members of Parliament could not be arrested for debt, but when he lost the election in 1813 he was sent temporarily to debtor's prison. His last play, *Pizarro*, had been produced 14 years earlier, and no more were forthcoming. Had his heart led him astray? Perhaps not. It had led him into a full life, and given the world such memorable characters as Mrs. Malaprop, Joseph Surface, and Lady Teazle.

As you turn the corner you will see the bust of:

ALFRED, LORD TENNYSON *b. August 6, 1809, Somersby, Lincolnshire; d. October 6, 1892, Haslemere, Surrey.* On the surface it could have been an idyllic life; a country pastor, his wife, and their 11 children living in a rectory nestled in a green landscape. It was anything but that. The Rev. Dr. George Tennyson was a violent alcoholic obsessed with having been disinherited by his father in favor of his younger brother. His brooding black moods overflowed with recriminations and a death wish. As his drinking increased he developed debilitating seizures which trapped the wary family into vigilance for his survival. This circumferential concern persisted until Alfred was at Cambridge University and his mother, out of fear and desperation, fled the house taking the remaining children with her.

If such paternal blackness were not enough, Tennyson's youth was saddled with the fanaticism of his Aunt Bourne who despairingly scolded, "Alfred, Alfred, when I look at you, I think of the words of Holy Scripture — 'Depart from me, ye cursed, into the everlasting fire.' " Neither maternal love nor sibling affection could overcome such gloom. It is not surprising that Tennyson, in recounting his childhood to his son Hallam, could find no light or gaiety.

Alfred was the third-oldest surviving child. He attended the village school and then a school at Louth that he detested so much he was unwilling to visit it even much later in life. Upon reaching 10 or 11, Frederick, the oldest, went to Eton. At the same age Charles and Alfred received personal tutoring, which would last seven years, from their father at the rectory. The Reverend was, at least, a learned man who played the harp and kept a well-stocked library. He encouraged Alfred's poetry, more than once predicting, with prescient bragging or rare fatherly enthusiasm, that his son would become England's greatest poet.

In 1827 Alfred and Charles published *Poems by Two Brothers*. Since four poems by Frederick were included the title understates the fraternal contribution. The book received little attention and did not mark Alfred as a poetic genius, raw or otherwise. His huge frame must have made its mark at Cambridge, but shy and depressed, Tennyson initially found the school almost as intolerable as Louth. Fortunately he formed a friendship with Arthur Hallam, a fellow poet who became his most ardent supporter. Both men were drawn into the small circle of undergraduates known as the "Apostles." This group broadened Tennyson's intellectual and political views and boosted his confidence. In 1829 he won the Chancellor's Gold Medal for his poem "Timbuctoo" and enjoyed the enthusiastic praise of his fellow Apostles.

Tennyson's father died of typhus in 1831. While the granting of his death wish may have been a relief for him and the rest of the family, the Reverend's death also served to seal and confirm the father and son's disappointing relationship. Tennyson became hypochondriacal about his eyesight and remained so in varying degrees for his entire life. Worse was to come, for in 1833 Arthur Hallam died unexpectedly. The blow to Tennyson was severe and sparked an inspired poetic outpouring culminating ultimately with *In Memoriam* (1850).

Much of Tennyson's best work was written in the two decades after Hallam's death. His poems of 1830 and 1832 were viewed as affected and had not been well received. The poems published in 1842 demonstrated a marked improvement and gained him substantial notice. *In Memoriam* confirmed his fame and garnered him the appointment of poet laureate. In turn, this lofty position provided Tennyson with the money he needed to marry Emily Sellwood, whom he had been courting since 1836.

Tennyson came to dominate poetry in the Victorian age; few poets have ever ruled their time so totally. Dressed in his wide-brimmed hat and cloak, the poet delivered thundering recitations of his poems before an adoring and awed public, much as Dylan Thomas would do a century later. Tennyson's opinions — and he had many on all manner of subjects — took on the air of authority with his readers. His critics were less impressed and many of his later poems came in for harsh comment. The generation following his death was especially adverse and the invocation of Tennyson's name alone invoked smirks and derisive laughter.

Subsequent years have been kinder and it is recognized that even near the end of his life Tennyson was capable of writing great poetry. "Crossing the Bar" (1889) is one such poem. The second stanza reads:

> But such a tide as moving seems asleep,
> Too full for sound and foam,
> When that which drew from out the boundless deep
> Turns again home.

Set to music by Sir Frederic Bridge the poem was sung at Tennyson's Westminster Abbey funeral service after the poet had crossed the bar in 1892.

Against the wall is a bust of **John Milton**, who is buried in St. Giles Cripplegate (see Chapter 6), as well as a memorial to **Thomas Gray**, who is interred in Buckinghamshire. There is also a nice monument to a forgotten poet, **Guglielmo Mason** (1725–1797). It shows a woman mourning over his oversized profile cameo, which rests on a stand.

In the corner by the door is the bust of Ben Jonson with "Oh Rare! Ben Jonson" under it, with three faces below the inscription. He is actually interred in the floor of the main sanctuary below the Parson's Window. According to legend, he was desperate to be buried in Westminster Abbey, but did not have the price then asked. Finally he was offered a small space in which he would have to be buried standing up. He accepted, saying that on Judgment Day he would have that much more of a headstart.

BEN JONSON *b. June 11, 1572, London; d. August 6, 1637, London.* There are reasons other than financial that Westminster Abbey might have preferred not to have Ben Jonson within its sacred walls. A scrapper by nature, Jonson murdered at least two men during his lifetime. The first was under the guise of war, but the murder of fellow actor Gabriel Spencer came after a violent quarrel. Though Jonson later tried to characterize it as a "duel," he was stripped of his possessions, and branded on his right thumb as a felon. He escaped being hung only by pleading the "right of clergy" because he could read and write.

The third death he was rumored to have caused seems more in keeping with the character of the mature Ben Jonson. Engaged in a drinking bout at the Mermaid Tavern with John Drayton and Jonson, William Shakespeare was said to have died from the aftereffects.

Thin-skinned, emotional, and ambitious, Jonson was born a month after his minister father's death. Ben's step-father, a master bricklayer, sent him to school and welcomed him into the Bricklayers' Union. But manual labor was not to Ben's taste. After serving in the army in Flanders, he worked as a talentless actor and began writing plays. *Every Man in His Humour* was performed at the Globe Theater in 1601, the humours referring to the body fluids defined by Greek physicians as blood, bile, phlegm, and choler. In his comedy Jonson explored the natural outcome of such humours as excessive choler and bilious envy, giving them life in such characters as Captain Bobadilla and Thorello, the jealous husband. The story line was Lorenzo's defense of poetry as a career to his objecting father.

There were other personal themes which persisted throughout Jonson's works. In his plays he appeared to punish his own aggressiveness by imprisoning quarrelsome types like himself, and to work out his sexual attraction to married women by creating triangles of amorous poets, wives, and angry cuckolded husbands. The rational poet, detached from the storm of such humours, was an image that Jonson admired but could never master himself.

Ben Jonson used his plays for revenge as well, lampooning other writers with whom he was on the outs. The royal family was not above his wit, and he was imprisoned several times for "treasonable" passages in works such as *The Isle of Dogs*, *Sejanus*, and *Eastward Ho* — the latter derogatory to Scots when James I was on the throne. During the controversy over *Sejanus* a story arose that Jonson's mother had acquired a dram of "lustie strong poison" to finish her boy off — whether to spare him the indignity of jail or to bring his embarrassing behavior to an end is not known.

Given his temperament, Jonson might not be expected to have had a happy marriage. He didn't. Married to Anne Lewis when he was 22, the relationship endured several separations before a final severance 19 years later in 1613. By then their four young children had all died. Before their deaths Ben had dreamed his famous dream in which his seven-year-old son Ben appeared grown to manhood, but with a bloody cross carved into his forehead. The cross was the symbol that was nailed to the doors of houses quarantined with bubonic plague. A letter came soon from Anne Jonson, confirming the boy's death from the plague. The loss inspired Jonson's moving poem, "On My First Son," reminiscent of "On My First Daughter," written when baby Mary died in 1601. In an age when many parents hesitated to form attachments in the face of widespread child mortality, Jonson loved his children dearly.

Jonson's works, unlike Shakespeare's, are rarely read or performed, with the exception of a few poems ("Drink to me only with thine eyes"), and the plays *Volpone* (1606) and *The Alchemist* (1610). A tragic fire destroyed all his books and manuscripts in 1623. In the next few years he suffered from paralytic strokes, and could barely drag his now-massive body to the Devil Tavern, where he still held forth brilliantly to the "sons of the Tribe of Benjamin."

By then his classical scholarship had been recognized as

well as his wit, and he was the unofficial poet laureate, receiving the pay for that position from the Crown, which included a "butt of canary." With recognition, he could finally integrate the "wilde Ben Jonson" with the measured poet he had always aspired to be. He could even warn, "Nay, we so insist in imitating others [that] we cannot (when it is necessary) returne to ourselves."

Close by is **Samuel Butler** (1612–1680), high in the air with a marble altar and his bust above it, with a wonderful epitaph based on Matthew, Chapter 7:

> The Poet's Fate is here in Emblem shown:
> He asked for Bread and he received a Stone.

He was interred in St. Paul's Church, Covent Garden.

Near Butler is **Edmund Spenser** (1553–1599). "The body of Edmund Spenser heare lyes (expecting the second coming of our Saviour Christ Jesus), the body of Edmund Spenser, prince of poets of his time whose divine spirit to ours needs noe othar witnesse than the works which he left behinde him. He was born in London in the yeare 1553 and died in the yeare 1598." When Spenser was buried, in the custom of the times his fellow poets composed funeral elegies then threw them and the pens with which they were written into the tomb.

Edmund Spenser calls to mind Miniver Cheevy who was born in the wrong century and lamented it, bottle in hand. But Spenser handled his displacement more constructively. The more life disappointed him, the more he allowed himself to live in the Golden Age of Chivalry, a dream world that compensated him for his exclusion from Elizabeth I's Court. Despite his poems to the Queen and satiric complaints such as "Mother Hubberd's Tale" in which the cupboard turned up bare as far as he was concerned, the most he ever received from the Queen was a stipend of £50 a year.

With this bounty he retreated to Ireland where he lived in Kilcolman Castle, leased after the confiscation of Roman Catholic property. He became Sheriff of Cork in 1598, but the next year during an uprising the property was seized and burned, his family barely escaping death. This shock was too harsh to be lost in daydreams. Spenser retreated to London where he collapsed at 46 and died.

He left behind *The Faerie Queen*, an epic which begins with King Arthur's Court and moves into the Elizabethan Age, detailing in soaring language and apt imagery his ideal society. He experimented with metrics, creating a rhyme scheme named after him. Despite certain inconsistencies, his work earned Spenser homage as "the poet's poet," stretching his influence to the Romantics of the nineteenth century.

The memorial to **Matthew Arnold** (1822–1888) looks new. "Let but the light appear. And thy transfigured walls be touched with flame." He is buried in Laleham, Surrey.

Just above Arnold is a modest bust to **Michael Drayton** (1563–1631), "A memorial poet of this age who changed his lavrell for a crown of glory, 1631."

His epitaph reads: "O pious marble, let thy readers know what they and what their children owe to Drayton's name: Whose sacred dust we recommend unto thy trust: Protect his memory and preserve his storye: Remain a lasting monument of his glory: And when thy ruins shall disclaim to be the treasurer of his name, his name that cannot fade shall be an everlasting monument to Thee." Drayton, seduced by the poetic fashions of his time, wrote sonnets, satires, historical epics, biblical paraphrases, myths, popular ballads, and poems on England's topography.

Moving into the larger area, to your right you will find Chaucer in a niche which can be easily missed. He has a simple carved chest tomb with an inscription in Latin and highlighted in white, with two shields with a plain gold and red design. A Purbeck marble canopy rests above it. The monument was erected by a lesser-known poet, Nicholas Brigham, in 1556 and does not contain the remains of Chaucer which are buried in the floor nearby.

GEOFFREY CHAUCER *b. ca. 1342, London; d. October 25, 1400, London.* Since the first written notation proving Chaucer's existence is dated 1357, only guesses can be made as to his childhood. Its backdrop appears vividly, however. The late Middle Ages in England were a litigious time marked by many gratuitous and fraudulent suits. It was also an age marked by death, not only with the Black Death of 1348–49, but with the violence that followed lengthy oaths of hatred and was punctuated for all to see by bodies swinging from gibbets and heads impaled on spikes.

In reaction to the ghastly gloom of the plague, which had claimed one-third to one-half of the population and which recurred at intervals, clothing fashions grew outlandish. Though the sleeves now draped to the ground, men's tunics grew shorter revealing the tight hose, each leg a different bright color, which emphasized the genitals and buttocks. For shoes they sported poulaines, whose pointed tips were sometimes so long that they had to be delicately chained to the calf in order to keep them up. Women, not allowed to wear drawers (the prohibition against a woman wearing anything between her legs would last until the nineteenth century), wore larger headdresses, plucked their eyebrows, and lowered their decolletage. Both sexes sported furs and jewels. The moral authorities, to little effect, railed against the middle class, who imitated royalty, who were themselves imitating the conquered French, the initiators of chivalry.

Geoffrey Chaucer was born and raised in a well-to-do merchant-class family in such a time. His father, John, was a vintner who enjoyed considerable status among his fellows. Their home, which housed the business, was located on Thames Street in the Vintry Ward. In school Chaucer was probably exposed to religion, grammar, arithmetic, Latin, and humanistic philosophy, which viewed man as more important than other creatures because of his ability to think and reason. He also learned French, if not at school then certainly at home, for it was the tongue of both royalty and tradesmen in England.

As befitted a boy of his station, at age 14 Chaucer was sent off to be a courtier for Elizabeth, wife of Prince Lionel. There he learned the civilities of court life, the skills and realities of warfare (it was not unusual for 14- or 15-year-old boys to so serve their king), poetry, the art of diplomacy and running international errands, and the ins and outs of law and business. Pages were chided to mind their manners: to not spit too far, pick their noses, or "fire their rear guns." In war Chaucer was probably responsible for protecting a knight, possibly Sir Lionel, by carrying his lance, procuring his food, and tending the campsite. At some point in 1359 or 1360 Chaucer was captured and held prisoner until he was freed for a ransom of £16 on March 1, 1360. Such ransoms were commonplace, with monies and personnel in frequent exchange.

In 1366, as arranged by Queen Philippa, Chaucer married Philippa Roet, the Queen's retainer. The couple would have three children (and possibly a fourth). Although the nature of the marriage is not clearly known, there is no obvious reason to assume as some have done that Chaucer was terribly unhappy in his union. Politically the picture is clearer, for John of Gaunt, son of King Edward III, later took Philippa Roet's sister, Katherine Swynford, as his mistress and much later as his wife. This arrangement did not hurt Chaucer's standing at Court.

By the time of his marriage Chaucer was already writing poetry. One of his first efforts was an ABC poem "in which each stanza begins with a successive letter of the alphabet." His translation of the *Roman de la Rose* into English also evolved early on and used the alliterative form of his literary forebears, although it is far from clear this style appealed to Chaucer since he eschewed it in *The Canterbury Tales*. The translation was a natural for not only was England under the chivalric influence of France, but Chaucer was under the influence of its poets, most notably Guillaume Machaut and Froissart. His first major work was *The Book of the Duchess*, written in honor of Duchess Blanche, who died in 1367.

Chaucer continued to travel in service of the Crown, most notably in 1373, when he made the treacherous Alpine winter crossing to negotiate with Genoese and Florentine merchants. Here he came under the influence of the works of Dante, and then Boccaccio and Petrarch. The secular focus of the latter two were indicative of the growing influence of humanistic philosophy. Chaucer's uncompleted *The House of Fame* grew directly out of his Italian experiences. When not traveling as emissary and mediator Chaucer occupied a variety of positions in London, such as "Controller of the King's Custom and Subsidy of Wools, Hides, and Wool Fells."

Of his later works Chaucer completed *Troilus and Criseyde* in 1386 and began *The Canterbury Tales* in the same year. Here he was able to combine his mastery of poetry with a secular tale told with comic skill. His characters are boldly and broadly brought to life. Their pious pursuits and bawdy talk, hypocrisies and passions are so clearly portrayed that they represent the best picture of the times that we have. Chaucer's achievement is most remarkable for its humanity and its psychological insight. The text we know was completed in three phases, but the outline called for far more to come.

Chaucer's wife died in 1387. Tending toward greater self-absorption as he grew older, and perhaps suffering from a later romantic disillusionment, he preferred the bachelor's life. In his last year, short on cash, he took up lodgings in the garden at Westminster Abbey. It was not the most desirable housing in town for the Abbey served as a sanctuary for criminals. The fact that Thieves Street was located near the Abbey's shadow was no coincidence, and it may be that Chaucer sought the apartment because it would bring him sanctuary from his creditors. Now in middle age,

Chaucer became preoccupied with death. Whether it was prescience or gloom he succumbed to an unknown illness and was buried at Westminster. Fittingly, as the first major poet in English history he has drawn his literary followers to his side to form Poets' Corner.

To your left is another cluster of in-floor plaques. On top of these is a memorial to **T.S. Eliot**, though the poet is buried in Somerset. His slab reads, "The communication of the dead is tongued with fire beyond the language of the living." Of the others, those actually interred here, beside Tennyson, include **John Masefield** (1878–1967), poet laureate, and Robert Browning, whose stone has a border of tan marble and a darker red center with a flower at the top and a fleur-de-lis at the bottom.

It is always charming to hear of an American connection in the lives of English writers; John Masefield worked for several years in a carpet mill in Yonkers, north of New York City. Orphaned at an early age, he sailed on the *Conway* at 13, and received an education in seamanship. By 17 he had traveled around America, working at odd jobs, and in 1897 he returned to London. He combined his love of poetry and the sea in *Salt Water Ballads* (1902).

Although he was well accepted, the barroom language and grittiness of Masefield's first major poem, *The Everlasting Mercy* (1911) came as a shock to some readers. He followed it up with *Dauber* (1913), and what many considered his masterpiece, *Reynard the Fox* (1919). But his homing signal was the sea. Masefield produced naval histories and novels with nautical themes, such as *The Bird of Dawning* (1933).

Masefield took his role as poet laureate seriously, producing poems to fit various occasions during his remaining 37 years. The lines from one of his earliest works, *Sea-Fever*, provide a fitting epitaph:

> I must down to the seas again, for the call of the running tide
> Is a wild call and a clear call that may not be denied.
> And all I ask is a merry yarn from a laughing fellow-rover,
> And quiet sleep and a sweet dream when the long trick's over.

ROBERT BROWNING *b. May 7, 1812, Camberwell; d. December 12, 1889, Venice.*

> God's in his heaven—all's right with the world.
> Ah, a man's reach should exceed his grasp, or what's a heaven for?
> Grow old along with me! The best is yet to be.
> Every joy is gain, and gain is gain, however small.

After Robert Browning's death, the above lines were mined from his poetry, and embroidered on needlework cases, samplers, and pillows. It had the effect of sentimentalizing him, of making people forget that "God's in his heaven" comes from *Pippa Passes*, a work which deals with forced prostitution, adultery, and murder. Yet Browning was no tortured Baudelaire or Byron. On the surface he was ebullient and optimistic, bouncing like a cork on the waters of Victorian society.

Robert Browning was the son of gentle and cultured older parents. As a young man his father had been sent by his own father to oversee the family estates in Jamaica. Sickened by plantation conditions, he freed the slaves and gave them farms. Browning's incensed grandfather sent his son a bill for all the expenses he had incurred, going back to those of his birth. These were duly paid, but it did not bankrupt the family. When young Robert asked, at 17, if there was enough family income for him to pursue "a life of pure culture," he was given an allowance and his father's blessing.

Spared from having to earn a living, Browning began writing poetry. His audience for works such as *Paracelsus* (1835) and *Bells and Pomegranates* (1841–46) was discriminating, and small. A friendship with the older actor William Macready detoured Browning into writing a number of plays such as *Strafford* (1837), *A Blot on the 'Scutcheon* (1843), and *Columbe's Birthday* (1853). These did not achieve notable success; the historical material bored audiences who were more at home with trained animal acts, and the matter-of-fact sexual relationships of the characters upset the Victorian press. Worse, Macready, for whose son Browning had written *The Pied Piper of Hamelin*, demanded rewrites, threw Browning's scripts on the floor in a rage, and termed him "very conceited." Their final quarrel was not resolved for years. Browning went back to poetry.

By 1842 he was ripe for matrimony. He began a correspondence with another poet, Elizabeth Barrett. There was no chance of an accidental meeting. Confined to her father's house on Wimpole Street, suffering from tuberculosis and consoling herself with muriate of morphine and her cocker spaniel, Flush, Elizabeth treated Browning's early protestations of love with alarm. Then, as love developed, her health began to improve, although her father's stranglehold on her life did not. In great secrecy Elizabeth went out for a rare drive, married Browning at St. Marylebone's Church, then raced back home. On September 21, 1846, her long childhood ended at 40 when the pair fled to Italy.

The love of Robert Browning and Elizabeth Barrett, his

"Ba," has been widely celebrated. The couple settled joyously in Florence, though Elizabeth suffered debilitating miscarriages. A son, Pen, was born in 1849. There were a few other shadows. Elizabeth was distressed at her husband's literary inactivity, and at his disclaimer that writing poetry was, for him, not what it was for Elizabeth and Tennyson. During that time he did produce *Love Among the Ruins* and *Childe Harolde to the Dark Tower Came*. But Browning was far happier modelling in clay and socializing with the Trollopes, artist Val Princep, Nathaniel Hawthorne, and the young American reformer Kate Field. Loud, jovial, anecdotal, in his eagerness to converse he would often run a woman right off the couch.

Elizabeth's health was already poor, and her death, from a burst abscess on her trachea on June 29, 1861, was the cruelest of blows. She was buried in Florence, a place to which Browning could never bear to return, and he and Pen left for his father's home in England. The poet handled Elizabeth's death characteristically, howling to a woman friend, "I want her! I want her!" yet writing to another friend three weeks later, "Do not fancy that I am 'prostrated.' " Always trying to put the best face on life, Browning immersed himself in London society with even more vigor, but never remarried. When he did propose in 1869 to one Lady Ashburton, he let her know that her place would be beneath the shadow of the divine Elizabeth, and that he was counting on her fortune to help launch Pen. Her outraged refusal made them permanent enemies.

It was around that time that Browning received his widest popularity with his epic, *The Ring and the Book*, based on the murder of a young Italian woman caught in adultery by her outraged husband. The work explored the complexities of the situation and psychological viewpoints of those involved, and was reviewed by one newspaper as "the most precious and profound spiritual treasure that England has produced since the days of Shakespeare." When he died of pneumonia at his son's home in Venice, there was no question as to where his remains would be headed. But with further burials at Ba's cemetery in Florence forbidden, Browning had to settle for Westminster Abbey.

To your left is a bust of **William Blake** which appears modern in design; he himself is in Bunhill Fields (see Chapter 6 on Bunhill Fields for the biography of William Blake).

Up against the wall is the bust of **John Dryden** (1632–1700). Because his works were so firmly rooted in the politics of his age, Dryden is almost lost to contemporary readers. His marker mirrors the image his own age had of him. Short, stolid, and laconic, with a noticeable mole on his cheek, Dryden would have been a disaster in group therapy. He saw no need to share his feelings, experiences, or beliefs. There was something peculiar about his wife, Lady Elizabeth Howard, but no one knew what; he kept the same mistress for years but nobody cared.

Dryden was accused of protecting his position as poet laureate, which had been granted in 1668, by changing his personal banners with each new regime. He elegized Cromwell, satirized the enemies of Charles II, and converted to Roman Catholicism when James II took the throne. He did not re-embrace Protestantism for William and Mary, however, and lost his laureateship and his pension.

Dryden's writing was lucid and unadorned. His satires, *Absalom and Achitophel* and *MacFlecknoe*, bludgeoned his points home. When he busied himself with the work of others—"scrubbing up" Chaucer, as he put it, and making an opera out of *Paradise Lost*—the results were sometimes unfortunate. But he excelled in his religious poetry, such as *The Hind and the Panther*, and in his tragic plays, *The Indian-Queen* and *Don Sebastian*. Besides these works, what lives on are the critical essays which preceded his plays and helped make Dryden a father of modern English prose.

As you exit the chapel to the outer area where materials for grave rubbings are sold, in the floor you will find the stone of Aphra Behn with the epitaph:

> Here lies a proof that wit can never be
> Defence against mortality.

APHRA BEHN *b. 1640, Canterbury; d. April 16, 1689, London.* According to Virginia Woolf in *A Room of One's Own*, "All women together ought to let flowers fall upon the tomb of Aphra Behn, for it was she who earned them the right to speak their minds." Yet her neglected grave reflects her position in society both in the 1600s and now. Buried outside the warm conviviality of Poets' Corner, her inscription has been worn clean by the careless feet of centuries. Behn's work has been virtually forgotten as well, although much of her writing deserves that fate.

Behn's plays were written for the Restoration era, a time in which sexuality was elevated to a minor religion. Language was frank—as explicit as any that has appeared in modern plays—and sexual coupling was constant. Women were allowed to have sexual appetites as voracious and promiscuous as men's, although there was the inevitable societal backlash. The mistress of Charles II, Nell Gwynn, and many other women were described in scornful and graphic language.

Into this atmosphere came Behn, determined to support herself by writing. She had had a short, undistinguished career as a Dutch spy, and a brief marriage to an older Dutch merchant who presumably died in the Great Plague of 1665–66. Florid, with reddish-brown sausage curls, snake-hooded eyes, and a slight double chin, Aphra was soon turning out bawdy plays and novels for Restoration society. *The Amorous Prince* (1671), *The Rover* (1677), and *The Lucky Chance* (1686) were all successfully staged, along with dozens of others. Characters in *The Rover* include Willmore, who believes in sex without responsibility; Angelica, the whore, who has resolved that "nothing but gold shall charm my heart"; and Hellena, who yearns for sexual freedom but is determined to avoid being stuck with "a cradle full of noise and mischief, with a pack of repentance at my back."

It was a dilemma that Aphra could not solve for herself. Unwilling to marry again, she took lovers, suffering the reputation of the "ruined woman," despite the freedom of the age. She railed against marriage for financial gain in works such as *The Forced Marriage*, and supported herself successfully by her writing alone, though she frequently had to importune publishers to give her what they owed her. A woman who supported herself by her pen was unprecedented.

Aphra did not always choose her lovers wisely. John Hoyle, presumed to be the author of her epitaph, was witty, cynical, and unable to commit himself to anyone. He explored every avenue of pleasure, and was arrested for homosexuality. Knowing that he feared both her tongue and her desires Aphra sometimes joked that she was "the Behn" of his existence. Yet some of her most touching poems were written to Hoyle. He was stabbed to death in a tavern brawl in 1692; the jury, citing his quarrelsomeness, returned a verdict of self-defense in favor of his assailant.

Aphra put up with the condescension of her male peers and the pain of having her work, her beauty, and her life lampooned in verse until she was 48. Then, suffering from arthritis and related ailments, she took her leave.

DIRECTIONS TO WESTMINSTER ABBEY: Take the District or Circle Line to the Westminster stop. Walk south one block to Victoria Street, and turn left. The Abbey will be ahead on your right.

CHAPTER 5

The Tower
of London

THE TOWER OF LONDON, even visited in bright sunshine,
can be a chilly proposition. Its numerous turrets and colorful flags give it the look of a toy left out on the lawn. But
despite its thousands of daily tourists, the Tower's dark
history lurks in its gray stone buildings. As night falls,
ghosts are said to walk, particularly in the Beauchamp
Tower and the Bloody Tower, and along Tower Green.
Sometimes they toss stones at the sentries patrolling; other times they simply appear in period costume and then
vanish.

Originally constructed as a fortress and palace for William the Conqueror, the structure reached its present size
of more than 20 towers by 1300. Coronations and royal
weddings took place here, but it was first an arsenal and a
defense. If you look up as you enter through Byward
Tower, you will see three "murder holes," from which
boiling oil and water could be poured on uninvited guests.
The tour of the Tower, offered at no charge by a Beefeater
guide, is fascinating. But for our purposes, we will move to
Tower Green and the Chapel of St. Peter ad Vincula (St.
Peter in Chains) where the bodies of the Tower's victims
were buried.

ST. PETER AD VINCULA AND TOWER GREEN

A few of the executions took place on Tower Green, but
many more were done on Trinity Green, the hill that rises
behind the Tower. Treated as festivals, they attracted
20,000 to 40,000 spectators to picnic and be entertained by
jesters and musicians. The condemned, who had their portraits painted just before dying, were allowed to make a
final statement. Noblemen had to give their executioners

The Tower from Tower Bridge

"severance pay," and the axemen also got to keep various pieces of apparel, such as Anne Boleyn's garters. Then the axe or sword fell on the condemned neck; as the masses cheered, the head was hoisted by the hair with the proclamation, "So end all traitors. God save the King!"

Not everyone imprisoned in the Tower died there, of course. Elizabeth I was kept confined temporarily by her half-sister, Mary Tudor, and Archbishop Thomas Cranmer was released (to be later burned at the stake in Oxford). Some of the Tower dead were buried elsewhere. Sir Walter Raleigh's body was taken to St. Margaret's Church in London and his head sent to West Horsley, Surrey, and Mary Queen of Scots is in Westminster Abbey, along with what are presumed to be the bones of the Little Princes. King Henry VI was murdered while at prayers in Wakefield Tower, but his body lies in St. George's Chapel, Windsor Castle.

Because of its history, the Tower has developed its own lore. **James Scot** (1649–1685), Duke of Monmouth, an illegitimate son of Charles II, tried to take the throne from his uncle, James II, by invading England at Dorset with a ragged band of believers. The rebellion was put down and Monmouth was imprisoned in the Tower and executed. But someone had forgotten to have his portrait painted; his head was hastily retrieved from where it had been impaled as an object lesson on London Bridge. The painting, completed in 24 hours, shows him wearing a scarf around his neck.

Margaret Pole (1471–1541), Countess of Salisbury, though blameless, was executed at 70 because Henry VIII could not get her son, the Roman Catholic Cardinal Reginald Pole, who railed against Henry's unique religious interpretations from the safety of France. In response, the King imprisoned and executed Pole's older brother, cousin, nephew, and a friend, Sir Edward Nevile, as well as Pole's mother. Proclaiming her innocence, Margaret refused to kneel at the block and challenged her executioner to "remove her head the best he could." He chased her around the scaffold on Tower Green, hacking her to death. According to witnesses, the ghostly scene has been reenacted on the anniversaries of her death.

Henry VIII was also responsible for the Tower death of **John Fisher**, Bishop of Rochester, who opposed his divorce from Katharine. Fisher, an old-fashioned cleric who slept on a straw mat, wore a hair shirt, and dined alone with a skull for company while being read religious homilies, was not impressed by wealth or power. For 14 months he was held with Sir Thomas More in the Bell Tower. After execution, Fisher's body was interred in Barking Abbey, Greater London. More was buried here in St. Peter ad Vincula.

Sir **Thomas More** (1478–1535), 13 years older than Henry VIII, had few illusions about the nature of his God-given king. Even as he traversed the royal gardens, discussing theology, astronomy, and mathematics with the excited youth, he gingerly rubbed the back of his neck from time to time, knowing it to be his most vulnerable part. His joke about Henry's willingness to sacrifice him for a castle in France seemed grounded in truth.

More, a dark-eyed man with an impressively jutting nose and steady chin, received a scholarly education at Oxford and came under the influence of the Renaissance humanism of John Colet and Erasmus. Described by a contemporary as "a man of angel's wit . . . of marvelous mirth and pastimes, and sometimes of sad gravity, a man for all seasons," More became a respected lawyer. He also authored *Utopia* (1516), his blueprint for an ideal state based on reason.

It was with some sense of self-preservation that More initially refused Henry's offer to become Lord Chancellor in 1529. But it was a command performance. Henry's Great Matter was already on the table, but the King assured More that he would not force him into the divorce controversy. The lawyer, he said, could "look first unto God, and after God unto him." But six years later when Henry, as described in the chapter on St. George's Chapel, made himself the Head of the Church of England rather than the Pope, he insisted that More sign an oath of agreement. Unwilling to do so, the Chancellor was imprisoned in the Tower with John Fisher for over a year. Their assent was seen as crucial to the new regime, a necessary divine blessing. But they would not give it.

On June 22, 1535, Thomas More went to the block over the tears of his daughter who begged him to change his mind. He stayed in good spirits; at the scaffold he commented to his executioners, "I pray thee see me safely up, and for my coming down let me shift for myself," and pushed his long white beard out from under his neck since "*it* had never committed treason." More, whose last words were, "I die the King's good servant, but God's first," was canonized as a saint by the Roman Catholic Church in 1935.

Turning to your left, move past the Tower Green to the Chapel. It is an attractive example of Tudor architecture though surprisingly small. Its foundation is held firmly by the weight of the 1,500 bodies shoved without ceremony beneath its paving stones. Queen Victoria had them all exhumed and properly reburied when she had the Chapel restored in 1876. After three years of work, 33 bodies were identified, including Anne Boleyn's.

The sanctuary proper contains a number of monuments of the families of Tower officers, parishioners, and other personnel. The monument of **John Holland**, Duke of Exeter, shows him and two of his wives. He was the inventor of the rack.

In the front of the Chapel, under the marble pavement in front of the altar, is buried the most famous person to die within the Tower precincts:

ANNE BOLEYN *b. ca. 1501–1507; d. May 29, 1536, London.* When Anne Boleyn was born, nobody cared. When she died, the eyes of the world were riveted on her slender neck. Public sentiment, which had condemned her as the whore "Nan Bullen," was shifting in her favor. The outwardly pious Henry was increasingly being perceived as a threat to human life. His complaints that Anne had "bewitched" him rang very hollow.

If true, the spell would have been a long one. Henry VIII first encountered Anne when she was a playful child with lustrous black hair and a deformed hand, acting as a lady-in-waiting to Queen Katharine. A few years later he was displeased to find that Anne had an "understanding" with young Henry Percy, and instructed Cardinal Wolsey and the boy's father to bully him out of it. Henry Percy wept, but capitulated. Anne, not knowing of the King's intervention, was sent home from Court seemingly in disgrace.

Henry caught up with her at her father's estate, and for the next ten years wooed her. Anne accepted his gifts and his company, but guarded her chastity. She would be nothing but Queen. Henry, unfortunately, already had one. So he began to wonder if his marriage of 18 years was legal. Katharine, after all, had been married to his older brother, Arthur, before being widowed, and that gave their union the taint of incest. Perhaps it was God's judgment on them that she had failed to give him a living male heir.

His pious concerns fooled no one. As Shakespeare slyly described it:

> Chamberlain: It seems the marriage with his brother's wife has crept too close to his conscience.
> Suffolk: No, his conscience has crept too near another lady.

That other lady did not need supernatural powers to know how to manage the King. By refusing to become his mistress, she remained unattainable. By expressing her temper and her whims freely, she kept Henry off balance. It was, perhaps, the intensity of his passion which suggested witchcraft to sixteenth-century Britons. There were other "signs" as well. Anne had been born with a strawberry-sized mole on her neck, known as the devil's paw print, and a rudimentary sixth finger on her right hand. She had a pet wolfhound named Urian—one of the esoteric names for Satan—who groveled around her like a familiar. It was easy to believe that she had struck a dark bargain in exchange for the throne of England.

The "annulment" from Katharine that Henry was seeking from the Church was foundering. He had cast around for clergy who would support his theological interpretation, and was waiting to hear from the pope—but the best voices said it would not be allowed. Henry had already beheaded one clergyman, Thomas Abell, for criticizing him. He was now infuriated

Anne knew when to make her next move. Ennobled by Henry as the Marquise of Pembroke and given the jewels of the Queen of England, she pulled back the covers and hoped to conceive a male heir. When the pregnancy was confirmed, the couple was secretly married in January 1533. It was a "hole-and-corner affair," that Henry promised would be redeemed by her coronation. Breaking with the Roman Catholic Church, Henry divorced Katharine and, with the Act of Supremacy, made his will the law of the land in 1534.

But the magic had already left the relationship. In addition to the inevitable letdown of having achieved his desire, Henry had also sacrificed his dignity, his religion, and several of his closest relationships—all for a woman his subjects barely tolerated. When Anne protested Henry's taking a mistress during her pregnancy, he told her to shut up and endure as "her betters [Katharine] had done." The lover who had signed his letters with hearts and had written love poems was disappearing.

There was still the "male heir" that Anne was carrying; but he turned out to be Elizabeth I. A string of miscarriages followed, always of baby boys, until Henry told Anne harshly, "You will get no more sons by me." What happened next is speculative. Knowing that her position depended on giving birth to a healthy male child, Anne may have bedded down with court musician Mark Smeaton in the hope of producing a hardier baby. Alternatively, she may have called him to her bedchamber only for his soothing melodies.

In any case, he was detained at the home of Cardinal Thomas Cromwell, and tortured until he confessed. Not only did he confess, but implicated four other men, including Anne's brother, George. One lover would have made Henry VIII a cuckold; five made her a nymphomaniac. Whisked away to the Tower, Anne and the five men were tried. There were no last-minute confessions of guilt on the scaffold. With her "lovers" dead, the Queen commended her soul to God and inclined her neck. Once severed, her head and body were quickly reunited in an old arrow box and taken to St. Peter ad Vincula.

Just before her death Anne (who had threatened seven years of drought in England if she died) left a message for Henry that no one dared deliver:

> Commend me to his majesty and tell him that he hath been ever constant in his career of advancing me; from a private gentlewoman he made me a Marchioness, from a Marchioness a Queen and now that hath left no higher degree of honour he gives my innocency the crown of martyrdom.

Henry VIII left another wife here, his fifth, though histo-

The Wakefield Tower (far left) and the White Tower

ry has agreed that she was more deserving of her fate than Anne Boleyn. **Catherine Howard** (ca. 1521–1542), Anne's first cousin, was a voluptuous 19-year-old who cheerfully flaunted her charms for His Majesty's pleasure. Unlike Anne, who held out for nine years, Catherine had never said no to anyone. But Henry was once again enchanted and covered the flirtatious teenager with diamonds and rubies, castles and lands.

In an interesting revenge against Henry, the matron of Catherine's suite, Lady Rochford (the widow of Anne's brother, George Boleyn, who was executed for "incest" with Anne), took delight in smuggling various lovers into the Queen's bedchamber. On a royal visit north it became a game, as one of Henry's courtiers, Thomas Culpepper, of whom Catherine had always been fond, slipped in and out of the room, narrowly averting being seen by the guards.

The fun ended when Thomas Cranmer finally confirmed that the rumors were true. The 50-year-old Henry had, at first, refused to believe the stories that his "rose without a thorn" had been already plucked when they were married.

But his council convinced him that her infidelity was on-going. Henry wept and Catherine left for the Tower. Standing at the executioner's block she announced defiantly, "I die a Queen, but I would rather die the wife of Culpepper."

Another young woman buried in St. Peter ad Vincula ran afoul of Henry's daughter:

JANE GREY *b. October, 1537, Lincolnshire; d. February 12, 1554, London.* The story of Lady Jane Grey is a sad one. She was bright, outspoken, and ardent in her faith, but those qualities could not save her. In the end the only thing that mattered was her bloodline, the accident of birth which brought her too close to the Tudor conflagration.

Jane, the niece of Henry VIII and therefore the cousin of Mary Tudor and Elizabeth I, got her first taste of Court life at nine when she was sent to live with her newly widowed aunt, Catherine Parr, Henry VIII's last wife. The tiny, freckled Jane had been sadly neglected by her own family; she blossomed under the former Queen's kindness. But when Catherine died six years later, Jane was returned to her parents.

She was quick to tell anyone who would listen that she considered their company hellish, complaining that if she didn't do everything "as perfectly as God made the world," she was "sharply taunted and cruelly threatened." She also joined with the resident chaplain, James Haddon, in criticizing them for compulsive gambling with cards and dice.

Within months the self-appointed critic was forced to submit to an arranged marriage with Guildford Dudley, the spoiled youngest son of the ambitious Duke of Northumberland. She protested loudly, but her parents were adamant. Jane was wed in a triple ceremony which included her 13-year-old sister, Catherine, and new sister-in-law, Catherine Dudley. Neither of Jane's Tudor cousins attended, and their brother Edward was too ill.

Once Jane became the property of the Dudleys, the Duke of Northumberland set to work. He influenced Edward on his deathbed to alter the line of succession, by-passing his half sisters, Mary and Elizabeth, and coming to rest on their cousin Jane. Warily Jane allowed herself to be proclaimed Queen on Edward's death. But she was not deceived by her position as a pawn. Her first official act as Queen was to deny Guildford the right to be crowned King, stating she would make him a duke instead. The Dudleys protested loudly—the whole point of the marriage had been to gain entrée to the royal line—but Jane stood firm.

She might have eventually yielded, but in nine days it

was all over. The people of England, who despised Northumberland and were attached to Mary Tudor, rebelled, rioting and proclaiming Mary Queen. Jane, who had been living in the Tower as Queen, was suddenly its prisoner. She wrote to her cousin Mary explaining the circumstances, and admitting that she never should have accepted the crown. Mary, believing her, had the Duke of Northumberland executed for his role, but was prepared to spare little Jane.

But Jane became a rallying point for the Protestants, making her a dangerous threat to the Catholic Mary. Jane's father, the Duke of Suffolk, was implicated in a plot to overthrow the Queen and restore his daughter to the throne. Always candid where her parents were concerned, Jane sent him a message of condolence when he was brought to the Tower, but added tartly that her death "was being hastened by one by whom my life should rather have been lengthened."

Guildford and his brothers were also imprisoned in the Tower. On the morning of February 12, 1554, Jane watched as her large, attractive husband was brought out of Beauchamp Tower, and refused to leave the window until she had witnessed the straw-filled cart returning from Trinity Green on its way to the chapel, his head wrapped crudely in a rag. Because of her royal blood, a private scaffold was being erected on Tower Green.

Dressed in black and dry-eyed, Jane quietly climbed the scaffold, accepting a handkerchief to place over her eyes. After proclaiming her Christian faith and washing her hands in symbolic innocence, the 16-year-old knelt on the straw to have her neck severed.

ST. MARY-AT-LAMBETH

A pleasant though not short walk from the Tower is St. Mary-at-Lambeth Church situated by the Albert Embankment and Lambeth Bridge.

Before entering, it is worth looking at the old tombstones by the church wall. Here you will find Mrs. **Jane Phillips**, "wife of William of this parish, butcher." On her stone is the couplet:

Adieu blest woman partner of my life
A tender mother and a faithful wife.

Nearby are the family of **William** and **Hannah Wood** whose stone sports a skull and crossbones.

The old church houses the Museum of Garden History, a tribute to the **Tradescant** family whose remains rest in the garden cemetery in the rear. The garden is a delightful, small oasis based on seventeenth-century patterns and is tended by the Friends of the Tradescant Trust.

Fittingly the most prominent memorial is the Tradescants'. At one end the large tomb pictures a multi-headed griffin and a skull flanked by trees. On one of the long sides is a scene of nature overtaking a past civilization. John Tradescant the Elder (d. 1637) and the Younger (1608–1662) were the foremost gardeners of their day, tending the gardens of the First Lord of Salisbury and of Charles I and Henrietta Maria. They made long, dangerous trips to North Africa, Russia, and America and brought back many plant species which now populate English gardens, such as rockrose, primula, Canadian columbine, trumpet honeysuckle, and the yucca plant. They introduced trees as well, including the honey locust, tulip, and swamp cypress.

Notable for its sculpted eternal flame is the monument to the most famous resident, **William Bligh** (1754–1817), Esquire, F.R.S., Vice Admiral of the Blue. Born in Cornwall, Bligh joined the navy as a cabin boy at the age of seven. Sailing with Captain James Cook on his second voyage (1772–1774) he was also master of the *Resolution* on Cook's final trip (1776–1780). A botanical thread led to Bligh commanding the H.M.S. *Bounty* in 1787, for the ship was to pick up breadfruit trees in Tahiti and carry them to the West Indies for transplanting. Near Tonga, on the way home from Tahiti, the crew mutinied under the command of Fletcher Christian and set Bligh and 18 followers adrift in a longboat. In a moment of compassion Christian gave Bligh a sextant. Incredibly Bligh used it to navigate the boat 3,600 miles in 48 days to Timor in the East Indies.

Christian and his men returned to Pitcairn Island, their colony undiscovered until 1808. Their descendants still reside on the island. Bligh returned quickly to command, again sailing to Tahiti to gather breadfruit. During the French Revolutionary Wars Bligh distinguished himself at the Battles of Camperdown in 1797 and at Copenhagen in 1801. He was appointed governor of New South Wales in 1805 but was again the subject of mutiny three years later. After a trial found the mutineers guilty, Bligh was promoted to rear admiral, and finally to vice admiral in 1814.

The question is, of course, what kind of man was Bligh? Was his behavior so tyrannical that it warranted mutiny? The answer is still unclear. There is no doubt that he was a man of courage and a great navigator. Similarly there is no doubt that his verbal abuse of subordinate officers and men was extreme. This abuse, coupled with his overbearing personality, certainly exacerbated the harsh conditions and dangers of life at sea. Beyond doubt Christian found Bligh's disparagement to be unbearable, although it is perhaps true that the notion of returning to Mauatua, his beautiful native lover on Tahiti, may have increased his resolve to mutiny. Caught between the hell that was Bligh's command and the temptations of Eden, Christian chose the voyage back in time. With Mauatua, eight mutineers and their eight kidnapped Tahitian "wives," six Polynesian men and three more Tahitian women, Christian eventually settled on Pitcairn Island. Paradise proved elusive from the start and four years later, angered at their mistreatment, the native men revolted in 1793, killing Christian in the process.

Tradescant memorial

DIRECTIONS TO THE TOWER AND ST. MARY'S: Take the District or Circle Line to the Tower Hill stop. Follow the signs along Tower Hill Road to the Tower. To reach St. Mary's, take the Bakerloo Line to the Lambeth North stop and walk down Kennington Road. Turn right on Lambeth Road, which will bring you to the church.

THE WORLD IS MY PARISH

...CTED ...WHITFUNDS COLLECTED
...CHILDREN OF METHODISM

WESLEY

Bunhill Fields

BUNHILL FIELDS IS a charming surprise in the heart of London, a park in which are buried a mixture of saints, sinners, and plague victims. This unlikely blend arises from the fact that the cemetery is unconsecrated ground. For the religious dissenters, such as Baptists and Quakers, it meant that they could be laid to rest here without the forced ministrations of an Anglican priest. For the others, a churchyard burial was either not allowed or thought not to do much good anyway.

Bunhill is a probable variation of Bone Hill, although the name was used even before it received its first infusion of bones from the charnel house connected with St. Paul's Churchyard. In 1666, the year of the Great Plague, over 5,000 bodies were buried weekly in the Great Plague Pit; eventually the plague toll buried here exceeded 120,000.

After the bombings of World War II some rearranging was done. The monuments of its most famous residents — John Bunyan, Daniel Defoe, and William Blake—were made more accessible and a garden was created in the northern area. Because of the danger of old stones falling, visitors are not allowed in the grassy areas. But you can get a good sense of Bunhill Fields by peering over the chain-link fence.

As you walk through the gates, look into the section to your right. In approximately the center is the stone bier of **Isaac Watts** (1674–1748), the father of English hymnody. He insisted on the modest inscription which explains that "after fifty years of feeble labours in the Gospel, interrupted by four years of tiresome sickness, [he] was at last dismissed to rest." Although Watts studied at the Dissenting Academy and was minister of a Nonconformist chapel for ten years, he is best known for his hymns "When I Survey the Wondrous Cross," "O God, Our Help in Ages Past," "Jesus Shall Reign Where'er the Sun," and "Joy to the World."

John Wesley

Walk into the open square. On your left is the memorial of John Bunyan, the author of *Pilgrim's Progress*. The reclining figure, which may or may not be Bunyan (the owner of the tomb, **John Strudwick**, was buried here first), is well worn. On one side of the monument is Christian, the pilgrim of *Pilgrim's Progress*, kneeling and holding up a cross; on the other side he is toiling with his "sacke of synne," leaning heavily on a staff. The inscription explains that the tomb was restored by public subscription in May 1862.

JOHN BUNYAN *b. November 30, 1628, Elstow, Bedfordshire; d. August 31, 1688, London.* To those who attended Sunday school, the name John Bunyan conjures up a flannelgraph memory of Pilgrim making his way through the pitfalls of Life, dazzled by Vanity Fair, despairing at the Slough of Despond. Like his alter ego, Christian, John Bunyan's life was a series of adventures. The son of a tinker, Bunyan received an education thin as a cup of gruel; at 16 he was drafted into the Parliamentary Army. Four years later, on his discharge, he took up his father's occupation of mending pots and pans, and found a wife. Marriage brought him a dowry of two books — *The Practice of Piety*, and *The Plaine Man's Pathway*.

The Plaine Man's Pathway, standard reading for every Puritan, was an instruction manual of 1,031 pages which reawakened in him terrifying childhood nightmares of burning in hell. Playing tipcat one Sunday afternoon on the village green, he was stopped in mid-toss by a voice which demanded, "Wilt thou leave thy sins and go to heaven or have thy sins and go to hell?"

Although his greatest transgression to that point had been swearing, Bunyan forswore that immediately for redemption. He joined a Baptist church in 1653 and zealously began lay preaching and writing theological pamphlets. It was an unpopular stance. With the demise of Oliver Cromwell and the Restoration, independent preachers had been outlawed for fear that they would incite rebellion against the state.

In 1660 Bunyan, whose only goal was to save souls from damnation as he had been saved, was arrested. Stubbornly, the large, ruddy man with a pear-shaped face, pageboy hair, and ungovernable moustache rejected offers of freedom in exchange for a promise that he would not preach again. Recently widowed and remarried, he left his new wife, Elizabeth, with his four young children. She supported him wholeheartedly, but neither of them realized that it would mean 12 years of imprisonment.

Prison life was unsanitary and grim, with a high mortality rate. In Bedford Prison there was no heat, washing facilities, nor means of disposing of human waste. Prisoners paid their jailers an annual fee for the cell's straw flooring on which they slept and the quarter loaf of bread they were fed each day. Yet Bunyan was allowed books and writing materials, and his eldest daughter, Blind Annie, brought him soup from home every day. As the jail's unofficial chaplain, Bunyan could occasionally hold services. He also published the story of his own conversion, *Grace Abounding to the Chief of Sinners*, during this time.

In 1672 Charles II, leaning toward Roman Catholicism, pardoned dissenting ministers, primarily Quakers, so that he could also free Catholic priests. Ironically, it was the Quakers, whom Bunyan had attacked so fiercely (and would so fiercely attack again), who generously suggested that his name and others be added to the Instrument of Pardon. Thus freed, and with a call to the Bedford Baptist Church, Bunyan settled down to become a country parson. But in 1675 the pardon was reversed, and Bunyan was returned to Bedford Prison for six months. From this confinement *Pilgrim's Progress* was born.

The tale of the quest, man's search for his destiny, did not originate with Bunyan, and the allegorical form was common in the seventeenth century. But the preacher wrote with color and suspense. From the beginning, in which Christian leaves the City of Destruction, sticking his fingers in his ears to muffle the cries of his wife and children and resisting the attempts of Obstinate and Pliable to hold him back physically, the plot moves quickly. Readers felt the hopelessness of the Slough of Despond and the temptations of Vanity Fair, and recognized such characters as Mr. Facing-both-Ways and Mrs. Diffidence. There was relief when Pilgrim was finally shown through the Wicker Gate.

There were real-life parallels, of course, in the way Bunyan had turned his back on his wife and children to go to prison for what he believed, refusing the compromises that would have made him a free man. Twelve years of harsh prison conditions would have given him many experiences on which to draw. Yet as if recognizing *Pilgrim's Progress* as his own story, in the sequel Bunyan sends his wife, family, and others on the same path, but gives them a more pleasant experience, and lets them travel together. It is his admission that all conversions are not equally intense.

In the last days of his life Bunyan mellowed still further. He wrote a number of charming rhymes for children along with his usual polemics, though he had no idea that his work would outlive him. At 59, riding 40 miles through a driving rain to preach in London, he became ill. Unable to shake what was probably pneumonia, he died at the home of a friend, John Strudwick, and was buried in the back of Bunhill Fields. When Strudwick died in 1695, John Bunyan's bones were transferred to his friend's vault.

After he wrote *Pilgrim's Progress*, Bunyan evidently polled his contemporaries before sending the allegory to the printer and reported their reaction in verse:

> Some said, John, print it; others said, not so;
> Some said, it might be good; others said, No.
> At last, I thought, since you are thus divided
> I print it will, and so the case decided.

Millions of children, whose Sunday mornings were brightened by Pilgrim's tribulations, say, "Amen."

At the other end of the open courtyard is another author, also famous among children but for a character who faced a different set of challenges. The obelisk to Daniel Defoe, creator of *Robinson Crusoe*, was erected in 1870 by young readers of the *Christian World Newspaper*.

Bunhill Fields

DANIEL DEFOE *b. Autumn 1660, London; d. April 26, 1731, London.* Defoe's London childhood was precarious for it entailed surviving both the Plague of 1665–66 and the Great Fire of 1666. Yet, though these momentous events left their mark on his youthful memory, he came through them healthy and unsinged. Of far greater consequence was the plague of religious persecution. Defoe's principled parents were Dissenters and while growing up he witnessed interrupted services, the arrest of ministers and members, the incursion of spies, and the harassment of the community. The courageous leadership and willing martyrdom of men like Rev. Samuel Annesley set for Defoe an example of aggressive independence and speech, cementing his belief in religious toleration.

His father, James Foe, was a successful merchant and a freeman in the City of London. Attracted to this world, Daniel put aside his ministerial studies for the excitement of commerce and politics, but did so only with great difficulty. He was already writing, and though his *Meditations* (1681) and *Historical Collections* (1682) did not gain widespread acclaim, they did attract the attention of Mary Tufley, the daughter of a cooper, whom he married on New Year's Day, 1684. As religious tensions rose in 1685, Defoe put work and family aside and joined the Duke of Monmouth's ill-fated rebellion against James II. He survived the rout at Sedgemoor and, just as importantly, evaded arrest at home before finally being pardoned by the King in 1687. Capture might well have meant death, torture, or deportation.

Initially Defoe's business as a hosier flourished. As it did he expanded his outlook and began trading in wine, beer, and cloth goods. Inexperienced, he was soon overextended and in serious debt. War with France in 1689 dried up trade. Defoe became desperate, invested in efforts to recover sunken treasure, and even imported civet cats, whose musk, used as a base for perfume, was extracted with a spatula from a sac located above the anus. Despising the cats and unable to pay for them, the sweet scent of a steady income turned sour. By 1692 Defoe was bankrupt and twice arrested for his debts.

To avoid debtor's prison Defoe schemed, renegotiated, lied, delayed, and cheated. He also took up the pen to earn extra money. Publishing one political and religious pamphlet after another, his opinions became increasingly vehement, and in 1702 his satiric *The Shortest Way with the Dissenters* exacted a warrant for his arrest for seditious libel. Defoe became seen all over town. Advertisements for his arrest described him as "middle siz'd [i.e., five feet four inches] . . . of brown complexion, and dark brown-colored hair, but wears a wig; a hooked nose, a sharp chin, grey eyes, and a large mole near his mouth" and offered a reward of £50 for his capture (this was notable, for most similar rewards were smaller and were based on conviction). For months Defoe avoided arrest, even brazenly attempting to bargain by letter and messsenger with his inquisitor, Nottingham, but by May 1703 he was found and sent to Newgate Prison.

Five months in wretched prison conditions were bad enough, but the pillory could mean death and, as if wishing to secure just that, Defoe was sentenced to stand it three times. Not only were the victim's head and hands imprisoned in a wooden frame but he was publicly ridiculed and pelted with stones, rotten eggs, filth, and live or dead cats. His clothes might have been stripped and he might have been beaten to death. Defoe fared better at the pillory than any man in history, for his friends and supporters surrounded him and insured that the only offerings were floral.

Defoe stood his punishment firmly, but was less conscience-stricken in his efforts to obtain release from jail. Currying favor with Robert Harley, the speaker of the House of Commons, Defoe was freed. In return he was to be a spy and propagandist. Because *The Shortest Way* had placed the Dissenters in an even more precarious position by making them appear yet more dangerous, Defoe was already being isolated by many of his fellows. His early release fooled no one and sealed his deteriorating relationship with the Dissenters.

With his bankruptcy, the undying stigma of the pillory, and his religious isolation, Defoe's natural sociability declined. He enjoyed the information-gathering trips to the countryside which Harley ordered, but such travel took him from his family and relations there grew and remained strained. Laden with guilt but freed by travel, Defoe reported on the political mood of various villages and on individuals who were pamphleteering and editorializing. In Scotland he spied and propagandized for the unification of England and Scotland.

Though a devout Whig, Defoe argued capably for the Tories when they were in power. In fairness he did not renounce his belief in religious toleration and political freedom and, influenced by Locke, he firmly held many of the ideals that fueled the American Revolution. Even in his political hack work he was ahead of the times in his ability to recognize special-interest groups and appeal to their specific needs.

And so his life went: a hired pen, pamphlets and newspapers of his own opinion, constant money problems, a large family to raise, economic strategems to ensure the supremacy of England (he prophetically advocated strong trade, colonization, and a powerful navy), poems, satire, sexual advice for the newly married, and finally the novel. Published when he was almost 60, Defoe's adventure story, *Robinson Crusoe* (1719), is credited by many as the first novel. More novels followed, such as *Moll Flanders* (1722) and *Roxana* (1724) as well as the fictionalized history, *A Journal of the Plague Year* (1722). Though slighted by polite society, his books were successful with the unpretentious and with commoners. In them Defoe was able to combine realistic detail and psychological insight, often incorporating his own isolation and the struggle between pragmatism and genuine piety that he waged in his own life.

Defoe was unchanged to the end. Dodging debt and jail he left his family in financial need and took up squalid lodgings in Rope Makers' Alley. Bitterly realizing that help from his successful son Daniel was not forthcoming, he sank "under the weight of an Affliction too heavy for my Strength, under the Load of Insupportable Sorrows." He died from a stroke, with no consolation from the generous eulogies published in the newspapers after his death.

Behind the obelisk and to the right is a plain marker which reads, "Nearby lie the remains of the poet-painter William Blake and of his wife **Catherine Sophia** (1762–1831)." His exact burial location is not known. Also buried here are Blake's father and his brothers, **Robert** and **James**.

WILLIAM BLAKE *b. November 28, 1757, London; d. August 12, 1827, London.*

> I must Create a System or be enslav'd by another Man's.
> I will not Reason & Compare: my business is to Create.

Blake was a man of religious vision and apocalyptic fervor; indeed he was a child of the same. At age four he saw God's head appearing at the window, and at eight or ten spied a tree filled with angels. His father wanted to beat these mischievous visions out of him but his mother, recognizing the boy's sincerity, intervened. As a young man he sat a death vigil for his beloved brother, Robert. At the moment of expiration he saw Robert's soul ascend "clapping its hands for joy" and from that time took dictation from

Robert in his writings as well as inspiration for a new print-ing technique for his illustrations. Such visions did not appear to be schizophrenic, for Blake was always aware of himself. He was grounded in reality, yet his mind operated through divine inspiration. Such polar extremes were typi-cal of his philosophy and psychology.

Blake was the third son of a London hosier. When he could hold a pencil he began to draw, and, because of his temper, was educated at home. Recognizing his artistic talent his parents supplied him with materials and encour-agement, and enrolled him in art school when he was ten. Apprenticeship to an artist, however desirable, was ruled out due to the expenses of the large Blake family, and at 14 William was apprenticed instead for seven years to James Basire, an engraver. He learned his craft well, though he typically shunned those artists currently in favor for those of his own liking. He not only knew his mind but spoke it, clearly, forcefully, and often satirically. To his elders and betters it was not his most endearing trait.

While studying engraving Blake drew sketches for Rich-ard Gough's *Sepulchral Monuments*. Since Westminster Abbey was a less proper place in those days, Blake could be found straddling the royal tombs so he could better see their details. But the Abbey also afforded him a place of quiet, reverence, and visions. He described Christ and the Apostles as being "organized and minutely articulated be-yond all that the mortal and perishing nature can produce."

Despite his fondness for Basire, Blake left in 1779 and enrolled in art at the newly formed Royal Academy. Along with his paintings he was producing poetry and prose. *Poetic Sketches*, a collection of his teenage work which he sometimes sang to his own melodies, was published in 1783.

Blake was not blind to more worldly pursuits. In fact he could not seem to escape them. In 1781, fleeing a soured infatuation, he visited Battersea only to fall in love with Catherine Boucher, his host's daughter. Illiterate, Cather-ine signed the marriage register with an "X" when they were married a year later. But she was sympathetic, sup-portive, intelligent, and pretty, and Blake, now a print-shop owner and engraver, soon taught her to read, write, and help with the printing.

Blake was drawn to extremes in his political beliefs. He was inspired by both the American and French revolutions, staunchly opposed slavery, and could not abide mistreat-ment of either people or animals. Not surprisingly his reli-gious beliefs were singular. Influenced briefly by Swedenborg he and Catherine helped to start the New Jerusalem Church, but they dropped out shortly thereafter and never joined another congregation. Blake decried established religion and Deism. He declared that "there is no Natural Religion," believing instead that all religions were one.

One of Blake's overriding themes was: "Without contraries there is no progression." *The Songs of Innocence* (1789) juxtaposed with the *Songs of Experience* (1789–94) and *The Marriage of Heaven and Hell* (1790–93) all dramatize this belief. The illustrations and decorations (etched in relief, printed, and then individually watercolored) with which he surrounded each poem supply yet more meaning and inspiration. The art is powerful — stylized human forms, apocalyptic themes, and superb color. Blake's work was of a piece and not meant for anthologizing in black and white print. For Blake art was religious; it was the expression of the divine in man.

In 1800 the Blakes moved to Felpham on the seacoast under the patronage of William Hayley. Patronage soon became patronization and the independent Blake moved back to London to work on his own. His later works such as *The Four Zoas* (1795–1804), *Milton* (1804–08), and *Jerusalem* (1804–20), were based on the Book of Revelation, and grew increasingly apocalyptic, using that theme as a metaphor for man's inner state of fall from grace.

Blake did poorly on his own and after a failed one-man art show in 1809 he all but passed into obscurity and poverty. By the 1820s he had given up poetry and concentrated on his art. He produced perhaps his finest work, illustrations of enormous strength for *Dante* (1825–27) and *The Book of Job* (1820–25). In his last years he enjoyed a revival and found himself surrounded by a coterie of young admirers. It gladdened him in his old age. But Blake might well have been happy anyway, for he was frequently heard singing his impromptu songs of praise. Lying in bed near death he announced, "Kate, you have been a good wife, I will draw your portrait." Two days later, just before he died, "his eyes brightened and he burst out into singing of the things he saw in heaven."

As you move away, notice the thin slate marker about five feet tall, with an ornate picture of what appears to be a workman tending a flame. Various tools are scattered around him—including a pickaxe with a skull lying near it on the ground.

Most of the other markers are not decorated and have religious and eulogistic inscriptions which are almost weathered away. The marker for **Sara Wheatley** is typical:

Sinners, prepare to meet your Judge, Your God.
His throne approach with faith in Jesus' blood.
Redemption's only price man's ransom paid
Long in affliction's night my soul afraid.
Triumphing in His cross her house of clay
Now cheerful quits for realms of endless day.

If you walk back to the next open area you will find the fascinating sarcophagus of a true martyr: "Here lyes Dame **Mary Page**, relict of Sir Gregory Page Bart. She departed this life March 4, 1728, in the 56th year of age." On the other side, her story is continued. "In 67 months she was tap'd 66 times had taken away 240 gallons of water without ever repining at her case or ever fearing the operation." At about 3.6 gallons per tapping she would have been a valued natural resource had there been a drought that year, but alas, she died of internal flooding.

Further down on the same path is the family grave of **Joseph Hardcastle** (1752–1819), a merchant of the City of London and founder of the British and Foreign Bible

Society, who worked with William Wilberforce to abolish slavery. To his right is the large rose granite stele of **Joseph Hart** (1712–1768), a prolific hymn writer whose funeral was attended by 20,000 mourners. A sample of his work, "Hymn Number 51," is given on the bottom:

Mercy is welcome news indeed
To those who guilty stand.
Wretches, who feel what help they need
Will bless the helping hand.

Nearby in this paved area is another musician, **William Shrubsole** (1799–1806), composer of the hymn tune "Miles Lane." The first few notes are engraved on the tomb.

Scattered through the cemetery is an interesting type of granite coffin, mummy-shaped and joining a larger headstone and smaller footstone.

Although their monuments are not accessible, others buried here range from the pious to the scandalous. At the top of that range is **Susannah Wesley** (1669–1742), mother of the Methodist reformers John and Charles as well as 17 other children. Her tombstone, re-erected in 1934, unfortunately reads "Samuel Wesley."

In the middle range are **Joseph Ritson** (1752–1803), a barrister who collected ballads and limited his diet to vegetables and milk, and **John Lettsom** (1744–1815), a Quaker physician who made his fortune in the West Indies, but whose most unique contribution was introducing the mangel wurzel—a large beet used to feed cattle—to England.

Down in the scandalous range are **Robert Tilling** (d. 1760), who was executed for murdering his master, and **Henry Fauntleroy** (1785–1824), a banker who embezzled £250,000 from his bank, spent it in riotous living, and was executed at Newgate. The rumor that he escaped death by inserting a silver tube in his throat was never substantiated.

WESLEY CHAPEL

Just across City Road is Wesley Chapel. In the front is a statue of the founder of the Methodist Church, John Wesley, done by J. A. Acton in 1891, but to see his resting place you must walk around to the tiny churchyard in back. There, reflected in the glass of a modern building, stands a tall, three-layered monument topped by an urn and bearing his name and dates on the base.

JOHN WESLEY *b. 1703, Epworth, Lincolnshire; d. March 2, 1791, London.* The stories about John Wesley as a child are charming, though they have an apocryphal ring.

As a small boy Wesley insisted on having all the facts before making a decision, deliberating until his father complained to his wife, "I profess, sweetheart, that our Jacky would not attend to the most pressing physical necessities of nature unless he could give a reason for it."

Perhaps it was only John's way of distinguishing himself from the 18 other children, living and dead, who competed for his parents' attention. At age five a Wesley child was allowed one day to learn the alphabet, then was expected to read. If any were whipped, they had been taught to cry softly. There was, however, some rebellion in the form of a poltergeist who made sounds like bottles being smashed or money being poured out, and who sometimes gave Mr. Wesley a good shove in the back. John Wesley was curious about otherworldly apparitions all his life, and even at the end did not discount them.

Growing up he loved knowledge for its own sake. Witty, gregarious, and passionate in conversation, at Oxford he frequented coffee houses, played court tennis, and slept late. It was an altogether satisfactory life, and he renounced it as soon as he could. His brother Charles had founded what became derisively known as the "Holy Club" and John quickly took the leadership. The young men studied the Bible, fasted rigorously, gave what they could to the poor, and preached in prisons.

In 1728 John Wesley was ordained as a priest in the Church of England. The learned clergy at Oxford were bemused, however, by someone who wept over his sins, prayed ceaselessly, and was rumored to open a vein on occasion to cool his hot blood. An intensity bordering on fanaticism seemed to be coming to the fore.

In 1736 the brothers left for America. John was hoping to serve as a missionary to the Indians, but in Georgia he became entangled with his own countrymen. His two years in Savannah and Frederica were marked by dissension, death threats, and emotional intrigues. The highlight of his stay was meeting a group of German Moravian missionaries who attracted him by their scriptural interpretations: personal salvation through the death of Jesus Christ, a vital faith, and infusion by the Holy Spirit. When he returned to England he tried to incorporate these into the Anglican Church.

But whereas the Moravians lived in quiet, hymn-singing colonies, Wesleyan services were dramatic and hysterical. Listeners fell writhing to the floor in a conversion process that would sometimes take days. John Wesley himself claimed to be newly saved, a position which shocked many, given his years as a clergyman. As John and Charles went from pulpit to pulpit as guest preachers, irate congregations demanded they be banned from ever returning.

This was the age of Hogarth, an age that loved dissension and rioting for any reason. Rumors that John Wesley was a papist spy plotting the overthrow of England and an illegal seller of gin gave excuse to attack him. He was often pummeled by rocks or dragged outside by mobs screaming, "Kill him! Hang him from the next tree!" Yet he survived everything and won many converts. As he aged, his implacable dogmatism gave way to the earlier charm of his boyhood.

Wesley was attractive — a compact five feet five inches with long auburn curls framing his face — but unlucky in love. He became involved several times with women who were informally engaged and hence unavailable, and had an excuse not to press his claim. At 48 he married a 40-year-old widow, Mrs. Vazeille. Mindful of his appeal to women, she was insanely jealous, rifling his pockets and following him everywhere. Charles commented succinctly, "My brother has married a ferret." When she left him 20 years later, Wesley took her defection philosophically, deciding that "the temptations of a calm hearth" were not meant to interfere with his mission.

By then his concern was the perpetuation of his beliefs. He had never wanted to break with the Church of England, but, as they would not ordain any Methodists as priests, he felt he had little choice. The name "Methodist" had arisen in the Wesleys' Oxford days when they vowed to conduct their religious lives by "rule and method." He began ordaining preachers, with the stipulation that only he could do it and only he could assign them to various posts. Neither Wesley brother believed they would not rule forever: Charles hung on until age 84, and John until 88. On his deathbed John uttered, "I'll praise, I'll praise," before dying. His portrait wearing a halo and a crown was stamped on biscuits and presented to the hundreds who came to mourn.

ST. GILES CRIPPLEGATE

Although St. Giles was the patron saint of "cripples, blacksmiths, and beggars," and is shown over the north outside door, he was brought to the church after the fact: the Anglo-Saxon word "crepelgeat" meant a covered way. Still, miracles were said to have occurred in the area, and the building has gone from a Norman church built in 1090 by Alfune to a medieval structure which was gutted by fire in 1545. St. Giles was badly damaged during World War II but has been restored, with the addition of some particularly beautiful stained glass windows.

Unfortunately many of the memorial monuments in St. Giles have been destroyed by fire or bombings. Those buried here include **John Foxe** (d. 1587), who graphically illustrated all manner of deaths in *Foxe's Book of Christian Martyrs*; Sir **Martin Frobisher** (ca. 1535–1594), the first British explorer to seek a passage between the Atlantic and Pacific through the Arctic; and historian and mapmaker **John Speed** (1552–1629).

If you walk down the center aisle, slightly to your left you will find a floor tablet signifying the burial of John Milton.

JOHN MILTON *b. December 9, 1608, London; d. November 8, 1674, London.* Born and raised on Bread Street, John Milton was the elder son of John and Sara Milton. His father, a scrivener whose father had disinherited him for his failure to follow the Catholic faith, took great delight in music. He composed popular songs as well as occasional pieces such as "In Nomine" which contained 40 parts, each voice being simultaneously independent. In this modest, musical home Milton was raised with gentility.

First tutored at home Milton later attended St. Paul's School where he learned under the heavy-handed tutelage of Alexander Gil, Sr., a master renowned for his "whipping fits." Gil advanced a plan for the standardization of spelling. While never adopted, it influenced Milton and accounts for many of his singular spellings. From the start Milton showed a remarkable talent for languages and poetry. But unlike his beloved Shakespeare, who blossomed full and early, Milton's great promise was more derivative than original.

At 16 Milton entered Christ's College, Cambridge. It was an unhappy time for him. Lonely, arrogant, and aloof, he had few friends. His fair complexion and chaste behavior earned him the sobriquet of "The Lady of Christ's College." Milton bore the title with little humor. But though pure in body, some early poems show him enthralled and mesmerized by the opposite sex.

Impatient with tradition, Milton balked at religious life and soon gave up the idea of being ordained. Indeed, after obtaining his master's degree in 1632, he found a patron and spent the next six years at his father's house reading the world's great works of literature in chronological order. He was also busy with poetry, publishing in that time *L'Allegro*, *Il Penseroso*, and a masque, *Comus*. But the

crowning glory was *Lycidas*, Milton's tribute to his classmate, Edward King, who had died at sea. For some people
this pastoral elegy is the most beautiful poem in English. If
anyone was surprised by Milton's level of achievement,
Milton himself was not one of them. Certain that he was
destined for greatness, this supreme egotist boasted in
Latin verse how his father's name would live on because of
his genius son. Nobody likes a braggart, but he was right.

After traveling to Europe and meeting an old and blind
Galileo, Milton immersed himself in politics and marriage,
backing Cromwell and marrying Mary Powell in 1642. During the time of Cromwell Milton published political propaganda, his first volume of poetry, *The Poems of Mr. John
Milton* (1645–46), and such prose works as *On Education*,
and *Areopagitica*, which called for complete religious tolerance. The naive Milton soon found the excesses of Cromwell's supporters to be as bad as those of the King and
Archbishop Laud. Tolerance was not in the air but still he
supported Cromwell and held hope for reform.

Milton's marriage fared poorly. Six weeks after their
wedding the 17-year-old Mary returned home. Did her
Royalist parents want her out of London, that hotbed of
political upheaval? Was she lonely? Did the young couple's
inexperience rule the night? In her absence Milton wrote
pamphlets advocating divorce, citing among other reasons, "a body impenetrable." Certainly rejection would
have been a severe blow to this older and egotistical man.
Whatever the reasons, Mary did not return for three years.
That the reconciliation was consummated there is no
doubt. Mary bore four children before dying shortly after
the birth of Deborah in 1652.

Possibly suffering from a tumor on the pituitary gland,
Milton began to be plagued by severe headaches and nau-
sea and gradually lost his sight. The pain and sickness
ceased only with his complete blindness in 1652. In *On His
Blindness* Milton fears he has been cast into darkness by
God for ignoring his divine calling and takes hope that,
"They also serve who only stand and wait."

Milton's woes did not end with his blindness. When the
Good Old Cause failed and Charles II resumed the throne,
Milton must have spent many restless days and nights won-
dering if he would be on the Crown's death list. Fortunate-
ly his friends, including Andrew Marvell in the House of
Commons, intervened and he was not exempted from the
King's pardon. Nevertheless, he spent a brief time in jail
and lost his house.

In 1663 Milton took Elizabeth Minshull as his third wife

John Milton

(his second wife, Katharine Woodcock, had died in chid-birth in 1658). Soon, finding inspiration in Homer and Virgil, Milton began to dictate his great epic poem, *Paradise Lost*. Published in 1667 its genius overrode Milton's troubled reputation and the objections of those pedants who decried its blank verse. The poem is a product of the traditions of both the Renaissance and the Reformation and places Milton in the line of Christian humanists. He followed this great achievement with *Paradise Regained* and the tragedy, *Samson Agonistes*, both published in 1671.

By 1674 Milton's health was in decline. Sunning himself in warm weather, he felt his blindness would be tolerable if he were free from the pain of his gout. Stricken with severe gout fever, his pain miraculously did ease before death for "his expiring was not perceived by those in the room."

DIRECTIONS TO BUNHILL FIELDS, WESLEY CHAPEL, AND ST. GILES: Take the Northern Line to the Old Street stop and walk south down City Road. Bunhill Fields will be on your right, John Wesley's Chapel on your left. To reach St. Giles, exit at the rear of Bunhill Fields onto Bunhill Row, and turn left. Cross Chiswell Street and continue into Moor Lane; when it ends at Fore Street, turn right. St. Giles is at the intersection of Fore and Wood Streets.

C H A P T E R   7

St. Paul's

IT IS SAID that St. Paul's Cathedral was burned down five times before Sir Christopher Wren got it right. The disasters which gutted the Cathedral between 962 and 1666, however, were due to Viking raids, lightning, and the Great Fire of 1666, which burned for five days and destroyed 89 other churches. Wren redesigned many of those churches as well as St. Paul's, which is his greatest achievement.

Built in the Renaissance style with two towers, the cathedral's 365-foot dome is second in size only to St. Peter's Cathedral in Rome. Wren insisted on a completely new design rather than renovation of the ruins, and hired skilled carvers such as Grinling Gibbons and ironworker Jean Tijou to make it magnificent. It was not created without conflict and meanness — Parliament withheld half of Wren's salary for the last 14 years to make him work faster — but as the inscription on his tomb in the crypt below notes, "Se monumentum requiris, circumspice" (If you wish to see his monument, look around you).

Pages could be written about the interior of St. Paul's Cathedral, but with one exception our interest is down in the crypt. The exception is just beyond the entrance to the crypt, which is to the right of the pulpit. Down the south choir aisle is the monument of John Donne, the only monument of significance to survive the Great Fire. It shows him as a delicate figure in a shroud, standing on a stone urn, carved by Nicholas Stone.

JOHN DONNE *b. 1572, London; d. March 31, 1631.* There is an eerie story about John Donne's monument. At 58, certain he would die soon, he got up from his sickbed and dressed in his shroud. After it was knotted at head and foot, Donne climbed onto a carved wooden urn and posed, eyes closed, for a life-sized sketch. It is said that he had the drawing hung beside his bed to remind himself of what was

St. Paul's Cathedral

to come. After his death, when it was transferred to marble, the ends of the shroud about his head were carved to resemble a crown.

John Donne was born on Bread Street where another poet, John Milton, would enter the world 36 years later. Donne's father, an ironmonger, died in 1576; his widow married a doctor soon after. The household was Roman Catholic at a time when persecution was starting to increase. John's brother, Henry, was convicted of hiding a young priest in his student quarters and was imprisoned in Newgate. He died there of the plague.

Donne's own life was not endangered, but his education was hampered by the persecution. He attended Oxford and Cambridge, but could not get a degree due to his refusal to take the Oath of Supremacy, which acknowledged Elizabeth I as the head of the Church and set forth other stipulations. After a brief military mission he returned to Lincoln's Inn to study law, but still could not take a degree.

One thing he could do was write poetry. His early work focused on secular philosophy, and the joys of love. It is startling to read an elegy written around 1600:

> Licence my roaving hands, and let them go,
> Before, behind, between, above, below.
> O my America! My new-found-land,
> My kingdome, safeliest when with one man man'd.
> How blest am I in this discovering thee.

The word "discovering" was a pun which could also be read as "dis-covering."

Donne obtained a post as chief secretary to Sir Thomas Egerton, Lord Keeper of the Great Seal. He lost it when he fell in love with Egerton's niece, Ann More, 12 years younger than he. They became lovers and were secretly married in 1601. When they revealed the union, Ann's enraged father had Donne imprisoned and wanted the marriage annulled. He relented finally, but Donne's post was gone.

Years of poverty and exile followed, children born and children lost, while Donne attempted to curry favor with the nobility. He hoped for any appointment with a comfortable wage, preferably in London. The only offer he got was to join the Protestant clergy. This he resisted, although he wrote a book, *Pseudo-Martyr* (1610), which urged Catholics to take the new Oath of Allegiance upholding Anglicanism. Donne presented a copy to James I; in 1614, seeing that he could not hope for anything better, he took holy orders and was made a Chaplain-in-Ordinary to the King.

He was pleased to be back in London, preaching at Lincoln Court and other churches. Gradually he grew into his new vocation and his poetry turned to spiritual themes. He came to regret his early poetry which had circulated in manuscript form. Finally comfortable, it was a terrible blow when Ann died in 1617 after giving birth to a stillborn child at 33. It was her 12th pregnancy in 15 years, not counting miscarriages.

A bill shows the charge for her death knell. In London when a citizen was dying, the church bells were rung to warn the population to pray for him while he was still living. After death the number of strokes told whether the deceased was a man, woman, or child—a custom which gives further meaning to Donne's words: "Any man's death diminishes me because I am involved in mankind. And therefore never send to know for whom the bell tolls; it tolls for thee."

In 1621 Donne was appointed Dean of St. Paul's Cathedral by James I. Like Jesus throwing the moneychangers out of the temple, Donne attempted to halt the commerce, job hiring, and business transactions which took place in its aisles. He was not completely successful, though he managed to quell some of the tourists who climbed to the leaded roof to carve their initials, and urinated in the corners.

The new dean was better able to oversee the large staff and a portion of the cathedral's finances. His sermons were magnificent—written out, memorized, and delivered by heart. He startled listeners by pointing out that the cathedral ground was holy, that "Every grain of dust that flies here is a piece of Christian." Death was a persistent theme, culminating in his final sermon at St. Paul's, "Death's Duel."

Though Donne's poetry and sermons were greatly admired by his generation and published after his death, for the next two hundred years his work fell out of favor. The wit and scientific allusions of his writings made them less than accessible. It took Coleridge, Browning, and, more recently, Auden and T.S. Eliot to restore him to the ranks of English poets and remind us of such charming verses as:

Go, and catch a falling star,
Get a child with mandrake root,
Tell me, where all past years are,
And who cleft the Devil's foot.

Return to the entrance to the crypt and go downstairs. As you enter the crypt, you will see on your left a gated area with a number of effigies in storage. These have lost var-

John Donne

ious limbs, but survived the Great Fire of 1666. Turn right and walk to the southeast corner. This will put you in Artists' Corner. In the floor is a marker to Sir **John Everett Millais** (1829–1896), eighth president of the Royal Academy. It is done in gold metal against black marble with his coat of arms at the top.

John Millais' parents were the first to recognize their son's extraordinary talent and place themselves in its service. While Millais attended classes at the Royal Academy from age 11, his mother researched the historical material he used as the background for his paintings. As he worked at home his mother read aloud to him, and his father, when not posing as a knight or a saint, entertained him on the guitar.

Despite such attentiveness, the teenager fell in with the wrong crowd. His friend William Holman Hunt introduced him to Dante Gabriel Rossetti, and the trio rebelled against the art establishment, scorning every painter after Raphael. They attracted followers and traded models and themes which harked back to medieval literature and the Bible. Their work was characterized by clear, bright colors and naturalistic detail.

One of the masterpieces of the five-year Pre-Raphaelite movement was Millais' *Ophelia* (1852). Lizzie Siddal Rossetti (see Chapter 10 on Highgate Cemetery) posed as the drowning maiden. Another enduring work was his *Portrait of John Ruskin* (1854), which, though successful, had some unexpected consequences. Ruskin insisted that Millais travel to Scotland with him and his wife, Effie, to execute the portrait. Millais and the unhappy Mrs. Ruskin — the marriage was never consummated, allegedly because Ruskin, used to the marble blandness of classical statues, was repulsed by his wife's pubic hair — fell in love. After some scandalous publicity and an annulment, Effie and Millais married in 1855.

Marriage brought artistic changes. As his family swelled, Millais no longer had time for the Pre-Raphaelite technique of painting on a wet, white-primed canvas. He churned out portraits and landscapes for which he was highly paid. Some were frankly sentimental; a pair of enraptured, newly declared lovers saying goodbye, the man holding his valise, was titled *Yes!* by Millais, but called "Have you put in my sponge bag and toothbrush?" by his family.

Despite the criticism that he had not lived up to his early promise, Millais was the most successful artist of his age, reaping titles and the presidency of the Royal Academy. Thomas Carlyle commented on first visiting the Millais' Kensington mansion, "Has paint done all this, Mr. Millais? It only shows how many fools there are in the world." But Carlyle's was a minority opinion. Millais painted steadily until 1892 when he began to suffer from throat cancer and a series of small strokes. Despite surgery, the Victorians' favorite artist died at 67.

Nearby is a granite memorial to **William Holman Hunt** (1827–1910) with the words, "Their bodies are buried in peace but their name liveth for evermore."

People who may not recognize Hunt's name are often familiar with his most famous painting, *The Light of the World*. It shows Jesus standing in a night forest, a lantern in his hand, knocking on the bramble-covered door of man's heart. The original is at Keble College, Oxford, but Hunt painted a larger version that is here at St. Paul's, upstairs in the south aisle.

Unlike his friend John Millais, Hunt had to convince his father, who had forced his son into business at 12, that he would only be happy pursuing art. Even so, he was rejected twice by the Royal Academy before being admitted to study. With Millais and Rossetti, he founded the Pre-Raphaelite Brotherhood, but was the only one who remained true to its principles.

In 1854 Hunt left for the Holy Land, planning to paint biblical scenes in the actual settings where they had occurred. From that trip came *The Finding of the Saviour in the Temple* (1854–60) and *The Scapegoat* (1854). The latter was a painting of an actual goat set against a Dead Sea background and, though ridiculed and puzzled over by many, brought Hunt £5,775.

The artist hoped to live an equally religious life, but his passions decreed otherwise. Enamored of barmaid Annie Miller, who modeled for him, Hunt tried to relive the Pygmalian myth by making a respectable lady out of her. He held out the bribe of marriage for her becoming educated, but, when she did, he reneged. She threatened to sue him for breach of promise and publish his letters. Fortunately for the artist, she soon married someone else.

In 1865 Hunt, now a financial success, married the above-reproach Fanny Waugh. She died after childbirth the following year. Then, despite a law against it, Hunt married Fanny's sister, Edith, in Switzerland. It was not until 1907 that the Deceased Wife's Sister's Marriage Act made their union legal in Britain.

Professionally Hunt suffered another slight from the Royal Academy in 1856 when they rejected his bid for membership by a vote of 39 to 1. The outraged painter would have nothing more to do with them. He set the record straight in his two-volume autobiography, published a few years before he died of complications from asthma.

To the right of Millais are the remains of Sir **Joshua Reynolds** (1723–1792). As a child Joshua Reynolds announced to his father that he "would rather be an apothecary than an ordinary painter." He need not have worried. In popularizing portrait painting by placing the sitter in the context of his interests and his times, he fulfilled his ambition admirably. Of course, like other artists of his age his true ambition was to be a painter of historical scenes. But he had never been taught how to draw properly—the drapery and distant landscapes in his portraits were usually done by someone else—and it is his vivid likenesses which have survived as masterpieces.

Reynolds was born into a family of 11 children, 6 of whom died in infancy or youth. He was the son of a pious, absentminded schoolmaster who could not settle on any one interest long enough to succeed. This experience may have helped focus young Joshua; when his portraits began to attract interest he organized his life around them. The ordinariness that he had feared in his painting emerged in his life instead. He never married or bothered with mistresses, and patterned his lifestyle on that of the gentry he painted.

Reynolds was intellectually ambitious, however, and in 1764 founded "The Club," a weekly conversational gathering, along with Samuel Johnson, Oliver Goldsmith, Edmund Burke, and others who met with them at the Turk's Head Tavern. The influence of Samuel Johnson may be seen in many of the ideas in Reynolds' *Discourses on Art*. Indeed, the artist credited Johnson with having "formed my mind, and to have brushed from it a great deal of rubbish." He repaid the author by incisive portraits which do not conceal Johnson's permanent squint, rugged features, and querulous expression.

The artist's other portraits are more conventional. The subjects smile wistfully or appear suitably grave; seen together they give a strong sense of an era. David Garrick is shown being pulled between two women representing Tragedy and Comedy, a tribute to the actor's versatility as well an acknowledgment of Reynolds' debt to painters such as Correggio and Titian. A number of women are portrayed in dramatic roles such as Cleopatra and the Tragic Muse. On meeting a commission, Reynolds would often follow the classical allusions the sitter evoked in him.

When the Royal Academy was founded in 1768, Reynolds

became its first president. He was knighted the following year. Three years before he died he lost his sight and stopped painting. His hearing had been poor for years. But he had obtained his goal. The ten pallbearers who carried him into St. Paul's were all nobility, a fact that would have pleased him greatly.

Behind Millais, to the left, is a raised dark slab that reads, "Here lyeth Sir Christopher Wren, builder of this cathedral, church of St. Paul, who dyed in the year of our Lord 1723 and of his age 91." In the Trophy Room in the back of the crypt is Wren's Great Model, a construction of a design for St. Paul's which was ultimately rejected.

CHRISTOPHER WREN *b. October 20, 1632, East Knoyle, Wiltshire; d. February 25, 1723, London.* It has been over three hundred years since Sir Christopher Wren designed the 51 churches which were rebuilt after the Great Fire of 1666, and for much of that time the spires of those churches, the glories of his architecture, dominated the skyline of London. Even today, though some have fallen to fire or bombs, and others have been crowded and obscured by modern neighbors, many of the churches still stand with prominence, handsomely decorating the streets of London while Wren sleeps on under his towering monument.

Wren grew up at Windsor, where his father was a clergyman, and he enjoyed the privileges of Court. Astronomy first drew his attention and did so through the sundial. When 15 or 16 he was asked to contribute a translation from English to Latin (the written and spoken language of the sciences) on "dialling" for William Oughtred's *Clavis Mathematicae*. Dialling is the use of geometry to understand "the relationship of the sun to the earth." More earthbound interests also drew the attention of his lively mind, including devices for measuring wind and rain, for writing in the dark, and a diplographic pen for duplicating one's writing. These comprised only a small number of Wren's inventions because, modest by nature and more inclined to hands-on work, he showed little inclination toward publishing his findings.

Working with his hands was his forte. He also constructed astronomical models, and when he served as an assistant demonstrator of anatomy for the famous doctor Charles Scarburgh, he constructed models of human musculature. Entering Oxford at 17 he graduated in two years, in 1651, and obtained his master's in 1653. Though trained in astronomy Wren continued to experiment with anatomy. Injecting opium into the vein of a dog's leg he was able to verify that poisons could be administered directly into the bloodstream. It was the first time that fluids had been injected into an animal's bloodstream under laboratory conditions. He later removed the spleen of a puppy. The dog "grew not only well but as sportive and as wanton as before" thus showing that removal of this organ, so puzzling to Galen, did not endanger life.

Among his other achievements Wren disproved Descartes' theory of the moon being responsible for tides through increased atmospheric pressure, addressed a thorny mathematical question of Pascal's, urged the keeping of weather records, did important work on cycloids, studied light and refraction, and used science to explain discrepancies in the Bible. Even without his architectural achievements Wren would have claimed a significant place in scientific history. Indeed, Newton listed Wren, Wallis, and Huygens as representing "the greatest geometers of our times."

In helping to start the Royal Society in 1660 Wren drew the attention of Charles II. Impressed with the man and his scientific and mathematical achievements, the King offered Wren responsibility for working on the fortification of Tangier. Wren turned the offer down and obtained his first architectural experience by designing the Sheldonian Theater at Oxford. Although the design elements are unremarkable, harkening back to the Rome of Vetruvius, his ingenious use of vertical trusses impressed his colleagues. In 1665 he traveled to Paris, fortuitously avoiding the Great Plague which was ravaging London, to study architecture firsthand, and was greatly impressed with the Louvre.

The following year brought the Great Fire and the need to immediately rebuild the city. Wren was ready; within five days he had drawn up a plan which emphasized broad avenues leading to certain fixed landmarks. Ultimately the plan was rejected due to practical considerations around property claims, but Wren was named to the committee of six appointed by the King and the City for the rebuilding process.

In 1669 romance finally caught up with Wren. Short, slight in build, with a sharp prominent nose, he was no physical prize but he appealed to Faith Coghill. They married and she bore him two children before she died five years later. Wren later married again; Lane Wren also gave birth to two children and died early.

In 1670 the King appointed Wren Surveyor of His Majesty's Works, a combined position of engineer and architect.

Both his offices and house were located in Whitehall. The 89 churches destroyed in the fire were consolidated into 51 parishes and Wren went to work, having a distinct hand in the design of every church. He worked with great speed. By 1671, 20 churches were started, by 1677, 30 were under construction, and by 1685 the job was finished. His overall success in design is extraordinary. Of particular note are the steeples for St. Mary-le-Bow and St. Bride's, but also Christ Church, Newgate Street, St. Vedast's, and St. Magnus the Martyr. Wren also busied himself with other illustrious projects, such as Chelsea Hospital and the Royal Naval Hospital in Greenwich.

St. Paul's Cathedral is unique, not only due to its size and beauty, but also because it was completed in 35 years under the guidance of one man. Wren's first plans, including the Great Model, were rejected. The "Warrant" plan passed muster and immediately Wren began to alter the plans so that the dome would bear much greater resemblance to the Great Model than the "Warrant" design. Building commenced in 1676. In 1697 the first service was held. By 1708 the dome was completed, with Wren's son, Christopher, laying the final stone in place on the lantern. With the official opening in 1711 Wren was able to lay claim to the missing half of his salary.

There are two sculptures facing each other on the walls of the crypt. The monument of **Randolph Caldecott** (1846–1886) shows a sculpture of a child in a simple gown holding a cameo of the artist, with the inscription, "An artist whose sweet and dainty grace has not been in its kind surpassed. Whose humor was as quaint as it was inexhaustible." Caldecott was the creator of a number of charming drawings of English country life. The Caldecott Medal for excellence in children's book illustration is named after him.

The carving facing Caldecott commemorates the only daughter of Christopher and Dame Lane Wren. It shows a woman playing a heavenly organ seated in the clouds with cherubs surrounding her.

As you walk toward the altar in the alcove you will find the marble bust of **Anthony Van Dyck** (1599–1641), "the Flemish master who in 1632 was made principal painter inordinary to King Charles I and Queen Henrietta Maria, having enriched England with many famous portraits, dyed at Blackfriars in the City on the ninth of December, 1641, and was buried in Old St. Paul's. His monument perished in the Great Fire but his name is imperishable."

There is a monument to **William Blake** on the opposite wall with his cameo and the epitaph, "Artist, Scholar, Mystic. To see a world in a grain of sand and a heaven in a wild flower, Hold infinity in the palm of your hand, and Eternity in an hour." (See Chapter 6 on Bunhill Fields for the biography of William Blake.)

Turning the corner you will come across a wall dedicated to another group of artists. The most striking memorial on it is a sculpture of a naked child holding a tiny Peter Pan in his hand. It is in memory of Sir **George Frampton** (1860–1928), who carved the statue of Peter Pan that stands in Kensington Gardens. The statue was commissioned and paid for by J.M. Barrie. Frampton also dotted the English landscape with statues of Queen Victoria.

George Frampton

Next to Frampton are the ashes of Sir **Edwin Landseer Lutyens** (1869–1944) under a coat of arms. Lutyens is the architect best known for the grand country houses he designed during the Edwardian years. He obtained his name from Sir Edwin Landseer (see below), who had offered to adopt him at birth. Proving that 11 children were not too many his mother turned Sir Edwin down but did honor his offer with the use of his name. Captain Lutyens, the boy's father, was known for his inventions in musketry and for his paintings of horses.

His father's artistic skill may have helped him develop his own eye, for Lutyens was educated at home due to his delicate health. While he learned much about building and style from a family friend, his lack of socialization only served to enhance his shyness. When he reached 16 he attended what would become the Royal College of Art, South Kensington. His first success was his design of Munstead Wood for Gertrude Jekyll. With it he gained a fast-rising reputation as an architect of genius. He went on to do the British Pavillion at the Paris Exhibition of 1900 and a string of country houses.

With his reputation preceding him, he found his style shifting to the classical, in part because he realized that larger commissions would come his way only if he could demonstrate his competence in this style. And he was right. Confirmation came with the design of the Viceroy's House in New Delhi in 1912–14. The residence, larger than Versailles, contained a mere 210,430 square feet. To Lutyens' credit he did more than imitate classical style; he was able to merge it with traditional Indian and Moslem influences to create a unique and beautiful structure.

Lutyens also engaged in designing large areas of flats, many of which were done in the traditional Edwardian manner. Though obviously not a member of the avant-garde he shifted in time to more abstract forms as in the Thiepval monument. Lutyens was knighted in 1918. Throughout his life he remained shy and inarticulate although he did exude a certain boyish charm. The elegant proportions of his buildings spoke for him. He died of bronchial cancer at his home in London.

Below Lutyens is Sir **Max Beerbohm** (1872–1956). In his seventies Sir Max commented, "I am what the writers of obituary notices call 'an interesting link with the past.' " Certainly the satirist preferred the past, freezing his style of dress at 1910. One of his caricatures, *And Only Just Thirteen!* shows a sinister-looking character, goggles shoved up to the hood of his black jumpsuit, striding by as a puzzled, rotund figure in granny glasses and a white-wigged, snuff-snorting companion look on. The drawing is subtitled, "The Grave Misgivings of the Nineteenth Century, and the wicked amusement of the Eighteenth, in watching the Progress (or whatever it is) of the Twentieth."

At any age Beerbohm himself was hard to pin down. Famous at 23 for his caricatures and witty essays, he held the post of drama critic for the *Saturday Review* for 12 years. Then in 1910 he married actress Florence Kahn and retreated to a villa in Rapallo, Italy, where he carefully cultivated his privacy. From behind his villa walls he posted drawings back to England. Readers were delighted at his depiction of Henry James waspishly inspecting a pair of men's and women's shoes outside a hotel room door waiting to be polished, and Oscar Wilde's plump hand grasping a walking stick, his fingers resembling a nest of piglets.

Beerbohm wrote one novel, *Zuleika Dobson*, about undergraduate life at Oxford, but his most successful work was miniature, on a level described as intimate. As one obituary writer pointed out, "He drew each reader aside, he murmured his neat, his apparently casual reflections into every private ear." The only time Beerbohm spoke to a larger audience was during World War II when he returned to London from Italy—he felt it bad manners not to be in one's own country during wartime—and gave a series of talks over the BBC. The topics covered everything from "Music Halls of My Youth" to "Advertisements" and sounded, according to Rebecca West, like "the voice of the last civilized man on earth." Just before his heart gave out at 83 and he slipped into a coma, the last civilized man thanked his doctor and his wife of three weeks for everything.

Nearby is another writer who died at 83, poet **Walter de la Mare** (1873–1956). He is recognized here as a "one-time choirboy of St. Paul's," with the epitaph:

> Where blooms the flower when her petals fade,
> Where sleepeth echo by earth's music made,
> Where all things transient to the changeless win,
> There waits the peace thy spirit dwelleth in.

When de la Mare suffered an earlier, close-to-fatal illness, a visiting daughter asked, "Is there nothing I could get for you, fruit or flowers?" The poet looked up weakly. "No, no, my dear; too late for fruit, too soon for flowers."

De la Mare attended the choir school at St. Paul's and also started the school paper there. Although he worked for many years for the Anglo-American Oil Company, he kept a child's perspective in his writing, delighting readers with such lines as:

> It's a very odd thing—
> As odd as can be—
> That whatever Miss T. eats
> Turns into Miss T.

Walter de la Mare's poems and stories were collected into numerous volumes and he was showered with honorary degrees. But perhaps the most heartfelt tribute came from a friend who commented that de la Mare "combined the best qualities of a man, of a woman, of a child, and of a dog."

In the center of the wall is a memorial to **E.V. Knox** (1881–1971), poet, satirist, and editor of *Punch*; he is actually buried in Hampstead Churchyard.

In the alcove across the way is a very pleasant monument to Sir **Edwin Landseer** (1802–1873), renowned animal painter. It was erected by his surviving brothers and sisters with the quote, "He hath made everything beautiful in his time." Carved in marble is an artist's palette, Landseer's larger-than-life cameo profile, and a coffin with a dog's head resting mournfully against it. Off to the right are a pair of spectacles lying on a book, along with slippers and a cane. If it is not taken from one of his creations, it is a scene he would have enjoyed painting.

Further along are plaques for sculptor **Henry Moore** (1898–1986) and a cameo of **Ivor Novello** (1893–1951). Novello is actually buried in Golders Green, but people sometimes bring a sprig of lilac to his memorial to commemorate his song, "When Lilacs Bloomed Around Us in the Spring."

There is a lovely dark sculpture to the memory of **Edward Robert Bulwer-Lytton** (1831–1891) which shows two large angels hovering over a portrait of him with a cherub beneath. Son of a novelist, Edward Robert was a diplomat to India and a poet.

On the opposite side are people who are of local or minor interest, such as aldermen, and plaques to artists and writers who are not here, such as **John Constable** (who is in the churchyard at Hampstead).

Alexander Fleming has a white marble tablet which reads, "Remember before God Sir Alexander Fleming F.R.S., discoverer of penicillin whose ashes rest beneath this plaque." Around the inscription is a thistle design, representing Scotland, and at each lower corner the fleur-de-lis of St Mary's Hospital, where he worked. The plaque's marble is allegedly from the same quarry in Greece that supplied the materials for the Parthenon. According to attendants at St. Paul's, Fleming's second wife, Amalia, kept bringing huge potted cheese plants to commemorate the spot. Although live plants were not permitted in the crypt, no one dared tell her not to leave them.

ALEXANDER FLEMING *b. August 6, 1881, Ayrshire, Scotland; d. March 11, 1955, London.* Alexander Fleming, an adept player of golf, billiards, and croquet, who often succeeded with deliberately unorthodox shots, had a puckish sense of humor, and enjoyed practical jokes. During World War I he often played golf with his commanding officer and on more than one occasion managed to surreptitiously place the colonel's tee shot in the cup. The unknowing colonel was delighted, and Fleming and other club members were the beneficiaries of his mandated largesse at the bar afterwards. Oddly, circumstance played a similar role in Fleming's life by twice dropping rare microbes on his petri dishes without his knowledge. It is to Fleming's everlasting credit that he was able to identify both these events as holes in one.

Fleming spent World War I in Boulogne seeing men die from wounds which should not have been fatal. He came home determined to find a way to make the immune system more effective. He first made the discovery of lysozyme, a naturally occurring enzyme with antibacterial properties which exists in most human and animal tissue and secretions. Lysozyme, which he obtained by swabbing his own nasal mucous, killed the bacteria with which it came in contact.

The particular bacterium growing in the petri dish must have blown in the window or the door for Fleming never saw it before or after. Yet this rare coccus was an ideal substance for the demonstration of the efficacy of lysozyme. For the next several years Fleming and his assistants worked at gaining a better knowledge of how bodily secretions helped to defend the body against a wide range of bacteria.

A similar confusion surrounds the discovery of penicillin. Was it a spore of mold from a loaf of bread or one from some beer froth that might have blown in the window? In truth it was probably nothing so delicious. But Fleming apparently did not know the origin of his experiment. Upon returning from his summer vacation, he checked his petri dishes. Those of no interest were stacked in a tray of lysol for cleaning. It was only after a chance second look that one of these discards, fortunately high and dry, showed an area of interest. The observed mold was staph-inhibiting. Further research demonstrated that the mold was a form of penicillia. But Fleming had not seeded his dish with this spore; in all likelihood it blew in Fleming's perpetually open door from La Touche's lab down the hall.

Fleming's own explanation was vague and could not be replicated. Other scientists struggled in vain to find ways to explain it, explanations which involved changes in weather conditions as well as the condition of the staph, but Fleming stuck to his mysterious version. He called his "mold juice" penicillin. It was to become the world's first wonder drug.

Over the next 12 years the bacteriologist presented his discovery in lectures and scientific papers but failed to attract attention, in large part because of his barely audible, unanimated delivery. Since penicillin failed to be effective when applied topically, it appears Fleming grew skeptical of its therapeutic value. He did not run animal tests in his lab or implore other scientists to take it any further. But one of them did anyway. Howard Florey, heading a team of researchers at Oxford, applied to the Medical Research Council and the Rockefeller Foundation in 1939 for funding to do therapeutic experimentation. Given five years of research money from the latter, he and an associate, Ernst Chain, ran lab tests and learned how to extract and purify a large enough quantity for use. They were startled when, in 1940, Fleming showed up at Oxford announcing, "I've come to see what you've been doing with my old penicillin."

In 1945 Chain, Florey, and Fleming shared the Nobel Prize in medicine for penicillin. But by then Fleming — without his intending so — had become a lifesaving symbol in the way Jonas Salk soon would. The public was not interested in the subtleties of scientific credit. They showered Fleming with 25 honorary degrees, 20 medals, 18 prizes, 13 decorations, and invitations to everywhere from India to Brazil. The bacteriologist grew to love the adulation.

Yet adulation changed him very little. Fleming never fitted the profile of a driven scientist — he enjoyed his hours at the Chelsea Arts Club too much — and after 1945 spent even less time in his lab. Though he enjoyed having other people around, he disliked having to make conversation and was considered unemotional. When he married Sarah McElroy in 1915 he had to bring wedding photos into the lab to prove to his incredulous colleagues that he had actually been able to make a personal connection.

What Alexander Fleming had, if not great originality of thought, was the ability to understand what he was seeing and to distinguish whether or not it was significant. And he only needed to do it twice to assure himself of a niche at St. Paul's.

Above Fleming is a plaque to **Gordon Hamilton Fairley** (1930–1975), with the words, "It matters not how a man dies, but how he lives." Dr. Fairley, an internationally known leukemia researcher and professor of medical oncology at St. Bartholomew's Hospital, was accidentally killed by a terrorist bomb while walking his dog. The bomb had been planted under the red Jaguar of Member of Parliament Hugh Fraser and his wife, writer Antonia Fraser, with whom Caroline Kennedy was staying. If Fraser had followed his normal routine instead of stopping to make a phone call, he and Caroline Kennedy would have been in the car on the way to her art class at Sotheby's when it exploded.

To Fleming's right is the bronze plaque of Sir **Arthur Sullivan** (1842–1900) with a bird and leaf border. At the top is a lyre. Originally scheduled to be held at Brompton Cemetery, Sir Arthur's burial service was changed at the last moment, with attendees being assured that their tickets to the Brompton service would be honored at St. Paul's.

Sullivan was, of course, the musical half of the great operetta team of Gilbert and Sullivan whose work still enjoys great popularity over one hundred years later. Sullivan was the musical whiz kid of his day, and was the first recipient of the Mendelssohn Scholarship at the Royal Academy of Music in 1856. The hopes for serious British music were pinned on him but he failed to deliver. Granted that he wrote a symphony, several oratorios, a grand opera

(*Ivanhoe*), hymns like "Onward Christian Soldiers," and songs such as "The Lost Chord," but they broke no new ground. The world did not need another stuffy oratorio.

In 1875 Richard D'Oyly Carte sought the services of Gilbert in writing a one-act piece as an opener to Offenbach's *La Perichole* at the Royalty Theater, and suggested that Gilbert seek out Sullivan to provide the music. Gilbert's reading left Sullivan in stitches and the partnership was born. The piece, *Trial by Jury*, was a hit and D'Oyly Carte wasted no time in forming the Comedy Opera Company and enlisting the talented team to provide the entertainment. *The Sorcerer* was next and then, in 1878, *H.M.S. Pinafore*. *Pinafore* was a phenomenon. It ran for seven hundred performances and rapidly became known wherever English was spoken. In America copyright requirements were blatantly ignored and it was performed in large cities and small towns, in churches, theaters, and halls. There were no barriers; black troupes sang it and it was translated into German for the German immigrant population.

With success guaranteed, the company moved in 1879 to the Savoy Theatre, newly built by D'Oyly Carte for Gilbert and Sullivan's shows, and thus the term "savoyard" was coined to describe aficionados of this music. The team followed with hit after hit including *The Pirates of Penzance* and *The Mikado*. Despite their success the partnership was not a happy one. Gilbert was not an easy man to get along with and their quarreling grew worse as the years passed. With the failure in 1896 of *The Grand Duke* their collaboration came to an end.

Sullivan was keenly aware that the operettas were considered by serious critics to be unworthy of his talents and efforts. Yet they made him rich and allowed him to move about in the best society, gamble at Monte Carlo, and maintain the odd mistress as well as two thoroughbreds. Serious or not Sullivan wrote unforgettable music marked by delicious wit and disarming melodies. Although history has shown his critics to be wrong, it is of no help to Sullivan, for he bore to the grave a nagging guilt about having sold his abilities for easy money.

To the left is a memorial plaque to **John Wyclif** (1328–1384). "Theologian, priest and preacher who inspired the first translation of the whole Bible into English. He was summoned here in 1377 to answer for his faith. Morning Star of the Reformation." Wyclif was actually brought up on charges of heresy at Old St. Paul's for espousing anticlerical views and other doctrines which led to the rise of Protes-

Stafford Cripps

tantism. He did not remain here after death, but was buried in Leicestershire until his ashes were exhumed and scattered on the Swift River.

At the back is the startling sculpture of statesman Sir **Stafford Cripps** (1889–1952) done by Jacob Epstein with the epitaph, "If man neglects the things of the spirit and puts aside the full armour of God he will seal the doom of future generations." The sculpture is startling in the way Cripps' clasped hands hang over the base, and in the apparent age in his face, which was not prettied up. He has a gaunt look and large staring eyes. In the beginning he wore glasses over those eyes but they kept being stolen. A pair of spectacles was cemented on, but they were purloined as well; now he gazes at visitors without optical aids.

Brilliant, impatient, visionary, Cripps first became a lawyer, able to isolate and unravel the intricacies of constitutional and corporate law. At 40, under the influence of his father and his uncle, Sidney Webb, he joined the Labour Party. Though he won a seat in Parliament, he was expelled from the party in 1939 for insisting on a united front with the Communists. Winston Churchill made him the ambassador to Russia the following year, and toward the end of his life Cripps was appointed minister of economic affairs; he helped to slow inflation and ease Britain's financial woes. At the end of his life he fought a spinal infection, then abdominal complications.

At this point you will be ready to go down several steps and look at the monument of Wellington. It is a large variegated rose-brown sarcophagus set at eye level with four sleepy lions as the cornerstones. It reads simply, "Arthur, Duke of Wellington," with his dates on the other side.

ARTHUR WELLESLEY, *First Duke of Wellington b. May 1, 1769, Dublin; d. September 14, 1851, Stratfield Saye.* Although much has been made of Wellington's adolescent awkwardness — his shyness, lack of intellectual achievement, and rawboned homeliness — like many leaders he just needed time to mature. The sixth child in his family, he mourned his father who died when he was 12, and felt rejected by his mother. It was she who decided when he was 16 that he was "fit food for [cannon] powder" and sent him to a military academy in Angiers, France.

Arthur, who had never contemplated a soldier's career, found himself drawn to many aspects of the military life. A loan from the sale of some family property bought him a commission as a major, and he carried out his first campaign at Boxtel, Netherlands, in 1793. He next distinguished himself in battle in India, culminating in his rout of the Mahratta armies. It was his obsessive attention to details of food and supplies which won the battle of Assaye as much as his campaign strategy. His men, who referred to him as "the long-nosed bugger," were secretly fond of him.

Wellington gradually grew into his long nose. He became handsome, with black curly hair, Irish-blue eyes, and a figure which stayed trim all his life. In between his Indian campaign and the battles against Napoleon's armies in 1814, he served in Denmark and Spain. He barely noticed his rise from knighthood in 1802 to viscount, earl, marquis, and finally duke in 1814. The news usually reached him in the field and was shrugged off. He paid more attention to his status when, after Napoleon's exile to Elba, a grateful nation voted him a gift of £400,000.

The following year, in which Napoleon escaped and raised a formidable army as he crossed France, brought the greatest battle of Wellington's career. He met Napoleon at Mont Saint Jean and Waterloo and, joined by the Prussian Marshal Blucher, defeated him after hours of agonizing battle. Placed in charge of the Army of the Occupation in

Paris, Wellington governed humanely, although at a reception when the French marshals turned their backs on him and an embarrassed Louis XVIII apologized, the Duke commented, "Sire, do not distress yourself. They've so got in the habit of showing me their backs that they can't get out of it."

A return to England in 1818 also meant a return to his wife, Kitty Pakenham. She had been his original inspiration to make good in the army so that he could support a family. But when he had returned from India in 1805 he could not find the girlish charmer he remembered in the compulsively chatty 33-year-old. Despite his whispered comment to a friend—"She is grown damned ugly, by Jove!"—he felt duty-bound to marry her the following spring. It was not a happy union. Kitty was always nervous, afraid of offending him, and Wellington was happy to escape to the battlefield.

The Duke, who always abhorred democratic gatherings and crowd sentiment, was unmoved by demonstrations of love or hate. After his French victories his popularity was profound, giving rise to Wellington boots, Wellington jackets, Wellington apples, and, no doubt, beef Wellington. When he had been home for a few years, however, and had served in a Tory cabinet as master general of the ordnance, progressing to prime minister in 1828, his conservatism became known. In his official capacity he had to allow the Catholic Emancipation Bill, but he opposed Parliamentary reform, arguing that by taking power out of the hands of the aristocratic few, anarchy was invited.

It was not a popular stance. As if to justify his fears about mob rule, demonstrators broke all the windows of his London home, Apsley House. They screamed at him when he rode into the city, pelted him with stones, and tried to pull him off his horse. He reacted with the stoicism he had cultivated all his life. When the tide changed and he was made chancellor of Oxford University and glorified as an elder statesman, he remained indifferent. He brushed off the crowds who gathered to shout, "God bless you, Duke!" with "For God's sake, people, let me get on my horse."

He was likewise indifferent to the adulation of his mother, the same mother who during his adolescence had considered him cannon fodder. He was more upset when his sturdy campaign horse, Copenhagen, died (and was buried with full military honors) than when his mother passed on at 90. It was her coldness to him as a sensitive child that had helped create the "Iron Duke." The iron shutters he ordered fitted on the windows of Apsley House were an emblem of the way he learned to shut his feelings away from the world. It was only with children, horses, and one or two old friends that he was able to show any emotion. Yet probably it was his imperviousness which helped make him the general that a young Queen Victoria eulogized as "the greatest man this country has produced."

The plaques on the wall around him are in memory of British leaders who distinguished themselves in subsequent wars.

Outside the room you will see the memorial to **Samuel James Browne** (1824–1901). It shows him in Indian uniform with a palm tree in the background. At 20 Browne was posted to Calcutta during the first Sikh War. In 1858, as he was pursuing a band of mutineers, his horse, Sheriff, veered, exposing Browne's left arm which was immediately hacked off by a native fighter. Browne continued his military career, commanding a division in 1878 during the Afghan War.

Also of interest is the marker of Major **Frederick George Jackson** (1860–1938), "Polar Explorer and Soldier, Commander of the Jackson-Harmsworth Polar Expedition 1894–1897." One of his greatest discoveries was that Franz Joseph Land, between Russia and the North Pole, was an archipelago and not a continent. Jackson mounted his first expedition to "run a polar show on his own," after Dr. Fridtjof Nansen refused to allow him to accompany the Norwegian expedition to the Arctic in a specially prepared vessel. In one of those particularly satisfying twists of fate, Jackson came across a stranded Nansen and another party member and conveyed them safely on one of his own ships. The carving on top of the memorial shows him in heavy clothing on skis with a husky by his side and a tent in the background.

Walking into the next alcove in the direction of Nelson's bier you will find a nice bas-relief of **Florence Nightingale** (1820–1910) attending a sick soldier. It is only a memorial to her since she is actually buried in St. Margaret's Churchyard in East Wellow, Hampshire.

After 1936 only ashes were permitted to be interred in St. Paul's. Admiral of the Fleet **John Rushworth Jellicoe** (1859–1935), in a separate alcove with his coat of arms as decoration, was the last coffin burial here. Jellicoe came from a long line of seafarers. His father was a captain and his mother's side boasted, among others, Admiral Philip Patton who was second sea lord during the Trafalgar campaign. From young boyhood on there was no doubt as to Jellicoe's love for things maritime. Excelling academically he became a midshipman and went to sea when he was 14.

IN MEMORY OF
MAJ. FREDERICK GEORGE JACKSON
EAST SURREY REGIMENT
POLAR EXPLORER AND SOLDIER.
COMMANDER OF THE JACKSON-HARMSWORTH
POLAR EXPEDITION, 1894~1897.
HE DISCOVERED, MAPPED-IN AND NAMED
THE GREATER PART OF FRANZ JOSEF LAND
AND RESCUED Dr NANSEN, WHO WAS LOST.
DIED 13TH MARCH 1938, AGED 78 YEARS.
SANS PEUR ET SANS REPROCHE.

"THEN THERE IS THE FEELING OF OWNERSHIP, THE RIGHT
OF POSSESSION, WHICH THE MAN EARNS WHO LIFTS A
NEW LAND OR A NEW SEA OUT OF THE DARKNESS OF
THE UNKNOWN, AND FIXES IT FOR EVER UPON THE CHART-
THE FEELING THAT THE SAVAGE, SPLENDID SCENE
BEFORE HIM IS HIS, BECAUSE HE HAS EARNED IT
BY WORK OF BRAIN AND BODY, WON IT BY SHEER
FORCE OF CLEAR HEAD AND CLEAN MUSCLE."
THE LURE OF THE NORTH POLE.

Jellicoe's first cruise lasted two and a half years, taking him to such ports as Gibraltar, Rio de Janeiro, Ascencion, Bombay, Hong Kong, Nagasaki, and Mauritius and giving him much experience. He rose rapidly in the ranks experiencing the usual illnesses (dysentery, Malta fever), adventure (delivering secret messages in Egypt disguised as a refugee), and danger (having his lung punctured by a bullet during the Boxer Rebellion). By 1910 he was vice admiral of the Atlantic fleet and three years later an admiral, commander-in-chief, Grand Fleet.

Jellicoe's reputation suffered badly with the indecisive battle of Jutland in 1916. He has since had his supporters, but at the time he was subjected to a barrage of hostile and demeaning criticism. Ironically, the armor-piercing shells that he had advocated for so long and which would have proved so useful against the heavily armored German ships at Jutland came into use after the battle. More controversy arose around the issue of employing the convoy system to protect British supply ships which were rapidly being sunk by German U-boats. Lloyd George became impatient with delays in implementing the convoys. The end result was that Jellicoe was fired, although here again his supporters feel he was discredited by men without sufficient knowledge for their actions.

After the war Jellicoe served with great popularity as governor-general of New Zealand from 1920 until 1924. Upon his return to England he busied himself with many volunteer activities. Chilled from planting poppies in November 1935, he died two weeks later when the infection spread to his lung.

Opposite Jellicoe is a plaque, "Here rest in God **Garnet Joseph Viscount Wolseley** (1833–1913), Field Marshall in His Majesty's Army, 1895–1900. His wife has placed this tablet to his memory, she now rests here with him." Her dates, 1843–1920, are given but no name.

The monument to Admiral Nelson is a sarcophagus set high off the ground with his name in gold. On top is a painted purple cushion with gold tassels, and a crown set with large pearls on top of it. An interesting mosaic on the floor shows anchors, sea lions, and stylized palm trees.

HORATIO NELSON *b. September 29, 1758, Burnham Thorpe, Norfolk; d. October 25, 1806, at sea off Cape Trafalgar, Spain.* "What hath poor Horatio done, who is so weak, that he should be sent to rough it out at sea?" Captain Suckling, the boy's uncle, inquired with heavy but affectionate teasing. Very small for his 12 years Horatio had done little, but he had suffered within one week at Christmas, 1767, the deaths of his mother and grandmother. Later at boarding school he had decided that a life at sea would be his career, and his father, rector of the local parish, arranged it to be so.

Nelson, for he hated the name Horatio, never reached five feet six inches as an adult. But at sea, fed on a diet of "beef which quite makes your throat cold in eating it, owing to the maggots which are very cold when you eat them," his love and knowledge of sailing grew rapidly and his cockiness blossomed. Traveling to the West Indies, the Arctic, and India, Nelson rose from captain's servant to midshipman by age 17. Nelson's ambitions congealed on his return trip from India. Sick with tropical fever and experiencing adolescent angst over his life's prospects, he experienced a febrile vision. "I will be a hero!" he exclaimed and described how "From that time a brilliant orb was suspended before my mind's eye."

In the immediate years that followed it appeared that Nelson's ambition might fall to simultaneous bouts of man-

Lord Nelson

chineel poisoning, yellow fever, and dysentery which left him skeletal, dehydrated, paralyzed, and precariously close to death. Recovery was long in coming, and Nelson had to forego a command while recuperating. In 1785 on the island of Nevis in the West Indies he met the widow Fanny Nisbet and her five-year-old son, Josiah. Two years later he was husband and stepfather.

Nelson's stay in Nevis was otherwise not too successful. His earnestness and blunt honesty proved an annoyance and embarrassment to his superiors, and when he returned to England with his family he found the penalty was to be unassigned to further command for five years. Those years put a great strain on a marriage that had quickly lost its early ardor. When he took to the seas again in 1793 as captain of the 64-gun *Agamemnon*, and with Josiah in tow, it was a relief for both husband and wife.

Nelson's command of the *Agamemnon* was noted for his victories at Bastia, Corsica, and Calvi where he lost the sight of his right eye. In 1795 with his defeat of the French warship *Ça Ira*, Nelson's fame increased. His praises were sung in doggerel by even the French Royalists. But Nelson's commands were not marked only by military success. His traits of authority coupled with sympathy, loyalty, courage, and expert seamanship brought him the most remarkable devotion from every crew he commanded and later the entire fleet.

In 1796 Nelson left his beloved *Agamemnon*, so worn that her hull was kept together by hawsers which ran about her midships, to take command of *Captain*. He was soon a commodore and, after capturing two Spanish ships simultaneously, he was promoted in 1797 to rear admiral. Shortly thereafter Nelson wrote to Fanny, "I have flattery enough to make me vain, and success enough to make me confident." These words proved to be a guide to the remainder of his life.

After losing his right arm and the battle of Tenerife Nelson was returned home. Whatever five years on shore had done to his marriage, four years at sea repaired; the next seven months proved to be the happiest he and Fanny would spend. In 1798 Nelson was back in the limelight with a victory at Aboukir Bay, Egypt. Landing at Naples Nelson found his fame had preceded him. Medals, speeches, fetes: all awaited. But the largest prize of all was Lady Emma Hamilton. Nelson accompanied Lord and Lady Hamilton everywhere and his affections for Emma soon became public knowledge. Emma, whose beautiful face sat atop a figure that lent new dimensions to plumpness, was strong-minded and loud-voiced, and was by many considered crude. For Nelson she was pure passion. He wrote to her of a dream in which "I kissed you fervently and we enjoyed the height of love." He rolled with Emma as he did at sea and never had with Fanny. By 1800 she was pregnant with their daughter, Horatia.

Nelson's return home was less spectacular. Sporting his foreign medals and the reputation of his affair, he was lionized by some but snubbed by the King and satirized in cartoons. Emma suffered, appropriately, satirical broadsides. The affair effectively ended Nelson's marriage. He could not now even be civil with Fanny and after an argument in January 1801, when he told her he would tolerate no ill speech toward Lady Hamilton, Fanny left him for good.

The sea and duty called again and this time took Nelson to Copenhagen where he earned one of his greatest victories against a strong Danish fleet in difficult waters. As the battle broke loose Admiral Parker lost faith; viewing the smoke from four miles' distance and considering the odds, he raised the flag for retreat. Nelson received word of the order as he paced the deck, his right arm stump twitching with nervous energy. After deliberation he declared that he had "a right to be blind sometimes." With that he put the telescope to his blind eye and brightly announced, "I really do not see the signal." What he ultimately saw and obtained was victory.

Nelson's greatest and final triumph came at Trafalgar. Now a lord and a vice admiral, Nelson commanded the H.M.S. *Victory*, a first-rate ship carrying 100 guns and 847 men. Splitting the line of French and Spanish warships, he led the way to a resounding victory which secured England's supremacy on the seas for the next 100 years. With *Victory* lashed to *Redoubtable* and crews exchanging grenades and engaging in hand-to-hand fighting, and with the ships' red-painted decks ill concealing the voluminous flow of blood, Nelson paced the quarterdeck and was there struck by a sniper's bullet fired from *Redoubtable*'s mizzen mast. Piercing the left lung and lodging in his spine the bullet left Nelson paralyzed from the chest down. Taken below, he suffered agonizing pain while he received reports of the battle. "Oh, Victory, Victory, how you distract my poor brain!" he murmured. His lungs filled with blood and after three hours he died.

The fleet was devastated. Sailor Sam wrote home, "All the men in our ship are such soft toads, they have done nothing but blast their eyes, and cry, ever since he was killed. God bless you! chaps that fought like the devil sit down and cry like a wench." The enlisted men who tended his casket had the last say at the funeral as well, for even Nelson's heroism and vanity were overwhelmed and lost in the multitude of official pomp. Of their own accord they ripped off a section of the tattered ensign that lay atop his coffin, each man taking a small piece for remembrance.

DIRECTIONS TO ST. PAUL'S CATHEDRAL: Take the Central Line to the St. Paul's stop. The cathedral will be in view.

AT REST

FLORENCE NELLIE CELLIER
BELOVED DAUGHTER OF THE ABOVE
WHO DIED 28th OCTOBER 1931
CREMATED AND ASHES SCATTERED

Brompton

BROMPTON CEMETERY IS a wonderful graveyard in which to wander, a place filled with Victorian vignettes. Here is Queen Victoria's pediatrician who left his practice to go dig up mummies; there the author of the melodrama *A Woman's Revenge* who died at 45 of typhoid fever. Newsworthy names — Emmeline Pankhurst, Brandon Thomas, and Richard Tauber — dot the grounds as do monuments which have been designated national treasures.

The 39-acre cemetery was opened in 1840. It is laid out in park-like avenues, culminating in the catacombs and chapel at the far end. As you enter through the main gate on Old Brompton Road, move briefly to your left at the first intersection. You'll see a draped urn to **John Snow** (1813–1858), M.D., a pioneer in the use of chloroform and ether. Dr. Snow was on hand to anesthetize Queen Victoria when her last two children, Leopold and Beatrice, were born, medical experiences that she rhapsodized about later as "soothing, quieting, and delightful beyond measure."

Dr. Snow's monument, "In remembrance of his great labours in science and of the excellence of his private life and character," is a replacement for the original which was destroyed during the Blitz in April 1941. It was erected by the Association of Anesthesiologists of Great Britain and Ireland in September 1951.

Another of Victoria's doctors, **Thomas Pettigrew** (1791–1865), is also in Brompton. In a then still-experimental procedure Pettigrew vaccinated Queen Victoria against smallpox when she was ten weeks old. Retiring from medicine at 63 to pursue his interest in Egyptology, he eventually published a book on embalming.

Moving back toward the center path you will see what appears to be a church door lying on the ground, complete to a keyhole. It has the words "From shadows and fancies to the truth," and commemorates **Squire Bancroft**

Augustus Henry Clossop

Brompton

A	Dr. John Snow	**J**	Blanche Roosevelt,
B	Squire Bancroft		Brandon Thomas
C	Henry Pettitt	**K**	Percy Lambert
D	Emmeline Pankhurst	**L**	Robert Coombs,
E	Richard Tauber		S. Leigh Sotheby
F	Soldiers Monument	**M**	Sir Samuel Cunard
G	Frederick Leyland	**N**	John Jackson
H	Reginald Alexander		
	John Warneford		

■ ■ ■

(1841–1926) and his wife, actress **Marie Wilton** (1840–1921). Bancroft was an actor whose patrician appearance—tall, white-haired, and sporting a monocle—provoked the comment that "no man ever was so distinguished as Sir Squire Bancroft looked." Later, as a theater owner he abolished the pit, causing a riot on opening night, and established morning performances which he called "matinées," after the French word *matin*.

On your left down the center path are a boy and girl in 1920s dress, their hands clasped behind their backs. They flank the marker of Major **Ronald Erne** (1882–1928). Such realistic statuary, often of deceased children, is especially poignant because the clothing is recognizable to us. The boy wears buckle shoes, knee socks, and a sailor's shirt and cap; the little girl, whose short, bobbed hair is topped with a large bow, has similar shoes, anklets, and a dress with a lace collar.

Across the way the Pettitt monument has an interesting bas-relief of playwright **Henry Pettitt** (1848–1893). He is shown with one hand on the side of his face, looking pensive and wearing a large Teddy Roosevelt moustache. Pettitt, who co-authored melodramas with titles such as *In the Ranks* and *A Woman's Revenge*, died at 45, not of vengeance but of typhoid fever.

Farther down on your left is a cross with a stylized figure of Christ with palms and a communion chalice held by two angels. It commemorates a person who made a lasting contribution to women's rights.

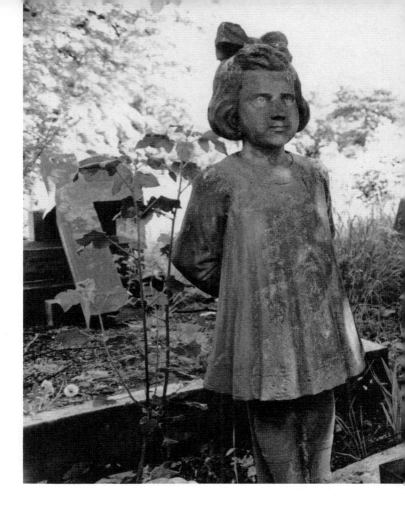

EMMELINE PANKHURST *b. July 14, 1858, Manchester; d. June 14, 1928, London.* Emmeline ("Burn the Barriers") Pankhurst was a more exciting person than her monument would indicate. Beautiful, charismatic, and often dictatorial, she embraced the cause of women's suffrage and never looked back, persevering, as one writer put it, "with the inflexibility of a hedgehog which having started to cross a road will not be diverted one degree from a straight course, even to avoid the wheel of a passing vehicle that will crush it to death." Growing up, she received a double message. Her Liberal party parents introduced her to women's suffrage meetings, but sent her to a Parisian finishing school. She was expected to make the family home attractive to her brothers until she had a dwelling of her own.

Emmeline escaped quickly into marriage with 42-year-old Richard Pankhurst, a brilliant, eccentric lawyer. His beliefs included abolition of the monarchy and the House

Maj. Ronald Erne

of Lords, and he was too busy with social causes to sustain a law practice. To help support their growing family, Emmeline initiated a series of gift shops which sold hand-painted knickknacks and home furnishings. The shops failed and soon after Richard, too busy with social issues to notice his health, died in 1898 from a perforated ulcer.

Devastated by his death, Emmeline turned to politics. She became obsessed by the idea that having the vote was women's key to reform. Only with the franchise could they elect leaders who would represent their causes. With the help of her daughters Sylvia and the militant Christabel, the Women's Social and Political Union (WSPU) was created in 1903.

The group worked for two years to get a women's suffrage bill before Parliament. When the bill finally came up for discussion, its time was filibustered away by arguments on the proposal ahead of it that horsecarts should have rear lights at night. One opponent of suffrage continued the issue by exhorting that washerwomen should also be ordered to wear red lights on their backs.

The Pankhursts, unamused, decided it was time for more aggressive action. White banners demanding "Votes for Women!" were unfurled with sudden rudeness like a flash of underwear. Women yelled out slogans in Parliamentary sessions and opera performances. When they were banned from gathering in public places, the suffragettes took to the streets and the battle turned grim.

Secret resentments toward women that had been building during the repressed Victorian era exploded. Suffragettes were gleefully punched, knocked to the ground, and had their clothes ripped off—by the police. Hooligans brandishing horsewhips also joined in. The fact that they were attacking educated and cultured women only seemed to excite the men more.

The Pankhursts soon realized that if they were arrested for vandalism rather than simply demonstrating—and their goal *was* to be arrested as well as attract attention—they would not be subjected to physical abuse. A new era of rock throwing began; no window in London was safe. A display case in the Tower was cracked open, paintings were slashed, a stadium was burned down. The suffragettes vowed that no human life would be destroyed, but that private property was fair game.

Sentenced and jailed, they came upon the technique of hunger striking. But the government fought back; it wanted no dead martyrs on its plate. Teams of prison wardens and doctors force-fed the women, clamping their mouths open with metal gags, and inserting tubes down their throats to pump in broth. No matter that the broth came right back up. As soon as they were weakened by fasting, the "Cat and Mouse Act" sent them home to fatten up, then re-arrested them as soon as they were stronger. Thus a six-month sentence could stretch out over several years.

Emmeline Pankhurst divided her time between hunger striking in prison, and giving brilliant lecture tours in the United States and Canada. Her body weakened and she would have died, but World War I put suffrage activities and hunger striking on hold. In an odd alliance with Lloyd George, Emmeline agreed to lead a demonstration "demanding" that women be allowed to work in munitions factories. They were so allowed; it is even possible that such work softened public opinion in regard to enfranchisement. In any case, on January 18, 1918, women over

30 were given the vote, and by the end of the year were allowed to run for seats in the House of Commons.

Thus Emmeline's mission was accomplished. At loose ends, she began the "English Teashop of Good Hope" on the French Riviera, which failed as her gift shops had. As a mother she fretted about her daughter Sylvia's illegitimate pregnancy by a socialist. She died quietly in a furnished room. Yet along with John Bunyan, Sir Thomas More, and other scofflaws of their times, Emmeline was quickly canonized. Two years after her burial at Brompton, the police band geared up to play "March of the Women," a suffragette war cry, and her statue was unveiled in the gardens outside the Houses of Parliament.

The tall monument that can be glimpsed by looking from here across the cemetery to your right is to honor 2,625 pensioners of the Royal Hospital, Chelsea, who were buried here between 1855 and 1893. The monument lists the battles in which they were engaged, from Mysore to Waterloo and Crimea. At each of the corners is a fiercely roaring bronze lion and an arrangement of five cannonballs. Superimposed against a shield on top are a collection of fallen bronze flags.

Continuing down the path, on your left you will find the in-ground monument of **Richard Tauber** (1891–1948). Winter or summer, flowers are left in his memory, but on his birthday, May 16, the site becomes a garden. On that day there is a letter from the Richard Tauber Foundation:

Dear Richard,

On the sixteenth of May we celebrate your birthday. Your birth was a God-given present to the world! Your heavenly voice and music sounds all the world over and grows stronger from day to day. Your golden heart, voice, and music shine like the stars of Heaven forever and ever. All greetings from the Tauber friends all over the world. God's blessings will be with you eternally.

Dirk Vandermeyden, Chairman.

Tauber was the out-of-wedlock child of a Jewish father and Christian mother. Raised in Austria as Richard Denemy or Richard Seiffert (his mother's maiden and married names) he had early exposure to the theater. His mother was a soubrette and his father, Richard Tauber, was an actor. Later, when he assumed his father's last name, he changed his first name to Carl on his early recordings to avoid confusion. Initially unimpressed with his son's voice, the elder Tauber became convinced of his son's talent after his son undertook voice lessons. Tauber made his operatic debut as Tamino in Mozart's *The Magic Flute* in 1913.

Immediately successful, he signed on with the Dresden Opera, starred in many leading tenor roles, and became one of the noted Mozart tenors of this century.

Somewhat like the Irish tenor John McCormack, Tauber switched his emphasis in mid-career and from 1925 on he concentrated on operetta. His favorite composer was his close friend, Franz Lehar, whom he claimed as brother "without the luxury of a blood relationship." Tauber was the quintessential tenor for Lehar's music and he bowled the public over. Never reluctant to sing encores for his adoring audiences, the song "Yours Is My Heart Alone" from *The Land of Smiles* (1929) became his signature piece, one he would vary by singing it *sotto voce* or in different languages.

Tauber suffered from severe arthritis which caused a disfigurement of his face and gave him a slight limp. As his career progressed he placed a strain on his voice through his ceaseless performances. His recordings show a refined singer whose voice fell somewhere between Caruso's and McCormack's in its timbre.

Because he was part Jewish, Tauber became *persona non grata* in Germany in 1933 and fled Austria in 1938. Ultimately he became a naturalized British citizen and aided the war effort by giving many recitals throughout the British Isles.

On the right hand side, several rows over, is a fenced-in area commemorating the soldiers of World War I and earlier conflicts. The area may be entered via a wrought-iron gate on the far side. The entry is a grassy aisle flanked with tall grave markers leading to the large cross placed high on a broad pedestal whose corners are marked by stacks of cannonballs. The individual markers are of particular interest, for each carries, in bas-relief, the insignia of the fallen man's company including cannon, horses, sheep, castles, maple leaves, harps, and thistles. They also bear the tragic information, e.g., "Died December 1914, Age 17."

Further down on the same side as Richard Tauber is the two-story **Albert Mellon** (1821–1867) monument. His eyes have a startled look as they gaze out toward the cemetery. The second tier has four columns of dark gray marble and a bronze violin now missing its strings. Mellon, an orchestral conductor, had just accepted conductorship of the Liverpool Philharmonic when he died at 46.

Nearby is the monument of architect **George Godwin** (1815–1888), flanked by two statues of women, one holding a scroll, the other reading a book. No doubt the book is one of his own. Godwin wrote two volumes on the churches of London, and two that deplored sanitary conditions that led to early death among the poor: *London Shadows* (1854) and *Another Blow for Life* (1864). In the center of the tomb the architect is shown in three-quarter profile, with measuring ciphers, blueprints, and other tools of his trade.

Across the way on your right is the **Frederick Leyland** (1831–1892) Arts and Crafts Movement monument. Enclosed by an iron gate, it appears to be a small house with the ends decorated by a stylized vine motif. On the broad sides the design changes to lilies. Created by Edward Burne-Jones, it is considered one of the finest surviving examples of Pre-Raphaelite sculpture in existence. The presence of this work of art in Brompton has not gone

Frederick Leyland

unnoticed. Of late there has been a movement to place it in the safety of a museum.

Frederick Leyland, a patron of the arts, was president of the National Telephone Company. He collapsed on the train between Mansion House and Blackfriars stations, and was carried into the waiting room where he died of heart failure.

Nearby are **Florence** (d. 1921) and **Valentine Prinsep** (1838–1904), Leyland's daughter and son-in-law. Because of the apostles in its niches, their monument, a pink planter on eight legs, has a medieval appearance. It is actually a fifteenth-century font brought from Siena by the artist to decorate his grave. Prinsep, a painter in his youth, also wrote novels and plays. His obituary chided him gently for being too versatile, pointing out that as "a rich man with all-round tastes and interests, he had not latterly been sufficiently a painter."

As you reach the colonnade area, look to your left for a wonderful monument to Flight Sub-Lieutenant **Reginald Alexander John Warneford** (1891–1915). It was "erected by readers of the *Daily Express* to commemorate the heroic exploits in destroying a zeppelin airship near Ghent on June 7, 1915." The bas-relief shows the zeppelin sinking with flames bursting from its top, and up in the right-hand corner flies a small airplane.

Even before the monument was erected, the young airman had caught the imagination of the British. Four hours before the funeral in Brompton Chapel thousands of people jammed the cemetery, spilling out onto the roads. Floral arrangements were almost as plentiful as mourners, including one in the form of an airplane from the staff and patients at the British Hospital in Versailles. Warneford was given a military burial including buglers and a 50-gun salute.

Across the way is a similar memorial to Admiral **Frederick Anstruther Herbert** (1827–1911). It is a sword with a tassel draped over a plain cross.

Also on this side is some nice turn-of-the-century sculpture. One shows the bust of a quintessential Victorian gentleman, **Augustus Henry Clossop** (1852–1896) with a woman in a simple gown reaching up to bid him adieu. On the side is a tangle of a violin, lyre, wreath, faces of Comedy and Tragedy, and a trumpet.

Another simpler but more touching memorial has a small rectangular bas-relief of a young boy lying on his deathbed with his mother and father looking on sorrowfully. It commemorates **Horace Lot Brass** (1880–1896).

Sub Lt. Reginald Alexander John Warneford

Lining the area and forming the perimeter of the Great Circle are the catacombs. As conceived by the architect Benjamin Baud, whose design won the competition to build the best cemetery, the catacombs were to extend the length of the cemetery and feature Roman Catholic and Nonconformist chapels as well. His design was severely cut back when the builders, West of London and Westminster Cemetery Company, swayed toward bankruptcy. Corners were cut on building specifications and Baud's designs truncated. But when defects in construction became apparent in 1844, the architect was blamed and fired.

The black iron gates to the mausoleum entrances echo the melancholy sense of disgrace and death. They show a pair of snakes facing each other, mouths gaping in salacious conversation, bodies wrapped around two downturned torches. Below, in a circle made by an asp, is a winged hourglass. All are symbols of life ended.

When you come to the circle, go straight down the middle. At the end is an American girl who made good. **Blanche Roosevelt** of Sandusky, Ohio, came to Europe to study music, and became the first American woman to sing Italian opera at Covent Garden. After other musical triumphs, she wrote several works of fiction and *The Life of Gustave Doré*, for which she was decorated by the French Academy. Married to the Marquis d'Alligri, Blanche died at 40 in 1898. Her statue shows a woman with short curly hair, wearing a simple gown and clutching a rose.

Blanche Roosevelt

Slightly behind Blanche Roosevelt is the plain black granite monument, surrounded by a gravel bed, in memory of **Brandon Thomas** (1850–1914). The actor and playwright once remarked plaintively, "I had hoped to go down to fame as a great actor. If I go at all, it will be as the author of *Charley's Aunt*." His prophecy came true. His epitaph adds that he was "the kindest man, the best condition'd and unwearied spirit in doing courtesies."

Across the path is a tall rose-colored stele in memory of **John Lionel Alexander Monckton** (1864–1924), a composer and music critic for the *Daily Telegraph*. He also wrote songs for musical comedies such as *The Geisha* and *The Shop Girl*.

Down beyond the circle is an interesting monument to **Gilbert Laye** (1866–1926). It shows a short-haired woman holding a lyre, gazing down at her chest with modest eyes with the words, "United Ever." On one side is a mask of Comedy with a robust grin; on the other side is a mask of Tragedy with a knife going in one side of its head and out the other.

Percy Lambert's (1881–1913) grave has a broken column and the epitaph: "A modest friend, fine gentleman and a thorough sportsman." Lambert, the first man to drive a car at 100 m.p.h., was killed at Brookland's Motor Racing Track while attempting to break his own record. On the 21st lap one of the outer tires burst, acting as a brake between the wheel and axle and tossing the car up an embankment. When it overturned and fell back, Lambert was thrown out. The night before, the 32-year-old racer had promised his fiancée that, successful or not, this would be his last attempt at breaking a record.

At the back wall of the cemetery, turn to your left and follow the perimeter. On your left is a startling bas-relief of what first appears to be a woman in mourning drapery holding a wreath; but as you get closer you see it is actually the face of Death. The inscription is worn away.

When you come to the exit gate, turn left back into the cemetery. The first monument of note you will come to is that of **Robert Coombs** (1808–1860), champion sculler who died insane. Sadly all four heads of the corner statues are missing; they appear to have been children or scullers dressed in different outfits. Coombs held his championship for seven years and was described as "the most finished and perfect sculler that ever lived"; if you look carefully you will see his upturned scull and draped jacket on top of the tomb.

Right behind Coombs is a cameo that shows the expulsion from the Garden of Eden by a stern angel. It is the monument of **S. Leigh Sotheby** (1805–1861) who founded the well-known auction house and drowned in the River Dart.

There are a number of cameos on upright slabs here in the oldest section of Brompton. Their subjects range from clasped hands to sailing ships.

John Jackson (1769–1845) has a large lion on top of his monument, paid for by public subscription. It is age, perhaps, which has given the lion an expression more puzzled than ferocious. On the right side of the monument is a well-worn cameo of the fighter, who was England's champion between 1795 and 1803. Afterwards he ran a boxing school attended by such notables as the Duke of Queensberry and Lord Byron.

From here walk back to the wall and turn right at the path. About six monuments down is the flat rose and gray granite marker of the **Cunard** family. "In memory of Sir Samuel Cunard (1788–1865), Baronet, who founded the Cunard Line."

Alfred John Priddell (1903–1942) has a poignant verse on his marker that sums up the experience of many in Brompton Cemetery:

> The call was so sudden, the shock severe.
> We never thought your end was so near.
> Only those who have lost you alone can tell
> The pain of parting without a farewell.

Also in Brompton

William Banting (1797–1878), a royal undertaker who wrote extensively about dieting. **Charles Collins** (1828–1873), the younger brother of Wilkie Collins, who married Charles Dickens' daughter, Kate. Also a writer, he produced a novel called *The Bar Sinister*. He suffered from ulcers and poor health all his life. Lady **Morgan Sydney** (1783–1859), whose tomb shows two of her books, *Wild Irish Girl*, and *France*. **Henry Richards** (1819–1885), a friend of Chopin, whose own best-known work was, "God Bless the Prince of Wales." Sir **Andrew Waugh** (1810–1878), a surveyor and astronomer who named Mount Everest after his colleague Sir George Everest. **Bennet Woodcroft** (1803–1879), inventor of the pitch screw propeller used in steamships.

DIRECTIONS TO BROMPTON: Take the District Line to the West Brompton stop. The cemetery is to your right on Old Brompton Road.

Hampstead Cemetery

NORTH LONDON

C H A P T E R 9

Kensal Green

WHEN LONDON'S NINETEENTH-CENTURY churchyards became dangerously overcrowded and malodorous, authors
quickly took up their pens to fight back. They wrote vividly
of "fatal miasmas" and described the long black flies which
crawled out of broken coffins and were called "body bugs"
by Sunday-school children. Dickens complained that "rot
and mildew and dead citizens formed the uppermost
scent" in the city, and one magazine pointed out that
"50,000 desecrated corpses are every year stacked in 150
limited pits of churchyards, and one talks of decent and
Christian burial!"

Kensal Green, licensed by an Act of Parliament in 1832,
was London's earliest private answer to this dilemma. The
General Cemetery Company had been formed several
years earlier, but it took the city's first cholera epidemic in
January 1832 to overcome resistance to non-church burials. *The Gentleman's Quarterly* was quick to assure its
audience that "the left hand road [of Kensal Green], as will
be anticipated, leads to the abodes of the Turks, Jews,
Infidels, Heretics, and 'unbaptised folk,' and the right hand
after passing among the beautiful and consecrated graves
of the faithful [Church of England], leads to the Episcopal
chapel." The Roman Catholics opted for their own cemetery, St. Mary's, which is adjacent to Kensal Green.

Enter through the main gates, turn to your right and take
the road off to the left, South Avenue. One of the first
monuments you will see is the 14-foot spire of **Feargus
O'Connor** (1794–1855) with the inscription, "While philanthropy is a virtue and patriotism not a crime will the
name of O'Connor be admired and this monument respected." Although his epitaph appears fit for a priest or
social reformer, O'Connor was actually a barrister who
gave much of his energy to the working classes. Unfortu-

Mary Austen Gibson

179

Kensal Green

A	Feargus O'Connor	**G**	Princess Sophia
B	William Makepeace Thackeray	**H**	Emile Blondin
		J	Wilkie Collins
C	Sir Marc Isambard Brunel	**K**	Anthony Trollope
		L	Leigh Hunt
D	William Mulready	**M**	Henry Russell
E	Andrew Ducrow		
F	Thomas Hood, Michael Balfe		

nately his death notice in the *London Times* deals entirely with the coroner's inquiry into his cause of death.

For the last three years of his life O'Connor, suffering from senility, had been a resident of Dr. Harrington Tuke's asylum. His sister brought him home for a visit and O'Connor, who could do no more than exclaim constantly, "I am your brother — you are my sister!" died 11 days later. At the hearing Miss O'Connor accused Dr. Tuke of keeping the former lawyer stupefied with brandy and of conspiring with a nephew to confine him at the asylum. She charged that the doctor bribed her nephew with half a sovereign, adding to the gathering's amusement, "Dr. Tuke was not so liberal as to give him money for nothing, for I heard that he only gave the sexton sixpence when he was married."

No charges were brought against Dr. Tuke. The cause of death was found to be "inflammation of the brain."

William Makepeace Thackeray, though prominent in life, is not easy to locate in death. To do so you will need to go down to the footpath along the canal, turn right, and look hard for the plain in-ground slab with the metal rail. Thackeray is buried here with his mother, **Anne Carmichael-Smyth**, who died in 1864 at age 72.

WILLIAM MAKEPEACE THACKERAY *b. July 18, 1811, Calcutta; d. December 21, 1863, London.* When William Makepeace Thackeray held a looking glass up to his contemporaries, Victorians recoiled. How could he mirror them as schemers, or portray sweet young women as having less-than-shiny hearts? And all done with a twinkle and rueful shake of the head! Many agreed with critic John Ruskin who complained that Thackeray "settled like a meat fly on what you were going to have for dinner and made you sick of it."

Yet even those who found Thackeray's writing unpalatable had to admit that the man was charming. His hulking, good-natured frame was a familiar sight around London. The head that had seemed enormous at birth had become less noticeable as the man stretched to six feet three inches, though his profile was not improved by a flattened nose, broken by an early critic at Charterhouse School. As an adult, a surfeit of wit and good humor overflowed the banks of his personality.

Thackeray's early life was not without drama. His mother, Anne Becher, was desperately in love with Henry Carmichael-Smyth, a young soldier; one day her pious grandmother came to her with the sad news that he had died of a fever. To cure her subsequent depression, Anne was sent to India where she met and married Richmond Thackeray.

When their son, William, was just a few months old, Richmond brought home "a delightful and interesting officer" who had just arrived in India: one Henry Carmichael-Smyth. When he and Anne had a chance to talk, Henry explained that his letters had been returned to him by the old lady, stating that Anne no longer cared for him. The Thackeray marriage was never the same. Richmond himself died of a fever three years later, and Anne and Carmichael-Smyth were married.

As was customary, William was sent back to England at age five to begin his education. Delicate, nearsighted, and consumed by reading novels, he disliked physical activity, preferring to form clubs to write and sketch satirically. At Cambridge he discovered the excitement of gambling and quickly lost most of his inheritance — an event he later detailed in *Pendennis* and *The Kickleberrys on the Rhine*. He made a stab at reading law, considered becoming a diplomat, studied art briefly, then spent the rest of his patrimony publishing *The National Standard of Literature, Science, Music, Theatricals, and the Fine Arts* — and supplying most of the copy himself. Despite the 22-year-old's best efforts, the paper went under.

After his paper folded, Thackeray earned a living writing book reviews and sketches for *Punch* and other magazines. The characters he created, such as the Hon. George Savage Fitz-Boodle, footman Charles James Yellowplush, and others, had distinct voices and developed their own followings. Thackeray's *Collected Sketches and Stories* were published in 1841 under the pseudonym M.(ichael) A.(ngelo) Titmarsh.

Vanity Fair, written under his own name, was first published in booklet form, several chapters a month, beginning on New Year's Day, 1847. Through the character of governess Becky Sharp (she of the ample chest and scheming heart), he took an unwavering look at English and Indian colonial society, and introduced the concept of character development. His idea that even the stupid or wicked could find redemption was controversial, however. The novel was praised as "brilliantly illuminated with the author's own candles," but caused conflagrations in many English drawing rooms. Phrases such as "them's my sentiments" and "I'm no angel" passed into the English language.

Pendennis (1849-50) was closer to autobiography, detailing some of Thackeray's unhappy experiences at Charterhouse. *Henry Esmond* (1852) was a departure in setting, a drama set in the late seventeenth century. But its true hold came from the timeless passions and domestic tragedies it described. Periodically Thackeray yearned for the luxury of time in which to lovingly craft novels (or to do nothing at all), instead of cranking out serials under the gun. But, as his success increased, so did his standard of living; at the end of his life, when he could have relaxed, he commissioned a huge red brick mansion and kept scribbling away to pay for it.

By then Thackeray's early levity had been tempered by the circumstances of his life. In 1836 he had married Isabella Shaw, a pale, red-haired young girl guarded by a dragon of a mother. He wooed her romantically and was thrilled to be married. But after giving birth to three daughters, one of whom died in infancy, Isabella tried to kill herself repeatedly. She suffered a breakdown and never recovered. Thackeray's two surviving daughters, Minnie and Annie, lived in Paris with his mother until he was able to establish a home in London. Anne Carmichael-Smyth, with her religiosity and her opinions, was never far away after that.

It was a situation that periodically depressed Thackeray. Isabella, pleasantly indifferent to her husband and children, boarded with various families for the rest of her life. Although he did not see her, he remained faithful to the idea of their marriage. He took advantage of his position to fall in love "platonically" with several women, however, and to take liberties with his friends' wives which would otherwise not be allowed. But that and the freedom to dine nightly at various favorite clubs, attend the theater, and conduct lecture tours around England and in America did not seem to be enough. As he ended *Vanity Fair*: "Which of us is happy in this world? Which of us has his desire? or, having it, is satisfied? — Come, children, let us shut up the box and the puppets, for our play is played out." Thackeray's life was played out when he died of a cerebral hemorrhage at 52.

Just off Center Avenue on the path before the next fork is the monument of Sir **Marc Isambard Brunel** (1769–1849), civil engineer. It is plain but points out, "He has raised his own monument by his public works at Portsmouth, Chatham and the Thames Tunnel." Brunel, jeopardized by the French Revolution because of his royalist sympathies, traveled to New York in 1793 where, in a six-year sojourn, he was named chief architect and engineer of the city. He moved on to England with an idea for mechanically manufacturing ships' blocks which revolutionized shipbuilding. He also invented a knitting machine, an air engine, and the concept of floating piers. But he was a poor businessman; Brunel spent six years in King's Bench Debtors Prison before his friends bailed him out. The strains of work on the tunnel under the Thames between Wapping and Rotherhithe broke his health, causing a series of strokes. He died six years later.

Sir Marc's son, **Isambard Kingdom Brunel** (1806–1859) is also here. An expert on railway traction, he engineered the Great Western Railway and the Clifton Suspension Bridge. His steamship, the *Great Western*, was the first transatlantic vessel, and the *Great Eastern* was the largest vessel of its time.

Return to Center Avenue and continue to the split where you'll be entering a leafy area with some fascinating monuments and mausoleums. On your left is the memorial of Major General **William Casement** (d. 1858) of the Bengal Army of the Supreme Council of India. It appears that he came home to die. The monument, sculpted by local artisan F.M. Lander, shows a bier which holds an oversized cloak and regimental helmet under a canopy. The bier is held up by four turbanned Indians. Casement's history is on the monument's base.

Just up the path on your right, **William Mulready** is laid out with the description "Artist, Royal Academician, Knight of the Legion of Honor, born at Inness, Ireland, 1786, died in London 1863." At the base of the six columns are instruments of his trade such as a painter's palette, writing script and quill, and a piece of parchment like a diploma. There are also roughly incised figures in a very light bas-relief. Mulready began his career by teaching art and illustrating children's books. He fell under the influence of the Dutch school and became an anecdotal painter whose works had titles such as *Snow Scene*, and *First Love*.

Two plots down from Mulready is the Corinthian temple of **Mary Austen Gibson** (1854–1872). It is topped by four angels yearning toward each other and has the verse, "Is it well with the child? And she answered, It is well." The verse, II Kings 4:26, refers to a young Shunnamite boy that the prophet Elisha restored to life.

The striking monument to **Andrew Ducrow** (1793–1842), which cost £3,000 to build and have decorated in 1837, has a beehive carved in the stone roof, a sphinx, broken columns with roses and wreaths, and, despite Christian angels on either side presenting the information, a strong Egyptian motif. Dedicated to "the Colossus of equestrians," the circus owner himself may have written the inscription: "This tomb erected by genius for the reception of its own remains."

William Mulready

Ducrow was born to an even more amazing father, Peter Ducrow, known as the "Flemish Hercules," who could lie on his back and support 18 grenadiers "armed and in marching order" on his hands and feet. Andrew preferred the tightrope and equestrian feats and eventually collected his own troupe and came to London. His popularity rivaled that of the Royal Theater. After one particularly well-received performance, women broke into his bedroom and strewed it with whips, silver spurs, and flowers.

When Ducrow's Royal Amphitheater burned down, it was a fatal loss. His obituary points out that "from this he had but partially recovered when the 'insatiate archer' changed the mode of his attack and by paralysis ended the mortal sufferings of one, of whom it may be truly said, that with the failings incident to humanity, he possessed the redeeming qualities of a kind heart."

Across the road is the memorial of patent-medicine purveyor **John St. John Long** (1798–1834). Underneath its dome stands a maiden, the work of Robert Sievier. The medical symbols of entwined serpents frame St. John Long's attempt to have the last word:

> It is the fate of most men to have many enemies, and few friends. This monumental pile is not intended to mark the career but to show how much its inhabitant was respected by those who knew his worth and the benefits derived from his remedial discovery. He is now at rest and far beyond the praises or censures of this world. Stranger, as you respect the receptacle for the dead (as one of many that will rest here), read the name of John St. John Long without comment.

Turn left on the road past Ducrow and you will come to the well-worn **Cooke** family monument which shows a horse with a small child resting trustingly against its front foreleg. The horse is looking down as if to see what the child holds in his hand.

Cooke family monument

Further down are the monuments of **William Grahame** (1761–1812), author of *The History of the United States of North America*, and **Thomas Hood** (1798–1845). His rose granite marker has been sadly defaced. Gone are the bronze bust of the author and the large cameo bronze scenes from his poem "The Song of the Shirt." The monument, by Matthew Noble, was judged "the best thing" in Kensal Green by the magazine *The Builder*. All that is left now is the epitaph, "He sang the song of the shirt."

"The Song of the Shirt," which appeared in the Christmas 1843 issue of *Punch*, was a melancholy indictment of the mills where women worked long hours; the poem contained such lines as, "O God! That bread should be so dear, And flesh and blood so cheap!" By then Hood had been writing for 20 years, sometimes anonymously in humor collections such as *Odes and Addresses to Great People* (1825), other times as with *Tylney Hall* (1834) and *Up the Rhine* (1840), under his own name. For several years he published a humor magazine, *Hood's Own*, trying to be a "lively Hood" to guarantee a "livelihood." Dogged all his life by poverty and bouts of illness, he suggested that his epitaph be: "Here lies one who spat more blood and made more puns than any man living."

Across the way from Hood is a plain stele to the Irish composer **Michael Balfe** (1808–1870). He moved to Italy as a young man and earned his reputation as a composer, but he also sang bass under the name of Balfi, going from Irish to Italian with the change of one vowel! In 1835 he was appointed the director of the National Opera of London and later became conductor of music to Her Majesty's Theatre. He wrote many operas, enjoying particular success with *The Bohemian Girl* and *The Puritan's Daughter*, but his music is rarely heard these days.

Return to Center Avenue and walk toward the church. On your left you will see the striking monument of Princess **Sophia**, a carved sarcophagus reaching high into the air with griffins on either side and "Sophia" at the top. The base reads, "Come unto me all that labour and are heavy laden and I will give you rest. Royal Highness Princess Sophia, Fifth Daughter of His Majesty King George III born November 3, 1777, died May 27, 1848."

One wonders why a princess of the royal family of Hanover is buried here in grand isolation, but during her youth George III was already suffering from bouts of porphyria, and behaved very peculiarly toward his daughters. None were allowed to marry before age 30, and he turned down proposals for them without their knowing, cloistering them in ways that led to melancholia and depressive illnesses. Sophia, a victim of an unhappy love affair, gave birth to the child of one of the royal horsemen, and was allowed to keep neither.

The large church is not open except by appointment, and the arrangements have to be made through the cemetery office, but if you walk around to the back you will find that the most interesting monuments here are in the two end niches. One shows a young woman on her death bed, "In loving remembrance of their daughter **Georgina Clementson** (1834–1868)." Below is a triple cameo that appears to show Georgina as a young girl, a young matron,

Sievier family

and a mature woman. It was executed by John Graham Lough.

In the other end niche is the monument of the sculptor **Robert Sievier** (1794–1865) and his wife, **Frances**. The statue shows a man on a chaise longue, legs covered by a blanket, his hand on the head of a woman kneeling in grief. In his other hand is a Bible open to a passage in Luke.

Robert Sievier began his career as a portrait engraver; he studied anatomy and modeling, and around 1823 turned to sculpture. He retained an interest in science but achieved popularity as an artist. His memorial sculpture includes the young woman on the monument of John St. John Long here in Kensal Green.

Across from Sievier, down the steps and along the dirt path is a nice sculpting of a helmet, sword, open book, and a collection of medals decorating the monument of General Sir **George Bell** (1794–1877). A fitting companion piece can be found down the next path and to the left, that of Admiral **Henry Collins Deacon** (1788–1869). It shows an entwining of naval accoutrements: sail, cannon, cannon-balls, broken mast, and a coil of rope.

Continue along West Center Road in Section 140 to the monument of **Emile Blondin** (1824–1897) who found fame as the first man to cross Niagara Falls on a tightrope. The following year, 1860, he crossed the falls on stilts, then made the trip three hundred more times with various impediments. At 65 he performed on the tightrope on Staten Island, walking it blindfolded, bicycling across, carrying his son and another man from one end to another, and setting up a stove in the middle of the rope where he cooked omelets for the audience.

Backtrack slightly from Blondin and take the dirt path to your right. A few monuments in is a plain granite cross over a planter commemorating writer **Wilkie Collins** (1824–1889). The marker identifies him as the author of *The Woman in White*. Collins was the son of a successful minor painter and religious martinet, William Collins, who made him consider the ministry, tea-importing, and the law as job possibilities before letting him settle on novel writing. Determined to produce bestsellers, Collins studied the conversation and characteristics of his contemporaries and married his findings to stories by writers he admired. *The Woman in White* was inspired by *La Dame Blanche*, a play by Eugene Scribe, and Collins' policeman in *The Moonstone* owes a decided debt to Dickens' Inspector Bucket from *Bleak House*.

Although this strategy was successful, dramatically raising the circulations of magazines which serialized his novels before publication, it was the only kind of marriage that he would accept. A small, handsome, nearsighted man whose love of gourmet food and fine wines ballooned him into obesity, Collins railed against "the danger from virtuous single ladies whose character is 'dearer to them than their lives.' " Instead of marriage he moved in with Caroline Graves and her daughter, Harriet. Caroline was euphemistically referred to as his "housekeeper" by his friends.

When Caroline married a plumber nine years later and was out of the house for several years, Collins had three children by a second mistress, Martha Rudd. But Caroline and Harriet returned, and Collins alternated between the two households. Caroline and/or Harriet, who became his private secretary and help in old age, are said to be also buried in this grave. "His affairs defy all prediction," his friend Dickens commented mildly. So did Collins' writing. Of his 30 novels, only *The Moonstone* has survived admirably, touted as the first full-length mystery story ever written.

Another writer whose work has survived can be located by going left off of West Center Road down the next dirt path. Resting under a horizontal cross of rose granite is Anthony Trollope with the epitaph, "He was a loving husband and a loving father and a true friend." On the side it reads, "Into thy hands I commend my spirit."

ANTHONY TROLLOPE *b. April 24, 1815, London; d. December 6, 1882, London.* Nathaniel Hawthorne praised Anthony Trollope's novels as being written on the inspiration of beef and ale, and "just as real as if some giant had hewn a great lump out of the earth, put it under a glass case, with all its inhabitants going about their daily business, and not suspecting they were being made a show of." If the gentry under glass served up by Trollope had known who their author was, they might have been even more confused. How could this quarrelsome postal employee, this brusque outdoorsman, understand the secrets of their hearts as he did?

As a boy Trollope gave little indication of his talents. He was neglected by parents who abandoned him when they went to America for three years, leaving his school bills at Winchester unpaid. Large and awkward, dressed in badly fitting, grimy clothes, Trollope felt unloved and condemned himself as ugly and uncouth. The family was struggling as well. A sister and a brother both had tuberculosis. Trollope's father suffered from what we would now call paranoia. His mother, Frances, was a cheery optimist, whose American sales venture, a general goods emporium in Cincinnati, failed, but whose first book, *Domestic Manners of the Americans*, met with great success. It inspired her to write to support her family.

But she never developed any interest in Anthony. She made arrangements for him to work in the post office at 19, which he did. When he announced to his family in 1845 that he had written a novel, their reaction was stupefaction. Unable to accept the fact that he was clever enough to create anything, they could never believe in his subsequent popularity.

Trollope kept writing. *The Macdermotts of Ballycloran* was well received, and he published another novel the following year. Compelled to continue, he wrote 47 more novels and 18 other books of travel and biography — and all while he was still working for the post office! In that capacity he laid out delivery routes in rural England, negotiated international contracts in America and elsewhere, and devised the first letter box. Hungry for the respect that had eluded him in his youth, Trollope took his civil servitude as seriously as his writing. When Thackeray was looking for an easy sinecure and proposed that he be given a position in the post office, Trollope was outraged at his presumption. Yet Trollope's working day at the post office, at least in later years, hardly seems arduous. He would get up and write from 5:30 A.M. to 9:30 A.M., then appear for work at

11:30 A.M., staying until around 5:00 P.M. when he left for tea at the Garrick Club. He also insisted on going hunting two afternoons a week. Charming with friends and family, in his official capacity Trollope remained abrasive to the end.

Barchester Towers (1857), Trollope's fifth and most enduring novel, continued the ecclesiastical theme initiated in *The Warden* (1856). The characters—Eleanor Bold, Archdeacon Grantly, Bishop and Mrs. Proudie—are thoroughly human. In his later fiction Trollope depended even less on plot and more on the psychological interplay of characters. He knew them all intimately, and at the end of every month made sure that they had grown 30 days older. In his *Autobiography* he asserted, "I know the tone of the voice, and the colour of the hair, every flame of the eye, the very clothes they wear. Of each man I could assert whether he would have said these or the other words; of every woman, whether she would then have smiled or so have frowned. When I shall feel that this intimacy ceases, then I shall know the old horse should be turned out to grass."

Trollope did not presume to know *why* his people behaved in certain ways or made the choices they did, only that they did. Admired by such disparate writers as Leo Tolstoi and Henry James, he was a master of dialogue, creating conversations and characters— Plantagenet Palliser, Lady Glencora, Reverend Crawley—which are still vivid to contemporary readers.

After he retired from the Civil Service in 1867, Trollope subsequently gave up hunting and his clubs and moved to a reconstructed farmhouse in the country. It was a mistake. Suffering from asthma and angina, feeling that his literary star was fading, Trollope wrote to his brother Tom that he wanted to die. It was at a dinner party in London, laughing uproariously at a funny story, that the author suffered the stroke which killed him a month later.

Along the same path is an interesting Celtic cross to **Gertrude Dacre** (1807–1883) which shows an angel, a griffin, a dragon—and a cow.

Continuing down the path and around to the left, you will intersect with Terrace Avenue. The monument of **James Henry Leigh Hunt** (1784–1859) is partially hidden by a large tree. It is a block about four feet tall showing a bas-relief of an urn with a flower branch over it and the words, "Write me as one that loves his fellow men," from his poem "Abou Ben Adhem." His white marble bust is no longer in evidence.

Leigh Hunt was an utterly charming, confidingly chatty gentleman, slow to take offense but uninhibited in his candor. He was also a force for free speech in his generation, at one point spending two years in jail for his description of George IV as a liar and "a fat Adonis of 50." The attack appeared in *The Examiner*, a weekly he and his brother, John, founded in 1808. The brothers also provoked controversy by their early championing of Shelley and Keats.

Possibly in gratitude, Shelley induced Lord Byron to include Hunt in a publishing venture, *The Liberal*, in Italy. Byron did so, but when Hunt, his alcoholic wife Marianne, and seven half-wild children descended on the poet, Byron fled to Greece as soon as he could. Stranded, without funds, the Hunts finally limped back to England where

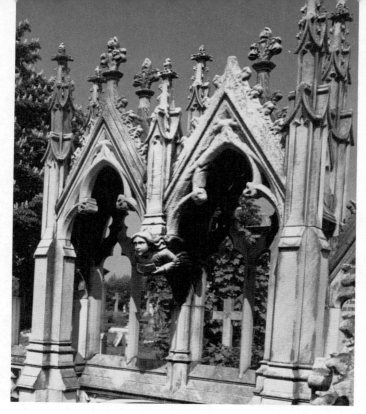

Shaw family

Leigh Hunt published a biography, *Lord Byron and Some of His Contemporaries* (1828) which shocked England by its indiscretions.

Hunt kept writing and founding journals, but it was not until his play, *A Legend of Florence* (1840), was admired by Queen Victoria that he found any financial security. This came in the form of royal grants and, in 1847, a pension of £200 — largely due to the pressure of Charles Dickens and other friends. It caused a rift later when Hunt continued to appeal to his friends for aid. It wasn't because of extravagance — he lived on bread, fruit, and water — but he had no sense of how to manage money, inspiring Dickens to use him as a model for Harold Skimpole in *Bleak House*. Still, improvidence seemed his only fault; when he died at 74 of "exhaustion," Hunt left behind a host of friends and the timeless poems "Abou Ben Adhem" and "Rondeau."

If you have time, return to Central Avenue. Just off it is the poignant monument of **Jonathan St. John Aubin** (b. London, 1928; d. New York, 1986) with the words, "When I get to my own country I will lie down and sleep." It is in the style of British and early American slate markers with a painter's palette in the top bas-relief and a cat incised in the lower left corner. A landmark on the way to help you find it is the chapel-style monument to the **Shaw** family.

193

Allingham family

In Section 166 on the corner is a sculpture showing
Alexandrina Allingham (1868–1904) lying in her coffin,
holding a bouquet of flowers and a sleeping dog. Above her
an angel-in-mourning rests on a podium, holding a wreath.

Near Allingham stands an armchair, the memorial of
Henry Russell (1812–1900). On the bottom of the chair
are the words:

I love it, I love it, and who shall dare
To chide me for loving this old arm chair.

Russell wrote the music for and performed over 800 songs,
including "A Good Time Coming, Boys," and "Woodman,
Spare That Tree."

Also in Kensal Green

"James" Barry (1788–1865), army surgeon and inspector general of the hospitals in 1858–1859 who had one last
surprise under his brass buttons. The embalmers made the
shocking discovery that Barry was a woman, England's first

female doctor. Sir **William Beatty** (d. 1842), the doctor who attended Lord Nelson at his death and saved the fatal shot, which he displayed on a gold mount. Sir **Michael Costa** (1810–1884), the first Englishman to conduct an orchestra with a baton rather than a violin bow. **Joseph Richardson** (1790–1855), creator of a musical instrument called the "Rock Harmonicon" which was played on stage by his sons. The Richardsons were not the forerunners of the Beatles; the rock components were pieces of mica that made sounds when clanked together. Major **Walter C. Wingfield** (1833–1912), the father of lawn tennis, who invented the original game "sphairistike" (Greek for ball-playing) in 1873. It was played on an hourglass-shaped court with the net in the narrowest part.

Henry Russell

DIRECTIONS TO KENSAL GREEN: Take the Bakerloo Line to the Kensal Green stop, then turn left and walk along Harrow Road to the cemetery entrance.

Highgate and St. Michael's

WHEN HIGHGATE CEMETERY was opened in 1839 it attracted an odd clientele. There was financier Julius Beer and his half-mad family; the poetic Rossettis, given to laudanum suicides and midnight exhumations; and, later, avowed lesbians Mabel Veronica Batten and Radclyffe Hall. There were also 166,000 people of lesser eccentricity laid to rest here although, given the secrets of the human heart, one might be hard-pressed to say who they are.

The early cemetery also drew atmosphere from its terraced layout, circuitous paths, and plantings from a greenhouse inside the cemetery which employed 28 gardeners. Architects Stephen Geary and J.B. Bunning and landscape gardener David Ramsey designed several features which set Highgate apart from such rivals as Kensal Green and Norwood. The first of these was Egyptian Avenue which was entered through an archway of massive lotus-decorated columns. Along the avenue were burial vaults carved into the hillside.

Egyptian Avenue led to the second innovation, the Circle of Lebanon, where below-ground vaults paid homage to a vast cedar tree which had been part of the original estate. Above the circle were the Terrace Catacombs where visitors could look down into the rest of the cemetery and out toward London. Here families could build mausoleums as massive as they liked.

Unfortunately, a cemetery of unbridled plantings and uneven terrain is self-destructive. In the beginning Highgate generated great income and could support a large caretaking staff. But as the cemetery filled and there were

Highgate angel

fewer new plots to bring in fresh money, the West Cemetery fell into disrepair. There were, as one writer lamented, a "vast army of Victorian merchants, officers, widows and judges gently crumbling into anonymity beneath ivy and saplings and lushly sinister mare's tales." Vandals operated freely, and graves were desecrated by the High Priest of the British Occult Society. This lofty figure broke into at least two dozen tombs and drove stakes through the hearts of the deceased. He received four years in jail for his anti-Dracula activities.

The West Cemetery, closed completely in 1975, has gradually been brought back by the Friends of Highgate Cemetery. Because the work of restoration is still underway, the only way to visit the West Cemetery is by a guided tour, conducted by one of the Friends. This restriction and the required donation have been criticized publicly. But whatever is collected goes toward further cemetery restoration — which will hopefully lead to more unsupervised wandering in the future.

Each West Cemetery tour differs slightly with its guide. Rather than suggest a route, we will describe what you might hope to see. For the East Cemetery, which is open to the public, we will give a route as usual.

WEST CEMETERY

At Swain's Lane enter through gates which still have the original name, London Cemetery. You will pass two brick chapels whose architecture has been described as Undertakers' Gothic, and enter the heart of the cemetery. With paths cleared for walking, it is easier to enjoy the half-buried monuments and ivy-shrouded angels.

On entering you will be near the monument of **James William Selby** (1843–1888), a noted coachman who died of exposure at age 45. The lower part of his tomb shows the whip and horn he used when he piloted his famous coach, "Old Times." In the year of his death, Selby won a bet by covering the 108-mile distance between London and Brighton in seven hours and fifty minutes. It is not surprising that he finally died of exposure; there were nights when the sleet froze his hat to his head, necessitating its removal by steam.

A number of other people buried on this side also have favorite objects displayed on their markers. **Frederick William Hobart** (1860–1927) has a three-dimensional concertina, or small accordion, at the base of his scroll. The hot-air balloon of **Charles Green Spencer** (1837–1890),

Note: Guided tours only.

Highgate West

A   James William Selby
B   Rossetti Family
C   George Wombwell
D   Thomas Sayers
E   Radclyffe Hall
F   Mrs. Henry Wood

G   Julius Beer
H   Dickens Family
J   Michael Faraday
K   Jacob Bronowski
L   Patrick Wymark

sporting a victory wreath on its gondola, is shown in bas-relief on his tomb. Spencer, known as "The Holloway Aeronaut," ascended to 23,000 feet. **Albert Prosser** (1862–1923), a sporting-goods merchant, displays his tennis racquets and cricket bats for all eternity.

Toward the front of the cemetery is the family plot of the Rossettis. The plain upright stones with a circular cross design betray little of the drama surrounding them. In 1854 the plot was first excavated to lay to rest patriarch **Gabriele Rossetti** (1783–1854), poet, scholar, and professor of Italian at Kings College, London.

The second opening was for **Elizabeth Siddal** (1832–1862), the tragic young wife of Dante Gabriel Rossetti. Lizzie, a classic 17-year-old beauty with red-gold hair, was discovered by the fledgling Pre-Raphaelite painters. Quickly she was transformed into John Stuart Millais' *Ophelia Drowning*, Holman Hunt's *Sylvia*, and Dante Gabriel Rossetti's *Beatrice*. Rossetti took charge of her artistic and romantic life as well. Yet despite her beauty and the mystique he created around Lizzie, Rossetti dragged his feet about their proposed marriage for ten years. By 1860 the situation had gone from hope to embarrassment to obligation. Lizzie was sickly and married Gabriel suspecting that he had found other attractions. A pregnancy that ended in a stillbirth undid her further and, on February 10, 1862, Lizzie died from an overdose of laudanum. Crushed with grief and guilt, Rossetti buried with her the sole copy of the poems he had written to her over several years, nestling it between her cheek and her hair.

In 1869, Dante Gabriel Rossetti was in a different frame of mind. Convinced — rightly — that his true gift was poetry rather than painting, he was suddenly desperate for proof. An exhumation order was signed and, by the glow of a wind-tossed fire, Lizzie's wooden coffin was dug up. A hand reached in and rescued the blue silk-covered volume along with a long strand of red-gold hair. Disinfected, the book appeared in 1870 as *Poems*.

Dante Gabriel Rossetti himself was buried in Birchington, Kent in 1882. The last poetic Rossetti to be buried in this plot was **Christina** (1830–1894), author of such classics as "Goblin Market," "When I Am Dead, My Dearest," and "My Heart Is Like a Singing Bird." Closely tied to her family and disappointed by love, her life had none of the drama of her brother's. She was a victim of Graves' disease, a thyroid condition which bulged her eyes and discolored her skin, marring her delicate beauty. But when she died at 64 it was from cancer that had begun in her breast and shoulder.

Another famous exhumation took place on this side of the cemetery nearly 40 years later when the heirs of one **Thomas Charles Druce**, shopkeeper, wished to prove that he had actually been the reclusive Duke of Portland. Their contention was that in 1864 the Duke, tired of his double role, had staged the funeral and burial. There was no doctor's signature on the death certificate and the heirs' hope was that the coffin would be filled with lead weights.

Unlike the secretive Rossetti exhumation, bystanders gathered outside the cemetery gates at dawn. To the disappointment of all, no doubt, but the Duke of Portland's heir, the body of an elderly bearded man was found in the lead-sealed casket. He was identified through photographs as Thomas Charles Druce.

Several wonderful animals guard their masters' graves. The lion of **George Wombwell** (1788–1850) came from his traveling animal show. Wombwell, who first exhibited the Elephant Man, started his traveling menagerie with a pair of boa constrictors. There is speculation that this lion, happily sleeping on his paws, is Nero whom Wombwell once unsuccessfully tried to engage in a fight against six bull mastiffs.

Nero atop Wombwell's tomb

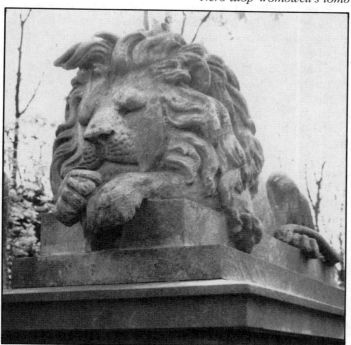

Lion, the dog of **Thomas Sayers** (1826–1865) looks far more watchful as he lies beneath a cameo of his master. Sayers was a bare-knuckle fighter who, at 35, went 42 rounds versus Heenan, a fight that lasted over two hours. His devoted fans raised £3,000 and presented it to him on the condition that he retire and not fight again. Perhaps because he had problems getting along with his wife, he was attached to Lion. In the funeral cortege the dog rode alone on the seat of Sayer's small carriage, a black mourning ruff around his neck.

Finally, there is the horse on the monument of **John Atcheler** (d. 1853). It appears to be grazing peacefully although its legs have been broken off, symbolizing at once the pastoral ideal and the cruel reality of Atcheler's occupation, "horse-slaughterer to Queen Victoria."

While Egyptian Avenue was meant to be impressive in its day, now it is mysterious as well. Entering the ivy-covered portal, with lotus buds on the flanking columns, you are at the "Gateway to the City of the Dead." This area is particularly overgrown and spooky. Holly trees have poignantly sprung up from Christmas wreaths left on graves. The family vaults along the avenue hold 12 coffins, with the larger ones stretching to 15. Along the row is one that is always decorated with flowers.

RADCLYFFE HALL *b. August 12, 1880, Bournemouth; d. October 6, 1943, London.* Although she wore her hair clipped short like a man's and dressed in a tie and jacket, it was her severe expression that made Radclyffe Hall look like one of the boys. A contemporary described her appearance as that of a retired admiral; another called her behavior in public "a British policeman act." The caricatures of Hall that appeared after she became famous focused on her aquiline nose, cigarette holder, and studied frown.

But life to John, as she was known, was serious business. She believed that she had been condemned to be an "invert" at birth; indeed, she believed that lesbianism could be predicted in infancy from the width of a baby's shoulders. Despite her own grim childhood, she gave no credence to the effects of environment, disregarding the fact that, after her shrewish Philadelphia-born mother rejected and beat her, she was ever after attracted to soft, motherly women. John's father, wealthy and Oxford-educated, had beaten a retreat even before his daughter's birth. She was only to see him a few times during her life, but from him came the inheritance which allowed her an independent life.

At 27 John formed a relationship with the kindly Mabel

Veronica Batten. Mabel, nicknamed Ladye, was 50 when they met, a noted singer and beauty who had been painted by John Singer Sargent. Her husband stepped aside discreetly, and John and Ladye spent eight wonderful years together.

In 1915 they met Una Troubridge, another soft, motherly woman to whom John was also attracted. Ladye resented the infatuation. In the middle of a bitter quarrel about Una, she suffered a fatal stroke, leaving John suffused with guilt. Seeking absolution, John and Una spent years visiting mediums, trying to communicate with Ladye's spirit. When Ladye told them she had forgiven everything and would look forward to their arrival, they were finally satisfied. But the ghost of the triangle was a permanent part of their relationship.

In 1924, after a number of successful volumes of poetry, John published her first two novels. *The Forge* was a social comedy about a couple who wanted to be artists but didn't have enough talent; *The Unlit Lamp* was a more serious work about the struggle between a domineering mother and a female tutor for control of a young girl's life. John's third book was even more successful. *Adam's Breed* won the Prix Femina and the James Tait Black Prize, and sold seven printings in its first year. It was, simply, the story of a waiter who becomes so revolted at the sight of people stuffing themselves with food that he chooses anorexia and disappears into the woods in a spiritual quest. Just before starving to death he has a vision of God.

With those three successes under her smoking jacket, John decided the time had come to explore the dominant theme of her life. *The Well of Loneliness* was thinly veiled autobiography. Its brief preface by psychologist Havelock Ellis bolstered the theme that lesbians could not avoid their condition and should be treated with consideration not scorn.

On publication day, July 24, 1928, John and Una made the rounds of the bookstores early to make sure that the book was being prominently displayed. It was, although the reviews were mixed; a number of critics felt that the story itself had been lost in polemic. Other prominent lesbians criticized its stereotyping and the idea that lesbian couples simply mirrored dominant-male/passive-female relationships. Vita Sackville-West felt that the definitive novel remained to be written and hoped to do so herself. But John received thousands of letters expressing agreement and gratitude, a response that made her feel that her effort had been worthwhile.

She might have simply turned her attention to her next book at that point had the *Sunday Express* not taken a sledgehammer to *The Well of Loneliness*, condemning its waters as "moral poison" and demanding that the home secretary ban the book. Home Secretary William Joynson-Hicks threatened the publisher, Jonathan Cape, with legal action if he did not withdraw the novel. Cape agreed, but smuggled the plates to Paris for publication. Shipments of the novel on their way back into England were seized, however, and the book was put on trial. Although no lewd passages could be cited, it was condemned as "obscene libel" for its subject alone and the book was banned in England.

It was John's last major work. She died of colon cancer in 1943 without seeing *The Well of Loneliness* reinstated. In 1949, when the novel was selling 100,000 copies a year outside England, Falcon Press reissued it without incident.

The Catacombs

In light of the earlier hysteria, it is startling to put Radclyffe Hall in the context of a contemporary of hers, Gertrude Stein. Just across the English Channel, Stein, six years older than John, was living unashamedly with Alice B. Toklas, holding court with Picasso and Joyce, and reveling in her sexual preference. Humorless and intense, it had taken all John's courage to creep out of the closet with the support of Havelock Ellis.

Yet history has a way of having the last word. Gertrude Stein's grave in Paris is overgrown with weeds and all but forgotten. Radclyffe Hall's mausoleum is never without fresh flowers.

Another remarkable woman writer is buried not far from Radclyffe Hall. **Mrs. Henry Wood** (1814–1887), author of *East Lynne*, has a plain piece of pink marble with "Mrs. Henry Wood" engraved on it. This simple grave does not reveal that, beginning at age 40, Mrs. Wood (born Ellen

Price) wrote 25 novels in 20 years. Her first novel, *Dune-berg House*, was awarded £100 by the Scottish Temperance League as the best novel illustrating the joys of abstinence; but it was her second book, *East Lynne*, that put her on the map.

From here you will no doubt proceed to the mausoleums above. The largest and most impressive is that of **Julius Beer** (1836–1880), German financier and owner of *The Observer*. The mausoleum was designed by John Oldrid Scott with a nod to King Mausolus' tomb in Halicarnassus, Turkey, which is known as one of the Seven Wonders of the World. Topped by a small cross on a spire, it is notable for a blue and gold mosaic roof and bas-relief statue inside it of a kneeling angel comforting a young girl who has her eyes shut. The sculpture, executed by H.H. Armstead, may represent Beer's daughter who died at age six of consumption.

When Beer died of apoplexy at 43 his son, Frederick, inherited the paper. Always delicate in body and mind, Frederick soon retreated into insanity. His talented wife, Rachel Sassoon, took over the editing of *The Observer* and *The Sunday Times* which she owned, ballooning circulation with such articles as an endorsement of cannibalism. Anticipating present grooming trends, she had Frederick's favorite poodle clipped in the pattern of the Beer family crest.

On the way out you will pass the plot of the Dickens family. **Catherine Dickens** (1815–1879), has a plain in-ground marker with a metal fence around it. Several of her children are also buried here. The grave mentions Charles Dickens' name as well, but he is buried in Poets' Corner in Westminster Abbey.

Along the north wall of the cemetery is the plain, peaked monument of scientist Michael Faraday. He is buried in the two acres of "unconsecrated ground" because he belonged to a sect called the Sandemanians, not recognized by the Church of England.

MICHAEL FARADAY *b. September 22, 1791, London; d. August 25, 1867, Hampton Court.* Modern physics owes a tremendous debt to Michael Faraday. In being responsible for the discovery of electric and magnetic fields, he set the groundwork for field theory's importance in understanding everything from the subatomic realm to intergalactic space. It is field theory which, according to Timothy Ferris, "portrays the entire material world as but a grand illusion, spun on the loom of the force fields."

Faraday's background was unique for a scientist. The

son of a blacksmith he was raised in poverty, his education consisting of no more than the basics taught in his common school. Raised in the Sandemanian Church, an offshoot of the Presbyterian Church, Faraday became first an errand boy and then, at 14, an apprentice to a local bookseller. It was his exposure at the store to scientific books, including *Mrs. Marcet's Conversations on Chemistry* and the *Encyclopaedia Britannica*, that stirred his imagination and interest. Watt's *Improvement of the Mind* urged him to greater discipline. To Faraday's great delight one of the store's customers arranged for him to hear a public lecture given by the great chemist Sir Humphry Davy. Faraday took detailed notes and upon his return home wrote them out, added illustrations, and had the whole package bound and sent off to Sir Humphry.

Davy was impressed enough to offer Faraday a job in 1813. Within seven months he was touring Europe with Sir Humphry and Lady Davy, serving as secretary and valet. Meeting and listening to some of the greatest scientists of Europe fueled Faraday's already burning interest. Staying on with Davy at the Royal Institute, Faraday began to make his own contributions. Eighteen twenty-one saw both the publication of his *Historical Sketch of Electromagnetism* and, more significantly, his demonstration of the continual rotational movement of a current around a magnet and the rotation of the magnet around a wire carrying current. This was, albeit primitive, the first electric motor. Two years later Faraday was made a member of the Royal Society over the objections of a jealous Davy.

In 1831 Faraday went on to demonstrate that a magnet could produce current and then, most importantly, showed that current could be produced without a battery. To do this Faraday attached the opposite poles of two bar magnets to either end of an iron bar wound with wire. When the far ends of the two magnets either made or broke contact current was generated. His achievement was popularized by a literary wag of the day:

Around the magnet Faraday
Was sure that Volta's lightnings play:
   But how to draw them from the wire?
He took a lesson from the heart:
'Tis when we meet, 'tis when we part,
   Breaks forth the celestial fire.

Faraday was able to reverse the process as well by substituting a battery for the magnet and achieving the same results. Hence the process of inducing a current was born. In this same banner year Faraday also produced the first dynamo.

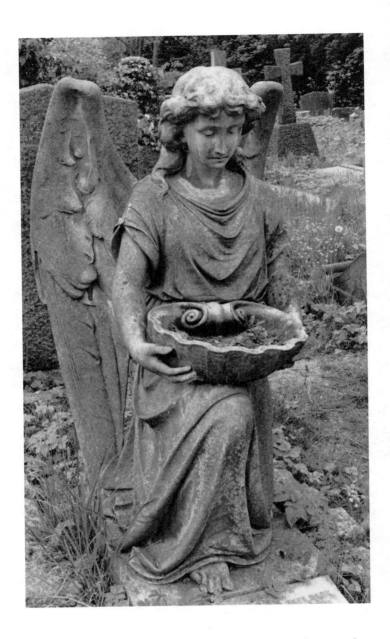

Faraday's electric motor and dynamo were later to be brought to more practical levels by other men. Most notable of these was James Clerk Maxwell who, with his superior mathematical skills, was able to quantify Faraday's experiments. Einstein likened the two to Galileo and Newton, one intuitive, the other mathematical.

Whether Faraday was handicapped by his lack of formal learning is hard to say. Certainly he lacked the mathematical knowledge that most scientists had. He substituted for it an intuition of the highest order and combined it with a dedication to work that could have served as the basis of Edison's dictum that genius is 1 percent inspiration and 99 percent perspiration. In his lifetime Faraday performed over 15,000 experiments ranging from the oft-repeated scattering of iron filings around a magnet to demonstrate the extent and form of its field to the revolutionary work already described.

Away from work Faraday enjoyed simple pleasures. With his wife he took pleasure in seeing Keene or attending a recital by Jenny Lind. He found the monkeys at the zoo hilarious and laughed until tears washed his cheeks. He rode his velocipede to Hampstead and around the Royal Institution when he had the chance. Perhaps he should have taken more of these pleasurable breaks, for at age 49 he suffered a nervous breakdown necessitating four years of convalescence. His memory never fully recovered. Indeed, it grew worse with the years and his work became increasingly limited. In 1858 Queen Victoria gave Faraday a house at Hampton Court. Realizing his "gentle decay" Faraday took to writing farewell letters to his friends ("Whether I shall recover — this condition — do not know. I will not write anymore. My love to you"). As his memory failed so did his force and energy. He spent his last two years in complete senility and died quietly while sitting in his chair.

Finally, you may come to an unexpectedly recent arrival. Known to modern audiences for his book and TV series, "The Ascent of Man," **Jacob Bronowski** (1908–1974) has a white marker whose plainness contrasts with his kaleidoscopic interests and achievements. It is now common wisdom, with the vast explosion of information in the twentieth century, that the Renaissance man has long been extinct. Successfully delving into and merging such diversified areas as science, mathematics, poetry, playwriting, history, and humanism, Bronowski belied the myth.

Bronowski's life was a peripatetic one. Born in Poland he spent the years of World War I in Germany, coming to England in 1920 and entering Cambridge in 1927. Studies and work continued there until 1933 when he moved to the University of Hull to teach. During the war years he applied his expertise in statistics to estimate the economic loss due to German bombing. In 1945, as scientific deputy to the British Chiefs of Staff Mission to Japan, he authored the classic report, "The Effects of the Atomic Bombs at Hiroshima and Nagasaki." After the war he shifted his mathematical focus to economic analysis and then, in 1950, became director of the Coal Research Establishment of the

National Coal Board. Under his direction researchers developed a new process for smokeless fuel. His work with the coal board continued until 1963.

By now Bronowski was 53 with achievement enough for most lifetimes. In his "spare" time he attended to the usual cares and concerns of marriage and of rearing four daughters. But there were also his books on literature, *The Poet's Defence* (1939) and *William Blake, A Man Without a Mask* (1944), his dramas for radio and television, including the prizewinning "The Face of Violence" (1950), his lectures for the BBC, and his book *The Common Sense of Science* (1951), which marked him as a leading proponent of scientific humanism. Inspired by the great age of science when Newton, Wren, and Dryden all actively participated in the Royal Academy, Bronowski proposed that such a broadbased view was still necessary and desirable in today's world. He argued that science was limited by humanness and that its goals should be those of serving mankind.

Bronowski, of course, did not stop there. He moved to the United States in 1964 where he shifted emphasis again, this time working at the Salk Institute for Biological Studies. He became the director of the Council for Biology in Human Affairs in 1970. The switch from physical to life science was one that he treasured enormously, expressing incredulity at his luck in being able to explore both areas in his lifetime. It was in gratitude for this that he wrote *The Ascent of Man*. His goal in this book, as in his other books, was not modest. In it he attempted "to create a philosophy for the twentieth century which shall be all of one piece." And he was clear that it was philosophy rather than history. Bronowski died suddenly of a heart attack at East Hampton, New York, in 1974.

If we were to create an epitaph to fill in this plain stone, Bronowski's words would surely serve best: "There cannot be a philosophy, there cannot even be a decent science, without humanity. . . . For me, the understanding of nature has as its goal the understanding of human nature and of the human condition within nature."

Also in this area is actor **Patrick Wymark** (1926–1970), best known to British audiences for his role as a ruthless tycoon in *The Planemakers* and *The Power Game*, shows portraying dynasties comparable to the Ewings of *Dallas*. While on tour in Melbourne, Australia, to star in a production of *Sleuth*, he was found dead in his hotel room of natural causes.

Highgate East

A   Richard Smith
B   George Eliot,
      George Henry Lewes
C   George Jacob Holyoake
D   Karl Marx
E   Herbert Spencer

F   Hewitt Henry Ravnor
G   Harry Thornton
H   Ralph Richardson
J   William Friese Green,
      Carl Mayer

EAST CEMETERY

As you cross Swain's Lane and enter through the gates, you may be surprised at the difference in terrain. The East Cemetery is on more level ground and more logically laid out. But what you miss in atmosphere will be made up for by interesting people and picturesque monuments.

As you continue along the main path, called Top Road, bear left at the fork. Just after the crosspath you will see a visual pun set back in the foliage on your right, a carved piece of rock with the nickname "Stony." It is the monument of **Richard Smith** (1836–1900) which explains, "After years of patient investigation he patented on the sixth of October 1887 his improved treatment of the wheat germ and broken wheat which made the manufacture of Hovis Bread possible."

The inventor of this type of brown bread would have been gratified to know that one hundred years later his product was still familiar; on behalf of his beautiful loaf, however, he might take exception to this portrait by Len Deighton from *The Ipcress File*: "He had a long thin nose, a moustache like flock wallpaper, sparse, carefully combed hair, and the complexion of a Hovis loaf."

Make a left onto the next path. A little way up on your right you will find George Eliot under a surprisingly austere gray granite stele, with the words, "Of those immortal dead who live again in minds made better by their presence."

GEORGE ELIOT *(MARY ANN EVANS) b. November 22, 1819, Warwickshire; d. December 22, 1880, London.* When she was 19 years old, George Eliot—then still Mary Ann Evans—wrote to a friend that she heard a voice inside telling her that "the bliss of reciprocated affection is not allotted to you under any form." It was a natural assumption. With a face that was all nose and little chin, plain dark hair and a grave manner, Mary Ann was no catch. She knew Latin, Greek, French, Italian, and German but, having been exiled to boarding school at age five, she had never experienced warm family relationships. Yet despite her prediction, she sought love everywhere; and it was not until she found it that she could settle down and complete her life's work.

After graduation Mary Ann returned to the home of her widowed father, but the following year she was invited to stay at the home of a 62-year-old scholar, Dr. Brabant, and learn from him. Rapturously she wrote another friend, "I am in a little heaven here, Dr. Brabant being its archangel." But paradise was flawed; Dr. Brabant's jealous sister-in-law and his blind wife intervened, and Mary Ann crept home.

She kept busy, translating *The Life of Christ* by David Friedrich Strauss from the German, for which she received £20 and no credit, and writing a number of articles for a local paper. But her real life did not begin until 1851 when, liberated by her father's death, she traveled to Germany and returned with a new identity. Offered a job in London as John Chapman's assistant on *The Westminster Review*, Marian, as she now called herself, was soon working with the most gifted minds of her time and further developing her own writing skills.

She fell in love again, first with John Chapman who was married and had a live-in mistress for good measure, then with the more available Herbert Spencer. She pursued the philosopher discreetly, first thanking him "for the few lumps of ice I carried with me from that tremendous glacier of yours," then more openly, "You will find that I can be satisfied with very little, if I am delivered from the dread of losing it," but in the end his timidity won out.

By then she had met George Henry Lewes, so small and homely that he had been nicknamed "Ape" by Jane Carlyle, but considered witty, personable, and charming. His personal life in 1853 was a disaster. Attempting a Shelleyan ideal of open marriage, Lewes and his friend, Thornton Hunt, had supported each other's early philandering and mingled their families. But the experiment created its own Frankenstein; Hunt, though living with his wife, became involved with Agnes Lewes and started fathering her children as well. At least twice the two women would give birth within a month of each other. Divorcing Agnes was impossible; the relationship that developed with Marian Evans offered him a second chance to be loved.

When the couple sailed for Germany in 1854 it was as husband and wife. A marriage based on love and commitment was *truly* moral, Marian insisted to skeptics, whereas a union of empty formality based on deception was not. Friends who wished to remain friends called her Mrs. Lewes. But Marian Evans was close to assuming her final identity; out of the secure soil of love and encouragement blossomed the novelist George Eliot. She adopted the masculine name to keep her writing from being immediately discounted through sexism or objections to her personal life, and to set it apart from the plethora of potboilers that "lady novelists" were turning out at that time.

Beginning with a short story, "The Sad Fortunes of Mr. Amos Barton," Eliot created a work called *Scenes of Clerical Life*, then went on to publish *Adam Bede* in 1859.

George Holyoake

Adam Bede was a sensation, selling a large number of copies in Europe and the United States as well, and surpassing *A Tale of Two Cities* and *The Virginian*. Her identity became known and had no dire effects on the reception of her next novels: *The Mill on the Floss* (1860), *Silas Marner* (1861), *Romula* (1862-63), and her masterpiece, *Middlemarch* (1871-72). By the time her final novel, *Daniel Deronda*, appeared in 1876, George Eliot was being called England's greatest living novelist. Her works were masterpieces of characterization, psychological insight, and drama set on a large scale. Years of studying life from the sidelines, of learning to decipher the human heart as a means of her own emotional survival, had paid rich dividends.

The end of her life was as unhappy as some of her plots. George Henry Lewes died unexpectedly in November 1878 from cancer, leaving her distraught. In the spring of 1880 Eliot married a family friend and comfort, John Cross, who was 20 years younger; but on a honeymoon trip to Venice he leaped out their window into the Grand Canal. He was fished out, but it upset his new bride who was already suffering a recurrence of renal problems. That December she succumbed to a heart attack. She was buried at Highgate, her plot just touching the corner of Lewes'.

Next to George Eliot is the rather curious marker of Elma Stuart "whom for eight-and-a-half blessed years George Eliot called by the sweet name of daughter." She was a pioneer in England of the Salisbury system of prevention and cure of diseases and author of *What Must I Do To Get Well and How Can I Keep So?* Elma, who had approached George Eliot by sending her a book-slide, mirror frame, and oak table richly carved with birds and flowers and their names intertwined, was only one of a number of young women who approached the novelist in a spirit of hero worship and were allowed to stay on as friends. Her rather wistful epitaph was perhaps written for George Eliot, since Elma herself had been married and had a child:

> What though thy name by no sad lips be spoken,
> And no fond heart shall keep thy memory green.
> Thou yet hast left thine own enduring token,
> T'is not as though thou ne'er had been.

Directly behind George Eliot under a long marble slab is **George Henry Lewes** with just his dates 1817–1878. Perhaps it is unfair to remember Lewes primarily as the man who encouraged George Eliot to write fiction and encouraged her during periods of doubt, but his critical and literary work has not weathered well. Lewes wrote extensively about Augustus Comte and positivism but his most notable work was *The Life of Goethe* (1855).

Behind Lewes is the bust of **George Jacob Holyoake** (1817–1906), "Co-operator and Social Reformer" whose granite monument was erected by the Co-operators of Great Britain. On the base are some quotes by Holyoake including "I have cared more for co-operation than for any other movement in which I have been engaged" and "Without honesty to principal there can be no progress in public affairs."

Holyoake, a disciple of the socialistic theories of Robert Owen, was the last person to be imprisoned for atheism in Great Britain, an incident that grew out of a debate after one of his lectures. He was also the last person to be indicted in England for publishing papers without a stamp; instead of being convicted, the Newspaper Stamp Act was repealed. Holyoake also traveled twice to America and Canada in an effort to induce their governments to publish guidebooks for immigrants.

It has been noted that Highgate provides yet another location for Marks and Spencer but the two fellows found here are wholly different indeed. Retrace your steps to Top Road and move along to the head of Karl Marx. The black metal bust shows the shaggy, bewhiskered philosopher and revolutionary staring ahead as if seeing some visionary future. Unfortunately the base of the monument is bulky and official, lacking the proportion and style which would do the bust justice. Beneath his chin is his clarion call, "Workers of all lands unite," and highlighted in gold, "The philosophers have only interpreted the world in various ways. The point however is to change it."

A small plaque tells who else is buried in the huge high vault beneath: **Jenny von Westphalen** (1814–1881), beloved wife of Karl Marx; **Harry Longuet** (1878–1883), their grandson; **Helene Demuth** (1823–1890), the family's governess and housekeeper; and **Eleanor Marx** (1855–1898), Karl Marx's daughter.

The family was moved to this plot from a more obscure location in 1954, another exhumation which took place secretly at night to avoid controversy and crowds. At that time the ashes of Eleanor "Tussy" Marx were reunited with her family. A brilliant but troubled young woman, she committed suicide in 1898 when she found that her longtime free-love husband, Edward Aveling, had secretly married an actress he had met the summer before. After death her ashes were kept at Communist Party headquarters in London. In a 1921 Scotland Yard raid the ashes were seized, held, and later given to the Marx Memorial Library in Clerkenwell.

KARL MARX *b. May 5, 1818, Trier, Germany; d. March 13, 1883, London.* To look at the cold, monumental Marx of his memorial gives little idea of the person, for Marx was a man of many faces. Asked by Queen Victoria's daughter to provide a firsthand account of Marx, Liberal M.P. Grant Duff had to report that he was not the man who ate babies in their cradles, as the police reported. Duff instead found the "Red-Terror-Doctor" to be a slightly cynical, highly learned gentleman who could discourse widely, who employed a dry wit, and who, while seeming sure of the past and present, was vague and uncertain as to the future.

From the outset Marx's life was marked by contradiction, for the great denouncer of the bourgeoisie was born into a middle-class family in Trier. Although the family's background was steeped in Jewish ancestry, Marx's parents were baptized in order that Heinrich Marx might retain his job. The children were thus raised as part of the small minority of two hundred Protestants in Catholic Trier.

As a young man Marx cut a dashing, romantic figure. He attended university at Bonn and then Berlin. As a student, he drank, was scarred above his left eye in a duel, and wrote love poems to his sweetheart, Jenny von Westphalen. Jenny was four years older and Marx was only 18 when they were engaged. Forced to wait seven years because of her family's objections, Marx immersed himself in his studies. Like many young men of the time he was a revolutionary, for such thought and fervor were in the air. The French Revolution, now a generation removed, held a golden aura for these young men.

Never one to think on a small scale Marx began to develop his own philosophy of history. Philosophy soon evolved into revolutionary politics. Marx saw work as the most noble expression of mankind. Freedom and change came about through work. But Marx saw capitalism as an infringement on the workers. The only answer lay in revolution.

After receiving his degree he became the editor of the liberal *Rheinische Zeitung*. Marx's personality soon dominated the paper's outlook. He became more outspoken and, for the first time, became aware of the importance of economic realities in determining the structure of society. The government, stung by his views, dispatched its censors to limit the damage. In 1843 the paper was to be shut down altogether and Marx, knowing his future in Germany was dim, set out for Paris.

Three important things happened to Marx in Paris. He married Jenny, he fell under the philosophical influence of Ludwig Feuerbach, and he met Friedrich Engels. Philosophically Marx grew apart from his early mentor, Hegel, claiming that Hegel had turned the dialectic on its head. Marx righted it by declaring that its basis lay not in ideas but in the material realm, hence dialectical materialism.

Paris saw friendships with others of revolutionary thought like the poet Heinrich Heine whom Marx aided in rewriting some of his poetry. In turn Heine saved the life of Marx's first child, Jenny, who was suffering convulsions. But superseding this friendship was Marx's relationship with Engels. In 1844 the two met at that famous rendezvous, Café de la Regence. History does not record their beverage of choice but there is no doubt that the talk was long, intense, and sympathetic. The friendship would last until Marx's death 39 years later.

The *Communist Manifesto* was the great product of this

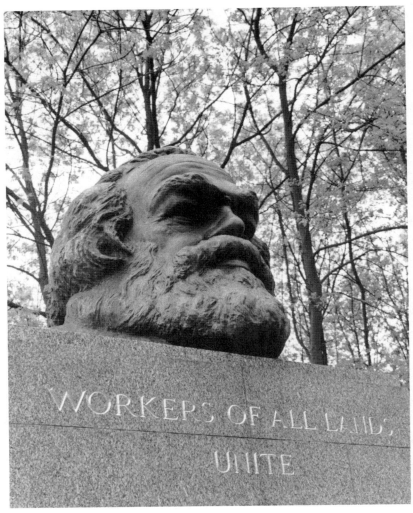

Karl Marx

friendship. Published in 1848 the *Manifesto* was at once philosophical, historical, and, in its predictions, inevitable. Communism would be the next step in the inexorable historical flow. "Workers of all lands, unite!" Seldom has a cause been espoused with such ringing intelligence and visionary fervor.

Ironically this work was not yet published when the 1848 revolution broke out in Frankfurt. Marx and Engels hurried back to Germany to give active support at the barricades but were too late. The revolt was all but dead. Because of his sympathies Marx quickly left with Jenny, but was arrested and briefly detained in Brussels. Fleeing to London they settled down to raise a large family in "bourgeois poverty" at 28 Dean Street, near Soho Square. The death of their first child added to the stress of their poverty. Marx sought solace in the bed of their housekeeper, Helene Demuth. A child resulted but, in order to avoid scandal for Marx, Engels accepted paternity before the infant was sent to a foster home. The family closed around the secret and it remained undiscovered for many decades.

Marx took on odd jobs such as the London correspondent for the *New York Tribune* and in his spare time could be found in the British Museum, where he performed extensive research and wrote his great economic analysis, *Capital*. The first volume of *Capital* was published in 1867. It had taken years, and not without a toll. Troubled by hemorrhoids in the latter stages of writing he could not sit down, lamenting, "I hope the bourgeoisie will remember my carbuncles."

In his last ten years Marx continued to be politically active but at a less intense level. The drafts of the next two volumes of *Capital* were prepared, but he was able to relax with his family and loved playing with his grandchildren as he had with his own children. His health began to deteriorate, and so did Jenny's. She was the first to go, dying in 1881. Marx was deeply affected. His daughter, Eleanor, was a solace and a companion but not a substitute. The final blow was the death of his oldest and favorite child, Jenny. Two months later, beset with bronchitis and an ulcerated lung, Marx died quietly in his sleep.

There are always flowers in all shades of red left at the tomb, though the monument has sometimes been defaced with red, white, and blue paint. Buried in the large plot are other revolutionaries such as **Claudia Vera Jones** (1915–1964), "Valiant fighter against racism and imperialism who dedicated her life to the progress of socialism and the liberation of her own black people."

Also in the vicinity is **Yusef Mohamed Dadoo** (1909–1983), chairman of the South African Communist Party. An Indian who studied medicine in Scotland then returned to South Africa to practice, Dadoo worked first on behalf of South African Indians, then on behalf of all non-whites. Sentenced to jail several times, he left South Africa through Botswana.

Across from Karl Marx in a plain gray granite sarcophagus are the ashes of **Herbert Spencer** (1820–1903). Spencer was born in Derby and came from a line of Nonconformists and Dissenters. He took his ancestry to heart for his work habits were unorthodox and his social relationships singular. All his life he worked on the edges of social norms. Though his family fairly reeked of teachers, he avoided studies, occupying himself instead in the most desultory fashion possible. He built watches, practiced civil engineering, wrote sociology, psychology, philosophy, biology, ethics, and politics. Yet despite his voluminous writings his preparation was slim and highly selective. For sociology he read no Comte; for ethics no Kant or Mill.

Spencer's gift and problem lay in his fertile mind, which pushed up ideas and theories in great profusion. Rather than being inspired by the work of others, Spencer's mind was self-pollinating. From his own ideas he neatly induced his theories. With so many observations at hand he felt obliged to explain the world to a waiting public. Built into such a profusion of thought is a certain degree of failure. According to his friend, Thomas Huxley, "Spencer's idea of a tragedy is a deduction killed by a fact."

Errors and omissions seemed not to faze him, and the ideas continued to flow. He was the greatest English philosopher of his day. Greatly influenced by Darwin's theory of evolution, he coined the phrase "survival of the fittest," and developed the basis for Social Darwinism which contended that the poorer (less materially successful) classes or races were obviously inferior in the daily battle and therefore should not be encouraged to reproduce. "The ultimate result of shielding men from folly is to fill the world with fools," Spencer declared. Still Spencer, who abhorred government in any form, valued the notion of charity as preached by the major religions, and could not acquiesce to laissez-faire treatment of the poor. He strongly advocated private charity which would lend comfort if not encouragement.

Spencer's dabbling produced a string of inventions, most of them failures. He tried vegetarianism and the opera and found both wanting. It took him until the age of 38 to decide that his life had been "miscellaneous" and to hit upon the idea that evolution existed in every science. He then spent the next 40 years elucidating his theory.

Spencer's personal life was marked by reclusive tendencies. Having but a few select friends he shunned unnecessary contact. The fair sex appealed to him sporadically, but affairs were short-lived and found Spencer scurrying back to the safety of his isolated bachelorhood. A phrenologist who examined him during his successful years labeled one bump "self-esteem very large." For Spencer it may have been superfluous verification. When George Eliot (one of his affairs) queried him as to why, since he thought so much, he had no wrinkles on his forehead, he replied, "I suppose it is because I am never puzzled." He was brilliant, knew it, and expressed it expansively and polysyllabically. That he might possess a sense of humor about himself never seemed to occur to him.

With age Spencer moderated his views, realizing that attacks against religion and politics were generally beyond the province of logic. Even so, his honesty precluded his acceptance by any one group and so he was shunned and castigated by all. His works fell into disfavor and Spencer was left feeling that he was a failure who would have been better served by seeking the simple pleasures of life. While there has been no major revival of Spencer's views, he nevertheless remains an important figure for his powerful influence on the philosophical and scientific thought of his day.

To Spencer's left is a stele commemorating **William Nassau Kennedy** (1839–1885) who died of smallpox on the return journey from the Nile. He was on his way home to Canada after commanding the Nile Voyagers, a group of Canadian boatmen who had been hired to guide Wolseley up the river to relieve Gordon at Khartoum.

On a tomb further down the path is a nearly faded quote from Rudyard Kipling, "The moving finger writes and having writ moves on. Nor all thy piety nor wit shall lure it back to cancel half a line, nor all thy tears wash out a word of it."

As you continue on what becomes Bottom Road, right before the intersection of Dog's head path (*sic*) is the flat slab of **Hewitt Henry Rayner** (1902–1957). His epitaph notes that he "made the famous drypoint during the Blitz of 1940, a protégé of W.R. Sickert." At the end of his tomb are the words "Artist — Mystic." Rayner's work was collected by the royal family and others, but a series of misadventures dogged the artist. His studio was destroyed during the war and he developed shell shock and asthma. His painting arm, broken in an accident, eventually healed, but he worked only occasionally after that. In 1957 Rayner gassed himself, leaving his wife a note that he "felt inadequate to be the head of the household."

The area around Dog's head path becomes overgrown in the spring and summer; you'll find the Queen Anne's Lace waist-high, making a search for a particular monument difficult. Hidden back in here is the marker of **William Henry Monk** (1823–1889), composer of the hymn "Abide with Me."

This area also has the most picturesque monuments in the East Cemetery. Dog's head path received its name from the monument to **Ann Jewson Crisp** (1800–1884) which

A crop of flowers and stones

shows an inset sculpture of a dog's head on its rose marble stele identified as "Her faithful dog Emperor." Possibly a mastiff, Emperor is a stocky, intimidating, though not hostile dog. Large, floppy ears and a leather collar, indicating that he might stay on a leash, help to put one at ease.

Along the next path, Babies head (*sic*), is the baby after whom it was named, a three-dimensional infant perched on a draped step and reaching up toward a cameo of an older man. The monument was erected "In loving memory of Charles John Griffiths, Captain 61st Gloucester Regiment, 1835–1910." The tiny naked baby is his little grandchild, Natica Violet Lily Claremont, who was born February 2 and died August 1, 1913. Along the way notice the poignant reminder of **Thomas Joseph Nighy** (1872–1930), a broken violin with no neck or strings.

A more dramatic instrument is located back on Main Road. On your right is the stone piano of **Harry Thornton** (d. 1918) which has unfortunately had its lid stolen. Along the side it has the sentiment, "Sweet thou art sleeping cradled on my heart, Safe in God's keeping while I must weep apart," a quote from Puccini. Thornton, a concert pianist, took time off to entertain troops during World War I. He died in the flu epidemic of 1918 which killed more people worldwide than the war had.

Harry Thornton

Further up the road is a charming bas-relief of five young angel faces set against a cross. All are individualized as if modeled on actual little girls, and each appears to be looking in a different direction with a different concern. They suggest a Sir Joshua Reynolds painting recast as sculpture. Below the faces is the epitaph, "And with the morn those angel-like faces smile."

Along Shaw's Path to your right are the remains of **Charles Green** (1785–1870). Green, a balloonist, reached a record altitude of 27,146 feet, nearly freezing to death from the cold and the 60–100 mph winds. Two years earlier Green's balloon, "Nassau," was used in a jump that proved fatal to another balloonist. Despite the risks Green took in his life, at 85 he went up to bed and died of clogged arteries.

Also in this area is Dr. **Reginald Harrison** (1837–1908) who introduced the idea of ambulances to speed emergency cases to the hospital.

About halfway up Main Road on your right you will find Sir **Ralph Richardson** (1902–1983), whose epitaph is "In treasured and tender memory." He is lying under a full-length cement slab which rises slightly at the end and curls under the way a pillow would.

Ralph Richardson was a career actor in a city where

longevity is encouraged. Although he first was attracted to the priesthood and then journalism, at 18 he got his first job in the theater, paying to belong to a small company which worked out of a bacon factory in Brighton. Richardson worked his way up through Shakespearian touring companies to the Old Vic, but his first major success came in *The Amazing Dr. Clitterhouse* in 1936. He returned to more classic drama at the Old Vic but took time out to make 40 films including *Long Day's Journey into Night* and *Rollerball*. Presumably he would be acting still, had not death pulled the curtain just before his 81st birthday.

Just past the fork in the road take the path to your left. At the end of it, near the wall on your left is the monument to **William Friese Green** (1855–1921). In contrast to some of the others, it is large and fairly easy to spot. It has a tall white spire which stands out against the fence, with pillars and a chancel decoration. The inscription identifies him as "the inventor of kinematography" (cinematography) and explains that "his genius bestowed upon humanity the boon of commercial kinematography of which he was the first inventor and patentee, June 21, 1889, Number 10301."

As often happens, the original inventor did not reap the financial rewards. Green spent £10,000 trying to interest others in his camera, eventually becoming bankrupt and having his effects sold at auction. In 1915, grappling with the idea of color film while living in poverty, he was rescued by some friends and employed at a film company. After addressing the film industry at a meeting in London, he collapsed from heart failure and died.

Right across from Green is an in-ground memorial to **Carl Mayer** (1894–1944). His epitaph reads that he was a "Pioneer in the art of the cinema. Erected by his friends and fellow workers." Mayer, who steadfastly refused all offers to come to Hollywood, co-authored the screenplay of *The Cabinet of Dr. Caligari*, as well as *The Last Laugh*, and an adaptation of *Tartuffe*.

Also in this area is an interesting modernistic bust of a woman clasping her hands, eyes shut.

Along the fence to your right is nightclub entertainer **Leslie A. Hutchison**, "Hutch" (d. 1969). He has a plain marker with a planted bed in front of it.

ST. MICHAEL'S CHURCH

On the hill above the cemetery, right in the village of Highgate, is the small parish church of St. Michael's. Built in 1832 by Lewis Vulliamy, its single spire is an area landmark. Look for the stained glass east window and the marker of Samuel Taylor Coleridge in the aisle. He is actually a new arrival, having been moved here in 1961 from the crypt of Highgate School.

SAMUEL TAYLOR COLERIDGE *b. October 21, 1772, Ottery St. Mary, Devonshire; d. July 25, 1834, Highgate, London.* Coleridge made an indelible impression on young William Hazlitt. Writing 25 years later Hazlitt described "a strange wildness in his aspect, a dusky obscurity. . . . His forehead was broad and high, light as if built of ivory, with large projecting eyebrows, and his eyes rolling beneath them. . . . His mouth was gross, voluptuous, open, eloquent; his chin good-humored and round; but his nose, the rudder of the face, the index of the will, was small, feeble, nothing-like what he had done."

In Wordsworth's poem *The Prelude*, he sympathizes with Coleridge for having been raised in the city away from beneficent nature. But Coleridge was in fact born and raised in a small country town in Devonshire and knew the countryside well. He was bookish, introverted, and a loner. When his father died in 1781 he was sent to school at Christ's Hospital in London. There he continued his solitary ways and habits. As a teen he would keep his clothes on while bathing in a local river. More than once he became sick from the chill of drying out and this practice may have led to the painful rheumatism he started to experience as a young man. It was to relieve that pain that he first started taking opium.

Coleridge's scholarly ways gained him entrance to Jesus College, Cambridge, in 1791, but he found himself unstimulated there. Falling almost immediately into debt while furnishing his rooms, his grades soon sank to the level of his slender bank account. Romantic escape beckoned and Coleridge enlisted in the Light Dragoons. His alias, Silas Tomkyn Comberbache, could not hide his total ineptitude on horseback. It was good fortune all around when his brothers rescued him from the army.

Returning to Cambridge in 1794 Coleridge became friendly with Robert Southey, then a student at Oxford. Both young men harbored poetic aspirations and radical political and religious ideas. They devised between them a plan for establishing a democratic utopian village in Pennsylvania which Coleridge called "Pantisocracy." A group of twelve men and women coalesced. Coleridge was without a mate and it was soon decided that Sarah Fricker, the sister of Southey's fiancée, would make a practical if nonromantic match. They were soon husband and wife.

Though the marriage was consummated, the Pantisocracy was not. The group never left England and the foundation of the marriage was all but removed.

Fortunately Coleridge found himself increasingly attracted to Sarah. The couple settled down at Nether Stowey, near Bristol, and Coleridge started a magazine called the *Watchman* which contained original poetry, political essays, and commentary. But his targets were too broad and his pot shots struck too many of his subscribers. After ten issues the *Watchman* was permanently off duty. Coleridge lamented biblically, "O Watchman! thou hast watched in vain."

In 1795 the Coleridges met the Wordsworths who had settled nearby. Coleridge planned to become a Unitarian minister but an annuity of £150 for life from Thomas and Josiah Wedgewood allowed him to pursue his writing instead. Wordsworth and Coleridge became friends and mutual inspirations. In 1798 they produced the *Lyrical Ballads*, which contained poetry by both men and included Coleridge's "The Rime of the Ancient Mariner." The reviews were mixed. Southey, with whom Coleridge's relations had considerably cooled, disliked the "Ancient Mariner," while Lamb declared, "It stung me into high pleasure through sufferings."

Also written at this time though not included in the book was "Kubla Khan," the poem Coleridge envisioned while in an opium dream. Upon awakening he found every word still fresh and immediately set to writing it down. In the midst of writing he was disturbed by a visitor for an hour and found upon his return to work that he could conjure up no more of the poem. Though incomplete the poem is considered a masterpiece.

Coleridge seemed incapable of sustained effort. Most of his work was produced in very short periods of time, even in a single sitting. More and more he turned to opium to relieve the pain of rheumatism and other ailments which, as Wordsworth described, would cause him "to throw himself down and writhe like a worm upon the ground." As his tolerance for opium grew so did the required dose. He was soon addicted. If drugs were not enough he was also in love again, this time with Sara Hutchinson. With his marriage and health in precarious condition he sought relief once more in escape, but after two years in Malta he returned in 1806 in even worse shape. Another crushing blow came with his bitter estrangement from Wordsworth in 1810.

Coleridge continued to write poetry as well as essays, plays, and criticism. Perhaps in reaction to his failed dreams, he was to become a spokesman for conservative politics and philosophy. John Stuart Mill labeled him "one of the two great seminal minds of England." He also lent his mind to discussions of literary theory and to liberal trinitarianism.

In 1816 he moved in with Dr. and Mrs. Gillman in Highgate. Though suffering nightmares and frequent relapses, he was still able to reduce his dosage of opium with Gillman's help and he enjoyed his best health in years. Coleridge eventually reconciled with Wordsworth and reached an amicable understanding with his wife. He entertained many visitors in his apartment, pouring forth his usual lengthy soliloquies. For some they were the essence of brilliance, for others total confusion. His death found a similar round of mixed reviews. Southey declared that Coleridge had long ceased to exist for him; for Wordsworth, he was "the most wonderful man that he had ever known."

DIRECTIONS TO HIGHGATE AND ST. MICHAEL'S: Take the Northern Line to the Archway stop. In the village locate Swain's Lane and walk downhill to the cemetery. On your way you will pass St. Michael's Church.

St. John-at-Hampstead

THE VILLAGE OF Hampstead, a charming mélange of bookstores, antique shops, and restaurants dominated by the Heath, has always attracted artists and writers. One would expect that the nearby churchyard, St. John-at-Hampstead, would attract creative and fascinating people—and one would be right. The first artist of note buried here was John Constable; since then personalities such as George Du Maurier, Herbert Beerbohm Tree, Hugh Gaitskell, and Kay Kendall have been laid to rest amid a collection of monuments and epitaphs which are fascinating in their own right.

The original St. John-at-Hampstead Church is believed to have been founded over a thousand years ago when Ethelred the Unready gave this area to the monks of Westminster, although this current structure was built in 1745–47. As on the Continent, the wealthy were buried in side vaults and beneath the church's paving stones, until the presence of the dead could no longer be concealed. The miasma of the remains of one's ancestors while worshipping lent grim religion an all too immediate reinforcement. Unlike Paris, however, where bones erupted from the earth each spring like devilish flowers, there was still plenty of land for outdoor burial here.

After you find the church, go through the gates on your left and follow the path toward the left side of the church. On the wall near the corner is the monument of someone who tried in vain to be buried *inside* the church before such interments were banned. The resentful remains of **William Taylor** (1684–1747), a page of the bedchamber to George I and George II, have perhaps the only marker to register a complaint as to their location. The epitaph points out that despite his characteristics as "careful, dili-

Eve Marie Hammersley

gent, and faithful," and despite the fact that he left money to his relatives and the poor and even sprung for £50 toward the rebuilding of the new church, he was still not allowed in. "Although he earnestly desired to be interred therein," his epitaph scolds, "although the utmost solicitations were made use of by his executors, that favor could not be obtained for his remains." Farther along the path that runs parallel to the church is someone who might have had more claim to an interior location. The large squared-off sandstone block is in memory of **John Harrison** (1693–1776), inventor of the timekeeper for ascertaining longitude at sea. His epitaph explains that "He was the Inventor of the Gridiron Pendulum and the Method of preventing the Effect of Heat and Cold upon Time keepers by Two Bars of different Metals fixed together. He introduced the Secondary Spring to keep them going while winding up: and was the Inventor of most (or all) of the Improvements in Clocks and Watches during his Time." His timekeeper, tested in sea trials in 1761 and 1764, won easily; collecting his £20,000 prize from Parliament and the Board of Longitude was considerably harder.

This monument was reconstructed by the Worshipful Company of Clockmakers of the City of London a century after his death.

A monument near Harrison's has the pleasant inscription, "I think of Heaven as a garden where I shall find again those dear ones who have made my world."

This churchyard has a number of the old upright slabs which one associates with early American churchyards, and quite a few chest tombs. Most of the headstones face east toward the rising sun. Thus, when the Day of Resurrection "dawns," those lying on their backs with their heads facing east will be able to see what is happening immediately.

As in American colonial churchyards, the older the marker the more likely it is to recount the deceased's occupation, his or her immediate survivors, and the commonplace and often accidental circumstance of death. In the area down the hill from the center path is the **Chapman** stone, commemorating **Elizabeth** (1752–1789), who "died of a Broken Heart" five weeks after her father passed away. Her son **Peter** (1777–1796) at 19 "fell a victim to the allurements of the ice, whilst skating on the Serpentine River."

Farther down the hill is another unlucky teenager, **Richard Mallard** (1786–1804) who "met his Fate by bathing in the Middle Pond on Hampstead Heath." Also in this churchyard are Sir **James MacIntosh** (1763–1832), a Scottish philosopher and barrister who choked to death on a chicken bone, **Abraham Sibthorp**'s two wives who died in childbirth 13 years apart, and **Daniel Sharpe** (1805–1856), president of the Geological Society, who perished after a fall from his horse.

Walking toward the bottom of the churchyard you will see a startling bier with two lamenting infant angels on a drape. At the bottom of the drape, peering out, is an unfriendly skull. On the end of this chest tomb is another skull draped in tassels. The monument is to the **Hart-Cary** family. William Hart (d. 1717), designated as a "Salter," was joined by Virginia merchant Robert Cary (1681–1751) and his family.

Continue to the bottom of the hill and turn left. Along the back wall is a fascinating sculpture done in Portland stone, "In loving memory of **John Hodgson** who died in 1858 in his 80th year, and his wife **Carolyn** who died in 1886 in her 98th year." It shows two angels, each with a hand supporting a scabbard which bears this information. At the bottom is an infant angel's face and wings. The banner beneath the angels reads, "Sleep on now and take your rest."

Finally in the back left corner, enclosed by an iron fence, is a limestone chest tomb, "Sacred to the memory of John Constable, Esquire, R.A., many years a resident in the parish." His wife, **Maria Elizabeth Constable** (1787–1828), left "seven infant children to lament her loss in common with their surviving parent." These children are also interred here with the exception of the Constables' eldest son, John Charles, who died in 1841 at age 23 and whose remains rest in the chapel of his school, Jesus College, Cambridge. He died at a young age, but by then he had buried his mother and father.

JOHN CONSTABLE *b. June 11, 1776, East Bergholt; d. March 31, 1837, London.* From the loveliness of the bucolic masterpieces he painted and his venerable English name, it is natural to picture John Constable as a pillar of the Royal Academy. His prickly nature, however, prevented him from playing this part. He was not elected to the academy until he was 53; and even then he was slighted. In one incident in which he was a judge for work submitted by outsiders for a Royal Academy exhibition, a painting of his was mistakenly put before the selection committee. He had to listen to comments which ranged from "It's very *green*," to "It's devilish bad — cross it!" before announcing to the company that it was his work. Despite their apologies, he insisted on withdrawing it.

Part of the problem was that landscapes were not yet considered "serious" art. Constable worked in the heyday of historical panoramas and portraits, and not to paint a biblical or classical theme was considered rebellion. But as a self-taught adolescent tramping around Dedham, sketching what he saw, Constable was never at home with the artificiality of fashionable painting. By his mid-twenties he had a firm idea of what he wanted to paint.

By then Constable's parents had become resigned to the fact that he would not be taking over the family mill, and had settled an income on him of £100 a year. But though living in London, Constable still had business back in Dedham. He had fallen in love with the wealthy rector's granddaughter, Maria Bicknell, a courtship which dragged on for seven years. The cause of the delay was the rector himself, Reverend Dr. Durand Rhudde, who had decided that he did not like Constable's prospects and threatened to cut Maria and her nervous father out of his will. For seven years he held the couple hostage until John finally convinced Maria in 1816 to marry him anyway. Ironically, though the rector did not carry out his financial blackmail, the fortune Rhudde left was less than anyone had assumed. He died, unlamented and quickly forgotten, in the village he had tyrannized, or as Constable's father wrote, "clean gone."

John and Maria Constable quickly had seven children, one for each year of delay. The painter adored them and showed endless tolerance in caring for them. But such a large family was ill-advised. Maria had inherited a disposition toward tuberculosis and, weakened by the stresses on her body, grew more and more ill. Lionel was born in January of 1828; by November the 41-year-old mother had been carried to Hampstead Churchyard.

In the 12 years of their marriage Constable did much of his best work, but looking over his *oeuvre* it is difficult for most viewers to judge which work is early, which is late. *Dedham Vale* (1802) is not dissimilar to *The Cenotaph* (1836) painted 34 years later. Firmly rooted in nature and the importance of balanced composition, Constable had a lifelong preoccupation with the effects of light on wet grass, reflections in water, and the changes caused by shade. After Maria's death his paintings seem less bucolic, yet he began to add rainbows to many of them. In a strange paradox, though his paintings never sold well, there were hosts of forgers flooding an indifferent market with more "Constables."

Even Constable copied himself. He thought nothing of selling a painting, then turning around and painting it over again, often in several different sizes. He was possessive toward the work he had sold, sometimes borrowing a painting back "temporarily" to exhibit or re-paint it, then refusing to return it except under duress. Several times when he was in dire need of cash for his family, he accepted commissions to paint anything he wished. Yet he found even those too constraining. "If I was bound with chains I would break them . . . if I felt a single hair round me I should feel uncomfortable," he wrote to a friend.

It is probable that Constable himself created some of the difficulty in the reception of his art. A difficult personality, seeing slights where none were intended, he could be heavily sarcastic to artists whose work he felt was inferior to his. He labored under the illusion that there was only so much adulation to go around. He was an archconservative, interested in protecting his inherited capital at the expense of reform, and considered the lower classes "the rabble and dregs of the people." That some of them showed up as idealized country folk in the scenes that he painted did not seem to him a contradiction.

Constable was true to his painting, his family, and a few friends, trying to balance an unpopular vision of art with caring for seven half-orphaned children. The elements in the artist that later generations have valued — his richness of color, the thick sensuousness of paint which was often applied with a palette knife, nostalgia for a more peaceable world — were not much in demand in his own time. In one last cruel blow John Constable died at 60 of severe indigestion, a death that doctors said could have been forestalled if there had been a drop of brandy in the house.

When you finish with the Constables, go back up the path. On your way notice the chest tomb halfway up on your left to **Joanna Baillie** (1762–1851), the leading woman dramatist of her time. Daughter of a Presbyterian minister, Baillie emigrated from Glasgow to Hampstead where she lived quietly with her sister, Agnes, and her widowed mother until, at 36, she conceived the idea of writing a series of plays. Each was based on a human emotion. *Plays on the Passions*, published anonymously, created a furor. One critic attributed the collection to Sir Walter Scott. Although the plays were more suitable for reading than acting, some of her later work was staged. Once her identity was revealed, Joanna and Agnes kept a constant open house, attracting friends by their wit and integrity. At 89

Baillie announced that she was tired of life, went to bed, and died.

The Churchyard Extension is back across Church Row. Although the graves in this section date back to 1812, the most interesting sculptures and epitaphs are, for a change, those of the twentieth century. Indeed, after Poets' Corner in Westminster Abbey, this churchyard may hold the greatest concentration of literary dust in London. It is the final resting place of poets, novelists, and men and women of letters, though with a sprinkling of other personalities such as Kay Kendall and Hugh Gaitskell.

After crossing Church Row, go around to Holly Walk and enter through the gate, then take the path to your left. About one-third of the way up is a small Celtic cross with a child's figure superimposed on it in a rudimentary modern design. The child, with his arms outstretched, becomes a cross within a cross. It is in memory of **James Tregaskis** (1850–1926), a well-known used-book collector and proprietor of the Caxton Head Bookshop, named, no doubt, after the fifteenth-century printer, William Caxton.

James Tregaskis

Further up the walk, under a granite canopy, is a bronze sculpture of a youthful seated angel clasping a small girl against his chest, his face resting gently on the top of her head. From her expression it appears to be the moment of her death. The statue was created by Royal Academy artist Harry Furse in memory of **Eve Marie Hammersley** (1891–1902). Her family was well acquainted with artists; Eve's mother, the former **Mary Grant** (1863–1911), was painted with her sisters by John Singer Sargent, Augustus John, and others. The Hammersleys had moved to Hampstead for Mary's health; she died of tuberculosis at 48.

Toward the back of the cemetery is a mass grave for girls. The Soldiers' Daughters monument was used between 1902–1941 for the residents of several local orphanages who were sent there after their fathers died in battle. The large marker gives information about each father's regiment as well as the name of the girl herself.

Move to the center of the churchyard and walk down the path toward the front. You will come across the singular marker of **Langford Reed** (1889–1954) with a small cross and the words:

There once was a fellow named Reed
Who knew that the world had a need
For limericks and fun
And all hearts he won
Since laughter and joy were his creed.

The laughter and joy will not die
As angels laugh with him on high
While we here on earth
Should cultivate mirth
'Tis better to laugh than to cry.

Although he was a journalist, Langford Reed's first love was the limerick. In 1924 he published a *Complete Limerick Book*, followed the next year by *The Indiscreet Limerick Book*, a collection of bawdy rejects from the first. It is felicitous for us, if not for Mr. Reed, that he passed away before 1962, when a handbook was published by the Church of England discouraging such exuberant epitaphs. It pompously reminds parishioners that, "the main object of the inscription is not to commemorate the dead person, but to indicate the place of his burial."

Continue all the way to the front fence, to the monument of **Hugh Todd Naylor Gaitskell** (1906–1963), leader of the Labour party from 1955 to 1963. It has a large urn, rather like a loving cup, and bears the motto "Fortitudo et Integritas." Hugh Gaitskell was one of those rare politicians who had the respect even of his foes. After a brief and moving ceremony marking his death, the House of Commons adjourned for 24 hours, an honor which hitherto had been granted only to those opposition leaders who had been prime minister.

Graduating from Oxford in 1927 with first-class honors in philosophy, economics, and politics, Gaitskell taught economics at University College of London University. He gradually moved into politics and was first elected to Parliament in 1945. His stay in the backbenches of the House of Commons was a momentary one. Soon he became minister of state for economic affairs and then Chancellor of the Exchequer. In 1955, only ten years after his election, he was leader of the Labour party, succeeding Clement Attlee. In 1960 the Labour party supported the platform of unilateral disarmament, a stance which if adopted would have forced Great Britain from the NATO alliance. Gaitskell was vehemently opposed to it and for the next year he tirelessly toured the country in his ultimately successful effort to get the Labour party to reverse its position. With his position solidified and conservative fortunes falling he had the prime ministership firmly in view, but his health, perhaps worn out by his ceaseless campaigning, failed him.

Basically shy, Gaitskell was headstrong, warm, and intellectual. Drew Middleton wrote that he "was no austere socialist. He liked good talk, a very dry martini, a swim in the sea, gardening and little friendly jokes." He mixed easily with all classes and made a point of visiting, talking, and debating with laborers throughout the country. Refusing to take their support for granted he wanted to know their views firsthand. It was that kind of energy, courage, and interest that won him such widespread respect.

Behind Gaitskell to the left you will find a large upright slate inscribed with the name **Kay Kendall Harrison** (1926–1959). It has a swirling design and reads "Deeply loved wife of Rex."

Although perhaps better known as Rex Harrison's wife at the time of her death, Kay Kendall was a statuesque beauty and comedienne who had been on the stage in one capacity or another since adolescence. Although some of the movies she made, such as *Lady Godiva Rides Again*, were dreadful, others such as *Genevieve* (1955), *Les Girls* (1957), and *The Reluctant Debutante* (1958) were well received. Neither her doctor nor Harrison, who had known for three years that she had leukemia, ever told her what her illness was.

Behind Kay Kendall is the statue of a woman that has been broken and repaired. She wears a classically draped gown and a pensive expression, her head shielded by a cloth. The statue commemorates Sir **Herbert Beerbohm Tree** (1853–1917) and his wife **Maud Tree** (1863–1937).

Herbert Beerbohm was working as a grain merchant with his father when he became successfully involved in amateur theatrics and decided to go on the stage. According to his half brother, Max (see Chapter 7 on St. Paul's), he added the name Tree because he could not imagine enthusiastic audiences yelling, "Beerbohm! Beerbohm!" Tree made his professional debut at age 25, but did not get any memorable roles until he began managing the Haymarket Theater in 1887. On that stage he appeared in *The Merry Wives of Windsor* and *Hamlet*, and played Svengali in *Trilby*, a role well-suited to his extravagant acting style and love of eccentric characterizations.

Tree, who died unexpectedly of heart failure while recovering from a knee operation, was most fond of the grand gesture, building large structures like His Majesty's Theater, and spending money freely. Max eulogized him as big. "His body was big and his nature big, and he did so love big things! Mountains, cathedrals, frescoes, Shakespeare, summer skies, Wagnerian opera — his spacious temperament welcomed everything of that sort. Things on a small scale, however exquisite, did not satisfy him."

Lady Maud Tree was an exception to his love of girth. She made her first stage appearance at 20 in *Sweethearts*, the same year that the Trees were married. She gained popularity by her portrayal of Lady Teazle in *School for Scandal*, and successfully played everything from Shakespeare and Greek tragedy to contemporary drama.

Another theatrical family in this section, the Du Mauriers, has a deadboard held by two Celtic crosses giving the family information. The first, **George Du Maurier** (1834–1896), was a cartoonist for *Punch*, then later in life an unexpectedly successful novelist. His best-known work, *Trilby*, added several words to our language. The book tells the story of the dark and mysterious Svengali who hypnotized Trilby into becoming the Continent's richest and most famous contralto. A subplot involves three young artists who knew her in her tone-deaf days as an artist's model, and fell in love with her beautiful feet.

England was soon obsessed with hypnotism and people calling their feet "trilbies," but oddly the name moved from the pedal extremities to the cranial, coming to mean a man's soft felt hat reminiscent of those often shown in Du Maurier's drawings. A Svengali became a villain who tries, with evil intentions, to control another. Already 60 when *Trilby* was published, Du Maurier felt that fame had come too late, though he was pleased that it boosted his first book, *Peter Ibbetson* (1891). He had just completed *The Martian* when he died of congestive heart failure. Du Maurier's epitaph is from the closing lines of *Trilby*:

> A little trust that when we die
> We reap our sowing—and so, goodbye!

George's son, Sir **Gerald Du Maurier** (1873–1934), was an actor who also managed Wyndham's Theater, and fathered author Daphne Du Maurier.

If you continue up this path almost to the wall you will find a poignant marker to **Michael Llewelyn Davies**, "an undergraduate drowned at Oxford while bathing, May 19, 1921, age 20." The design on the stone has been badly weathered. Michael was one of J.M. Barrie's "Lost Boys" in *Peter Pan*. Barrie had become the guardian of Michael and his four brothers on the deaths of their parents, Arthur Llewelyn Davies and Sylvia Du Maurier Davies, who both died from cancer at age 44. (They are buried in the plot of her father, George Du Maurier).

The drowning death of Michael and his best friend, Rupert Buxton, was shrouded in mystery. A witness described Sandford Pool in Oxford as being as still as a millpond that day and said that the boys were "clasped." But whether this was a panic grip by Michael, who could not swim, or a mutual suicide pact was unknown. Michael's younger brother, Nicholas, who characterized him as exceptionally clever but often depressed, felt that the deaths were deliberate.

Nearby is a stone sarcophagus, a memorial to another boy who died young, **Alexander Packe Thomas** (1910–1921). His epitaph reads:

> Death cannot long divide.
> For is it not as though
> The rose that climbed my garden wall
> Had blossomed on the other side?
> Death doth hide but not divide;
> Thou art but on Christ's other side.

Against the brick wall as you turn the corner is the interesting epitaph of **Edward Harry William Meyerstein** (1889–1952):

> Memoriae sacrum
> Ask not who he was!
> Transparent was his character as glass.
> Words were his love, a verbal grace his aim.
> This stone records an unremembered name.

In case you *do* ask, Edward Meyerstein was a novelist, poet, and biographer, and in fact had a memoir written about him by John Wain in *Sprightly Running*. Meyerstein's works include 14 volumes of poetry, plays, a biography of Thomas Chatterton, several short story collections, and novels including *Terence Duke* and *Robin Wastraw*.

At the back of the cemetery on this side is the simple marker of **Sara Jackson** (1910–1982), "Poetess, Wife of **Stephen Thomas**," with the words, "Dark with no sorrow" and a stylized bird on the top. The same bird is on his stone with his dates, 1897–1961, and the words, "The wind blew, my love, and you were there. The wind blows, I have not any fear its changing current could transport us where love was not knowledge of the strangest air."

Two plots down is **Valentina Aksarova-Sturtz** (1894–1959), a Russian opera singer who died at age 65. At the bottom is a Shakespearian quote:

> So long as men can breathe or eyes can see,
> So long lives this and this gives life to thee.

Between these two graves is a monument to a seven-year-old boy with a beautiful bas-relief of two rabbits frolicking in a field of flowers.

Several monuments down is **Peter Baylis** (1910–1973), whose marker says simply, "Filmmaker." A good friend of Orson Welles, Baylis was a maker of documentaries whose pictures concentrated less on the subject than on the look and mood. The winner of numerous European and British awards, three of Baylis' movies—*High Journeys*, *The Finest Hours*, and *See You at the Pillar*—were nominated for Oscars.

Teresa Necom (d. 1926) has a monument shaped like a triumphal arch with a crazy-quilt pattern of paving stones in front. Her epitaph reads:

> You were a summer's day all warm and true,
> Your soul a harbour dark beneath the moon,
> And flashing with soft lights of sympathy.
>
> —Maurice Baring.

On the flat marker of **Alfred Richard Orage** (1873–1934) is a starlike configuration, an image of what he called "a picture of man," and the words, "Thou grievest for those that should not be grieved for. The wise grieve neither for the living nor for the dead. Never at any time was I not nor thou nor these princes of men nor shall we ever cease to be hereafter. The unreal has no being, the real never ceaseth to be." A scholar of Nietzsche and other philosophers, A.R. Orage was also a lecturer and editor of *New Age*.

Randolph Schwabe

Against the back wall is a modernistic statue of a woman in Greek dress, holding a scroll. It commemorates artist **Randolph Schwabe** (1885–1948) and was created by Alan Lydiat Durst. According to his obituary Schwabe's domed forehead, long straight hair, and glasses destined him to be a professor; but inside the professor was an artist squirming to get out. As Slade Professor of Fine Art at University College in London and principal of the art school, his work moved from line drawings reinforced by monochromatic washes to the riotous use of color to create atmosphere.

Also against the back wall is a stone memorial, white as pearl, inscribed, as on tasseled velvet, to **Bert Matthews** (1884–1970) and **Rebecca Matthews** (1884–1963), "Pearly King and Queen of Hampstead, by whose efforts all charities gained." When he wasn't reigning, Bert was the rat catcher for Hampstead Council for 40 years.

Nearby is the marker of **E.V. Knox "Evoe"** (1881–1971), "Poet and Satirist, Editor of Punch from 1932 to 1949." An exceedingly private man, his obituary pointed out that "few men, writing so regularly for so long a period, have revealed so little of themselves in print." Evoe was an excellent poet and parodist, but was less comfortable as an editor. He was rumored to have asked when a longtime contributor sent up his card to see him, "What on earth can the man want?" There is also the image of Knox during the Blitz, wandering around bombed areas with a bottle of whiskey in his coat, looking for people who might need it.

Knox's marker has the quote, "Still are thy pleasant voices, thy nightingales awake," a line from the William Johnson Cory poem, "Heraclitus, Paraphrase from Callimachus." The closing line of the poem, not quoted, is "For Death, he taketh all away, but them he cannot take." There is the sense here that man's creative work lives on after him.

It is a fitting epitaph for the many gifted who lie here.

DIRECTIONS TO ST. JOHN-AT-HAMPSTEAD: Take the Northern Line to the Hampstead stop. Turn left on Heath Street, then, several blocks down, turn right on Church Row. St. John's is on your left.

IN DEAR REMEMBRANCE OF
MARTHE
DAND DEAR DAUGHTER
OF REV. WILLIAM LOW
1928

Hampstead

IN A SENSE, Hampstead Cemetery suffers from being too well rounded. It has fascinating monuments, including a pipe organ complete with music and bench, sculpture by William Goscombe John, and a poignant bas-relief of a woman who died in childbirth. There are interesting minor characters here, such as Horace Short who was captured by cannibals and later worshipped as their king, and ventriloquist Arthur Prince. And there are names that are very well known: Joseph Lister, Kate Greenaway, Pamela Frankau, Dame Gladys Cooper, Sebastian de Ferranti, and Dennis Brain. The cemetery, opened in 1876, is well maintained, with pleasant paths for strolling.

As you enter through the main gate and walk down the road toward the chapel, you will soon see the monument of poet **Arthur Frankau** (1849–1904). It is rather extraordinary, a bronze urn about three feet high with a decoration of wings on a globe on its lid. Coiled around the urn is a large snake with its tongue out.

Across the way and down the road is the rose granite stele of **John Kensit**, "A martyr for the cause of Christ who fell asleep October 8, 1902, age 49, having been struck down by the missile of an assassin in Birkenhead. Raised of God to defend the Protestant faith and the liberties secured at the blessed Reformation, he laboured throughout England for over thirty years." On the base is written, "The Bible and the Bible only is the religion of Protestants."

John Kensit, a London bookseller, objected to "ritualism" in Church of England services. With a group of followers and the battle cry "No Popery!" he created disturbances in churches across England. One of the most dramatic came on a Good Friday when he was protesting the "Adoration of the Cross." It was after a meeting that he was attacked with a chisel and died of pneumonia resulting from complications of the wound.

Marthe John

Sporting
Ground

Chapel

Public   Footpath

Office

Fortune   Green   Road

Hampstead

A   John Kensit
B   Marthe &
     William Goscombe John
C   Horace Short
D   Sebastian Ziani
     de Ferranti
E   Joseph Baron Lister
F   Kate Greenaway

G   Dame Gladys Cooper,
     Fred Terry
H   Marie Lloyd
J   Barritt pipe organ
K   Bianchi Family
L   Dennis Brain
M   Pamela Frankau

■ ■ ■

On your right is a small Egyptian temple with six fat columns and the asp-and-wings design. Although the Egyptian motif can be seen in cemeteries from New York to California, here for once it is appropriate. "Here is laid to rest the body of **James Wilson** (1831–1906), Pasha, Engineer who was for forty-three years in the Egyptian government's service."

Across the way is a Celtic cross with a floral design, the memorial of **Frederick Charles Hengler** (1827–1887). It has the verse, "Behold, He taketh away; who can hinder Him? Who will say unto Him what dost Thou?" from Job 9:12. Hengler, a circus owner, taught riding to the royal family. He was found dead in bed.

Between Hengler and the green iron gates of the public footpath are two attractive monuments. One, to **Eleanor Jane Adkey Edgar** (1854–1926), is a bas-relief of a woman with a fully sculpted head and arms, looking down as smoke from a lamp rises behind her. The other, to **George Storey** (1834–1919), shows a young woman with her legs together, arms outspread, her hair fanning out as she descends. Storey found early success as a Pre-Raphaelite painter with such works as *The Bride's Burial*.

Just behind Storey is the plain massive marker with a cross on top of Grand Duke of Russia **Michael Michaelovitch** (1861–1929) who left Russia following his marriage to **Sophie** (1868–1927), Countess de Torry. She is buried here as well.

Toward the chapel on your left is an attractive woman in mourning, head on her arms, in three-quarter size. It is in memory of **Herbert Thomas Maxwell** (1869–1925), "One of God's Best."

Move around the circle to your right and slightly off the path to the beautiful bronze statue "In dear remembrance of **Marthe John** (1863–1923)." The sculpture shows a woman in classical drapery with her hand to her mouth,

George Storey

looking back over her right shoulder and down, as if not entirely pleased. The statue was created by her husband, Sir **William Goscombe John** (1860–1952), who was later buried there as well.

John, a charming Welshman, whose works combined a delicate realism with flights of fancy, also created the memorial of Sir Arthur Sullivan in St. Paul's Cathedral. His bread-and-butter work included designing medals and commemorative seals for royal occasions.

Across the way in two beds of grass with marble and granite borders are **Horace Short** (1872–1917) and **Albert Eustace Short** (1875–1932). Their minimalist sites belie the interesting lives these brothers led. Horace, a world traveler, was captured by South Sea Island cannibals who later worshipped him as their king. When he returned he wrote about his experiences, and became an aircraft designer. Albert was a manufacturer of planes and balloons; he died in the cockpit of one of his seaplanes after safely landing it.

Continue around the circle and back onto the main path to the granite cross covering the family vault of **Sebastian Ziani de Ferranti** (1864–1930). De Ferranti's fascination with science began early when he would escape from his nurse in order to watch the nearby steam engines. By the age of 11 he had built a small, electric arc lamp, and in college he constructed a small dynamo. Oddly, however, book learning was not congenial to him, and he relied on Pepper's *Playbook of Science* and Ganot's *Physics* for the basis of his knowledge. In 1881 de Ferranti aided Sir William Siemens in his experiments with the electric steel furnace. The following year he developed the Ferranti alternator which produced far more electricity than its rivals.

In 1886 his help was enlisted at the Grosvenor Gallery station to efficiently increase the output needed for growing demand. From this project emerged the London Electric Supply Corporation and the first long-distance transmission of electricity (eight miles from the Deptford station). De Ferranti's work was revolutionary both in the voltage used and in the development of cables capable of carrying this increased current. In later years de Ferranti foresaw a system of generating stations which would supply all demands for heat, power, and light. More fancifully he also suggested the control of sunshine and rain through electrical means.

As you continue along the path you will find an interesting poem on the monument of **H. McNaughton-Jones** (1869–1949), M.D.:

> Through mist and cloud the race of life is run.
> The goal we do not see till it is won.
> Unknown the track, our only signposts years,
> The past is shrouded in a mist of tears:
> The future lies across an unknown waste.
> The present seems the past—with such hot haste
> We strive the noiseless steeds of life to ride.
> Our passions, hopes, and fears: Since side by side
> Run love and hate lashed by ambition's whip
> In vain of her who knows her rider's grip.
> For pain sits ever tight on pleasure's back
> With lifted spur a shadow on her track.
> Yet mid all-shrouding mists and forward gloom
> Or whatsoe'er athwart our path may loom
> One keeps the course with lifted lamp above
> To cast its beam o'er all—the light of love.
> Thus may love guide us through the years to come
> And when the race is over call us home.

On top of this monument is a very shallow bas-relief of an angel holding a staff in her hand.

On the way to the monument of Joseph Lister you can see on the right, about eight rows back, a marker which says, "In Affectionate Remembrance of **Henry Stevens**, Lover of Books, born at Barnet, Vermont August 24, 1819, the volume of whose earthly labor was closed in London 28 February 1886 in the 67th year of his age. And another book was opened, which is the Book of Life." The granite monument was made in Montpelier, Vermont, about 30 miles from his birthplace.

Stevens, who studied law at Harvard, gave writing lessons to support himself as an undergraduate. In 1845 he arrived in London with "a few Yankee notions in his head and nearly 40 sovereigns in his pocket." He used both to become an outstanding rare-book dealer, and worked with the British Museum to procure American titles.

Joseph Baron Lister (1827–1912) is in a pale granite sarcophagus. No other information about him is given on his monument. But we know from our school days and a well-known bottle of mouthwash that Lister is synonymous with antiseptic medicine. Born in Essex, Lister practiced surgery in Glasgow, Edinburgh, and London. His contemporary, Louis Pasteur, inspired Lister with his germ theory of disease and a paper on putrefaction. For 1700 years Galen's theory of laudable pus (that suppuration or the formation of pus was beneficial) was accepted. With Pasteur's work at hand Lister thought otherwise. For him hospital conditions were horrifying. Surgeons wore their blood and pus-encrusted aprons as badges of honor and displayed their similarly infected saws and scalpels as trophies. They were, in fact, a prime cause of the high mortality rate after surgery, due largely to hospital gangrene.

Lister's answer was to insist on the sterilization of hands, instruments, and gowns prior to operating. He then introduced a spray of carbolic acid in the vicinity of the incision as a means of killing germs, and followed up with a bandage soaked in carbolic acid. In time, because the acid irritated the skin, he reduced its strength and ultimately placed a pad between the dressing and the wound. The reduction in the number of deaths from fatal infections was remarkable. Patients now survived operations which had been guarantors of death. Nevertheless it took many disbelieving surgeons years to lay aside their honored relics of septic surgery and adopt Lister's methods.

A highlight of Lister's life occurred in Paris in 1892 when he attended, as the honored guest, a celebration of Pasteur's 70th birthday. There, before a large audience packed with dignitaries and fellow doctors, the two men emotionally embraced.

Lister's antiseptic methods have since been refined by the introduction of aseptic surgery, in which germs are excluded from the operating room rather than killed.

Behind Lister is a poignant cameo of a young soldier in a World War I uniform, Lieutenant **Robert Newman**, "RFC (Bobby), killed while flying May 27, 1916 age 21."

During most of the year the area where **Kate Greenaway** (1846–1901) is supposed to have been buried is overgrown and difficult to negotiate. There is a delicate statue that could be one of her illustrations lying on the ground, but it has no names or dates.

Kate Greenaway's children, innocents with rosebud expressions, developed out of a classical art education. After her first exhibition she was overwhelmed by requests for Christmas cards of her watercolors. John Ruskin encouraged her to stay true to her own style of outlining and filling in with flat pastel shades, rather than modeling forms with a full palette in the conventional way.

Greenaway's first illustrated book, *Under the Window*, was published when she was 33. She followed it up with a rainbow of others, including *The Language of Flowers*, *Mother Goose*, and *Kate Greenaway's Alphabet*. In later years she developed a line of children's clothing as well. Living quietly with her parents, she died at 55 and was cremated at Woking.

Back on the main path is the monument to **Bannister Fletcher** (1833–1899), a large four-pillared canopy with two women in classical drapery; one holds a cross, the other a wreath. His epitaph explains that he was "Professor of Architecture at King's College and Master of the Worshipful Company of Carpenters from 1889 to 1890." He was also the author of *A History of Architecture on the Comparative Method*.

Go back past the public footpath and make a left to follow the fence until you reach the third path on your right. Dame **Gladys Cooper** (1888–1971) is buried there with her parents and two younger sisters. On the bottom of the marker is a quote from Spenser, "Sleepe after toyle, port after stormie seas, ease after warre, death after life, dost greatly please."

Gladys Cooper had to overcome her father's adamant objections to her plan to enter the theater. This she did by the age of 17 when she played in *Bluebell in Fairyland*. By 1906 she was in London on the chorus line of the glamorous *Gaiety Girls*. And by World War I she was trying to expand her scope from light musicals to drama. Above all she was the favorite pinup of the British army, with innumerable soldiers carrying her photo abroad to the trenches.

In 1922 her career in drama took a major step forward when she starred in Piñero's *The Second Mrs. Tanqueray*.

Cooper continued to work in London and New York, and toured the United States before settling down in California. Propinquity bred roles in movies including *Rebecca*, *The Song of Bernadette*, and *Mrs. Parkington*, and later on as Professor Higgins' mother in *My Fair Lady*. She also appeared to much acclaim in a television series, "The Rogues." Gladys Cooper was made a Dame Commander in 1967.

Three rows down is a rough pale granite monument with a green bronze wreath to actor **Fred Terry** (1863–1933), younger brother of Ellen Terry. It has the sentiment, "Memory will be my happiness, you are enshrined there." The opinion of Terry's obituary was that his acting was much better than the plays he appeared in. He and his wife, actress **Julia Neilson** (1868–1957), formed a partnership in 1900 and did middle-brow comic melodramas such as *Sweet Nell of Old Drury* and *The Scarlet Pimpernel*. Neilson's marker has the Shakespearian quote, "I have done my errand, now I go."

Bannister Fletcher

IN
LOVING AND EVERGREEN MEMORY OF
· OUR DARLING ·
CHIEF MRS. VICTORIA MODUPE
SMITH
IYA-ALATE OF AGO OKO, ABEOKUTA
IYA-ALATE OF EGBA-OKEONA, ABEOKUTA
MORIYUN OF IKIJA, ABEOKUTA
IYA-ALAJE OF IDO EKITI
28 NOVEMBER 1937 – 25 APRIL 1984
R·I·P

The nearby monument to the **Arnold** family is attractive because the mourning woman on top of it is half-dressed in ivy.

Continuing up the path you will come to a striking bas-relief of an African woman, her head covered. "In loving and evergreen memory of our darling chief, Mrs. **Victoria Modupe Smith** (1937–1984)."

Further up is a plain granite monument with the Robert Frost quote, "I had a lover's quarrel with the world."

Actress **Marie Lloyd** (1870–1922) has a plain Celtic cross with an ivy design, erected by her family, and the verse:

> Tired was she and she wouldn't show it.
> Suffering was she and hoped we didn't know it.
> But he who loved her knew, and understanding all
> Prescribed long rest and gave the final call.

Marie Lloyd, born Matilda Alice Victoria Wood, was the oldest of 11 children born to an artificial-flower maker. Interested in performing, she soon organized a troupe of little girls into the Fairy Bell Minstrels to sing in schools and mission halls. At 14 she was on the music-hall stage and soon earning £100 a week. The combination of her golden good looks and vaudeville naughtiness captivated audiences.

She had wit and acting skill as well. Lloyd's career began with girlish numbers such as her hit, "The Boy I Love Sits up in the Gallery," and continued with deliberately stylish portrayals of women of her era. At the end she did humorous and poignant impressions of women cast aside by society. Although successful, Marie was worn down by overwork and the stress of three marriages. She collapsed on stage at 52 and died soon after.

Up at the top of the slope from the footpath is the wonderful Charles Herbert Barritt sculpture made in 1929, a miniature pipe organ with a bench in front. The detail work is so exact that you can read the notes on the sheet music.

Nearby is a dark stone with three unhappy figures, one covering his ears, one covering his eyes, and one raising his arms upward. "For here we have no continuing city but we seek one to come" (Hebrews 13:14). "This memorial has been provided by art lovers here and abroad for **Harry Robert Fischer** (1903–April 12, 1977). Born in Vienna, died in London."

From here you can also see the awesome monument of the **Bianchi** family at the end of the path. Over the gate and name stands an angel with her arms upraised imperiously, her wings unfurled behind her. The bas-relief to the left shows a couple on a stone bench. He is wearing a suit, she has her head on his shoulder, eyes closed, and appears to be in 1930s garb — her shoe is a sturdy pump with a strap and a bow. She holds a baby in her arms with its mouth near her breast. Beneath it reads, "Oh for the touch of a vanished hand and the sound of a voice that is still."

On the other side is a more conventional bas-relief of three women. The figure in the center is being escorted heavenward by the other two. All three are dressed in classical robes. Although there are no dates, on the flat sarcophagus below it reads:

> To my Mattie in Heaven.
> Thou ling'ring star with lessening way
> That lov'st to greet the early morn
> Why to ush'reth in the day
> My Mattie from my soul so cruelly torn.
> Oh lassie, dear departed shade,
> Where is thy place of blissful rest
> See'st how thy laddie lowly laid
> Hear'st thou the groans that rend his breast.
> Those sacred years can I forget
> Can I forget your Scottish hills
> Where by the winding birn we met
> To love and live in a peaceful idyll.
> Eternity cannot efface
> Those records, dear, of transports past,
> Thy image at our last embrace.
> Ah, to think that God made it our last.

Charles Barritt

The monument was erected by a restaurant owner in memory of his wife, an opera singer, who is said to have died in childbirth in the 1930s.

Dennis Brain (1921–1957), the great French-horn player, has a plain white marble marker in the next-to-last row as you walk back toward the entrance gate. The inscription, from Hindemith, reads, "My call transforms the hall to autumn-tinted groves, what is into what has been."

Brain was a child prodigy with a supportive and gifted family background. His father and teacher, Aubrey Brain, was principal horn in the BBC Symphony, and his grandfather and two uncles were also talented horn players. At the Royal Academy of Music, Brain would entertain and astonish his friends by tossing off "The Flight of the Bumblebee" or Paganini's "Moto Perpetuo" with seamless ease on his notoriously difficult instrument. This trademark virtuosity combined with his great sensitivity to the music caused Hindemith and Britten to compose works for him. In lighter moments he could be found playing the garden hose during comic performances at the Hoffnung Festivals.

Brain loved fast sports cars. During a recording session for his classic recordings of the Mozart Horn Concertos he was found playing from memory with a copy of the *Autocar* propped up on his music stand. He was killed when he lost control of his favorite sports car while driving overnight to London.

At the corner where the path meets the road, **Pamela Frankau** (1908–1967) has a small marker with a rounded top and stylized cross, and the words, "Greatly loving — deeply loved." She is here with her sister **Ursula Frankau** (1906–1980).

Pamela Frankau inherited her literary gifts from her paternal relatives, and a mordant wit from both sides. She wrote her first novel, *The Marriage of Harlequin* (1927) while commuting, using paper stolen from her office and a reed fountain pen given her by her father. Thus encouraged, she bought her own paper and penned 29 more, including *The Willow Cabin* (1949) and *Ask Me No More* (1958). She also encouraged herself to write three thousand words daily by muttering, "Get on with it, you rat." Her novels were witty and fast-paced with the requisite love interest, but grew in their psychological insights and morality as she became more mature.

Among the many others here are two worth noting: **Fred Archer** (1857–1886), a young jockey who won the Derby five times, but who ruined his health by trying to keep his weight down and shot himself in despair; and **Arthur Prince** (1881–1948), a ventriloquist who was the first to perfect the technique of drinking water while his dummy talked. His dummy is buried here with him.

DIRECTIONS TO HAMPSTEAD: Take the Metropolitan or Jubilee Line to the Finchley Road stop. Take the bus going north up Finchley Road to the junction of Fortune Green Road and follow it a half block to the cemetery.

Golders Green and St. Marylebone

ALTHOUGH CREMATION WAS used in ancient Greece and Rome, the practice was not popular in England until the early twentieth century. There had been a widespread belief in Christendom that to enter Heaven a person had to have all his body parts, and present them at the gate for admission. For centuries only the corpses of criminals were dissected to train medical students. Yet crowded churchyards and widespread epidemics began to create the need for other solutions; by the turn of the century, up to 50 bodies a day were being transported south by train from London to the crematory at Woking.

Golders Green built its own crematorium in 1902 as well as the West Chapel for services, then followed with the Ernest George Columbarium, named after the architect of the project. Other chapels and a smaller columbarium were added gradually. The grounds are very beautiful, particularly in spring.

Enter through the main gate. As you emerge to the expanse of lawn, you will see an interesting array of plaques on the building behind you, signaling niches, with a variety of shapes and carvings. Facing the colonnade, in the fourth grouping from the left you will see a blue-green and gold plaque at the top with the words, "The ashes of **Edith**, the wife and comrade of **Havelock Ellis** (1859–1939), were scattered over this garden on the 18th of September, 1916, and his ashes also were scattered here on the 13th of July, 1939."

The Ellises were a fascinating couple, a pair of psychologists and writers who held what the British termed "ad-

'Into the Silent Land'

vanced views" about life and marriage. Both defended birth control and open marriage. Havelock Ellis felt that if couples could afford it they should have separate residences, and at one point the couple lived next door to each other. His work was considered as unorthodox as his living arrangements. In 1897, when he published his first volume of *Studies in the Psychology of Sex*, it was banned as obscene, with ire particularly directed at the sections on homosexuality. Gradually the times caught up with Ellis, who had moved on to other works on sexuality and philosophy.

Edith Lees Ellis (d. 1916) concentrated on writing novels and memoirs, such as *Love-Acre* and *My Cornish Neighbors*. She died of pneumonia; her death was blamed on a cold she caught while watching a zeppelin attack.

When you come to the end of the arched passageway you will see a small brick building across the way. In front of it is a lilac bush planted as a memorial to **Ivor Novello** (1893–1951). It has the words, "Till you are home once more," a paraphrase of the last line of his politically stirring "Keep the Home Fires Burning" (1914). That song was the first hit for the classically trained Novello, who also wrote clever punchline songs such as "And Her Mother Came Too." When not composing, the multi-talented Novello wrote comedies and dramas and starred in movies. Indeed, his real fame came first as one of the most handsome male leads in silent movies, and then as the composer of many unredeemably romantic operettas. Though he left the singing to better voices, he assumed the hero's role. So as not to be upstaged, he inserted the tenor's songs in the story within the story. Novello's lush, beautiful melodies carried the often weaker lyrics.

Walk up the path beside the rose garden. To the left of the stone bench, almost to the corner, is the rose bush (#39802) of Peter Sellers with the inscription, "My darling husband I will always love you," placed there by his fourth wife, Lynne Frederick. On the back wall opposite Peter Sellers is a plaque which reads, "Life is a state of mind. With everloving memories, Peter Sellers."

PETER SELLERS *b. September 8, 1925, Southsea; d. July 24, 1980, London.* When Peter Sellers died it was a multiple casualty. Not only did the world lose a gifted if unpredictable actor, it was also deprived of Inspector Clouseau, Dr. Strangelove, Major Bloodnok, Chance the Gardener, and other characters who had come to life on their own. As Derek Sylvester pointed out, "There was quite a high death toll on that July day in 1980."

It is no surprise, given his early life, that Peter Sellers

Peter Sellers' plaque

turned out exactly as he did. As the only living child of Peg and Bill Sellers (talk of an earlier sibling who died at birth was forbidden), Peter was outrageously spoiled. Yet his needs were subordinated to show business. His maternal grandmother, Welcome Mendoza, alias Ma Ray, put her ten children on the circuit, and introduced on-stage aquatic shows in oversized fish tanks. Submerged beauties suggestively nibbled bananas in reviews called "Splash Me!" and "Have a Dip!" For the first five years of his life Peter slept in a basket in the wings, then was left with whoever was free to care for him while the show went on.

When Peter finally started school he was at first obstreperous, then embarrassed by his academic deficiencies. Despite being Protestant-Jewish, he was placed in a Catholic school where his performance was mediocre and he was not well liked. He exhibited a gift for mimicry, however, and a retentive memory for dialogue and mannerisms, but when he left school at 14 he spent several years as a drummer.

On being drafted for World War II, Sellers was able to use both his talents as drummer and mimic to tour in what were known as RAF Gang Shows. Off-stage he impersonated high-ranking officers, "inspecting" barracks and giving

259

pep talks—masquerades for which he would have been court-martialed and imprisoned if discovered. He was so convincing that he could show up in the mess hall an hour later, sans general's uniform and moustache, and not be recognized by anyone.

Gang Shows gave way to Goon Shows. As a civilian Sellers met up with Harry Secombe, Spike Milligan, and Michael Bentine, and on May 28, 1951, the first of their comedy shows was broadcast on the BBC. The locations were exotic—from Africa to Devil's Island—and the characters memorable. Sellers' Major Bloodnok who, in response to an innocent "Hello" would bluster, "How dare you accuse me of robbing the regimental cashbox!" was soon being imitated everywhere.

In 1951 Sellers made *Penny Points to Paradise*, the first of his 55 films. These varied widely as to quality and success. For every *Ladykillers* (1955) and *The Mouse That Roared* (1959), there were four or five other less memorable pictures. The quality improved with *The Pink Panther* (1972) and *Dr. Strangelove* (1973), but there were still occasional disasters such as *Soft Beds, Hard Battles* (1973) which was set in a French brothel, and *Ghost in the Noonday Sun* (1973), described as a poor man's *Treasure Island*.

Sellers' life off-screen was uneven as well. The spoiled child inside him insisted on having every fancy car he saw (he bought a Rolls Royce and sold it the same day when he could not get it out of a narrow street). He had no idea how to share attention with his three children, and his relationships with them were stormy. Sellers could move all too quickly from being the charming father they yearned for, to taking umbrage at some slight and announcing that the relationship was over.

The same insecurity and self-centeredness dominated his four marriages. He choked his first wife, Anne Hayes, and ripped off her clothing when he did not want her to go out; at the close of the marriage he rampaged through the house, overturning bookcases, smashing art objects, and shattering antique furniture. Britt Eckland, his second wife, suffered from similar treatment. Furious at a comment made by wife number three, Miranda Quarry, the actor deliberately rammed his car in traffic into the one in front, then reversed to smash the car behind. (He was arrested and held overnight until he promised to pay for the damage.) And, angry with Lynne Fredericks, he announced to a newspaper columnist that their marriage was over.

Peter Sellers saw the role of Chance, the simple gardener

who becomes president in Jerzy Kosinski's *Being There*, as a way of redeeming himself personally and professionally. He spent years trying to create enough interest to get the film made, and when he did he felt it was his masterpiece. Nominated for an Oscar as best actor, Sellers lost to Dustin Hoffman but gained critical acclaim. It was a good note to go out on, though he didn't feel himself ready. But later that year Sellers suffered the fatal heart attack he had been warned about. At the service here the organ played the "hymn" he had selected for such an occasion, "In the Mood." The world mourned Peter Sellers and the extravagant congregation of characters he took with him.

Continue down the path deeper into the cemetery to the series of rose bushes. On the front, about ten feet back from the path, is a rose bush "In loving memory of **Kathleen Ferrier** (1912–1953)." Born on April 22, 1912, in Higher Walton, Lancashire, Kathleen Ferrier was one of the world's most beloved singers. Her father was a local schoolmaster who sang in a local choral society and many of her relatives exhibited a strong interest and involvement with music. Her first interest and talent lay with the piano, and by the age of 18 she had won competitions in Manchester and Liverpool. At this point she was working as a telephone operator, but if anyone noticed her rich contralto voice it went without comment.

At 23 she decided to take voice lessons from Thomas Duerdon in Blackburn, surprising the teacher by usurping his place at the accompanying piano. Any annoyance quickly turned to awe at the richness of her voice, the evenness of her tone, and her range. Immediately Duerdon knew she had a rare talent. Two years later she entered and won the piano competition at Carlisle. While there she overheard some of the vocal competition and commented to her friend that she could sing better than they. For the wager of a shilling, she entered the contralto division, sang Roger Quilter's "To Daisies," and won the Rose Bowl, emblematic of the best aspiring singer in northern England.

From there she went on to London to study with Roy Henderson, and her career got underway. She made her operatic debut singing the title role in Benjamin Britten's *The Rape of Lucretia* at Glyndebourne in 1946 and followed with Gluck's *Orfeo* under Sir John Barbarolli. Her lieder recitals were frequently accompanied by Gerald Moore, but perhaps most famous were her performances of Mahler's song cycles under Bruno Walter's direction.

Tall and lanky and described by her mother as plain, Ferrier developed into a beautiful woman who adapted quickly to the larger world as her career quickly expanded. But she never lost her dislike of affectation and snobbery. She remembered her roots and, not at all prudish, enjoyed a dirty joke or story. Her fine ear allowed her to hilariously mimic twittering sopranos at an exquisitely painful quarter pitch off.

Ferrier's records keep her voice alive. Whether singing Brahms' "Alto Rhapsody," Schumann's "Frauenliebe und Leben," or Bach's "St. Matthew Passion" she brought great intelligence and emotion to her portrayals. She also had a special knack for the English folk songs with which she ended virtually all her recitals. Not overpowering the songs as many trained singers do, she could convey the humor of "The Stuttering Lovers," the regret in "Down by the Sally Gardens," and in a poignant a cappella version, the lost love of "Blow the Wind Southerly."

Ferrier's career was cut short by cancer at the age of 41. In her last photographic portrait, Douglas Glass captured magnificently the humanity of this handsome woman, her seriousness of purpose, and the tragedy of her early death.

Walk on to the Keats rose bed. In the second row back, the first plaque facing you from the road is in memory of popular bandleader **Victor Sylvester**, O.B.E., 1917 Italian Bronze Medal for Valor, who died in 1978.

On the opposite side of the garden, to the right of the path of the **Godfrey** family monument is the rosebush of pop singer **Marc Bolan**. The plaque is not usually there, since fans keep removing the replacements. Bolan gained popularity with his heavy metal group, Tyrannosaurus Rex (later shortened to T-Rex), and such songs as "Ride a White Swan." He was killed in a car driven by the American singer Gloria Jones.

On the grass is a large statue of what appears to be a contemporary guru, **Ghanshyamdas Birla** (1894–1983). The front of the monument reads, "What we call life is a wonderful journey full of purpose. When the mission is realized the person passes away. This is the eternal law of nature." On the side is a quotation from the Bhagavad Gita: "Ever engaged in actions, always taking refuge in me by my grace my devotee attains the eternal imperishable abode."

But Birla was no mere mystic. He was the wealthiest man in India, and one of the main funders of Mahatma Gandhi's struggle for Indian independence; it was in the garden of his home in Delhi that Gandhi was assassinated in 1948. Birla's empire was built initially on cotton and sugar, then expanded to include motors and textiles machinery. A publishing mogul, he owned newspapers and journals, and

Ghanshyamdas Birla

turned his remote village, Pilani, into a great educational center.

In order to visit the columbariums you will need to get a key from the office. As you enter the larger of the two, the Ernest George Columbarium, turn right and walk all the way into the tower. Against the far wall is the urn of Anna Pavlova, draped with her pink dancing shoes.

ANNA PAVLOVA *b. January 31, 1881, St. Petersburg; d. January 12, 1931, The Hague.* Anna Pavlova was the most popular ballerina of her time, cultivating a charm that captivated the world. The tiny, black-eyed dancer made an early agreement with her public; if they would remain loyal, she would live for them completely, renouncing any

Philipson mausoleum

attempts at a personal life. Instead of becoming involved in relationships, she poured her soul into her portrayals of Aziade, Aurora from *The Sleeping Beauty*, and Fenella in *The Dumb Girl of Portici*. She was rewarded by being made into a legend.

Part of her public personality was a girlish innocence and a bubbling vivacity which embraced new experiences. When she was eight years old, Pavlova was taken to the Maryinsky Theater to see *The Sleeping Beauty* and told that she was "going to see the country of the fairies." Completely enchanted, she began her studies at the Imperial School in St. Petersburg two years later and further honed her technique by hiring a private Italian teacher. Her reward was a coveted role in *La Bayadère* in 1902. A year later she brought to a performance of *Giselle* a fragile romanticism that had been missing in the era of sturdy acrobatic Russian ballerinas.

Shortly after, Pavlova began a lifelong tour of the world. Unwilling to be tied down in one dance company, she danced in theaters, palaces, music halls, and bull rings. A classmate of hers from the Imperial School, Michel Fokine, created for her a short solo, *The Dying Swan*, which became one of her trademarks, along with *Giselle* and *Chopiniana*. Throughout her life, Pavlova excelled in shorter, slice-of-life dances rather than formal ballet roles; her repertoire included 23 ballets and 80 divertissements.

Pavlova also believed that male dancers were subordinate to her talent. In 1911 Michel Mordkin refused to dance with her any longer after she slapped his face in public because she felt he had partnered her badly. She temporarily lost Laurent Novikoff in 1913 when she slapped him and pummeled his shoulder after he explained that his doctor had ordered him to take a long rest rather than accompany her to America. Her attitude toward men was singular. Touring America, she railed against "that hideous phrase, 'equal rights!'" believing that it meant that women had to give up their position of superiority.

Although she felt that marriage was incompatible with her gifts, she traveled with Victor Dandre, an aristocratic admirer who had left Russia when she did and thereafter managed her company. On occasion she referred to Dandre, a large, smooth-faced blond given to black bowler hats and English attire, as her husband, and allowed Sol Hurok to announce their "marriage" in 1924. No marriage license was ever found, and when Dandre had to leave Russia permanently in 1911 because he was charged in St. Petersburg with "appropriating vast sums of government money," Pavlova never returned to live there either. Instead they purchased Ivy House in Golders Green, a paradise of gardens, ponds, exotic birds, with a greenhouse, and studio where she taught.

Agelessly, Pavlova continued to dance and tour. She made a film in 1915, *The Dumb Girl of Portici*, which disappointed her and drew mixed reviews. But in person she remained magnificent, performing in India, Japan, Australia, and South Africa. At age 49, arriving in The Hague to begin another tour, she collapsed in a Dutch hotel room with a temperature of 104°. To drain the fluid that was collecting in her lungs, Pavlova was "bled" from the back. She slipped into unconsciousness and died of blood poisoning several hours later. Knowing her wish for absolute control over her body, it is difficult to believe she did not acquiesce to her death, deciding to leave while the footlights were still on.

Retrace your steps to the front door then go to your left, continuing into the next room. Make another left and you will find a tall marble pedestal with the names Sigmund Freud and **Martha Freud** (1861–1951). On top of the pedestal is a Grecian urn containing their ashes.

SIGMUND FREUD *b. May 6, 1856, Freiberg; d. September 23, 1939, London.* Oedipus complex . . . castration anxiety . . . Freudian slip . . . survivor guilt. No one in the last century has given mankind so much to worry about as Sigmund Freud. Almost singlehandedly he brought us out of Eden and into the country of repressions, sublimations, and the meaning of dreams. To carry us there he invented the vehicle of psychoanalysis.

The son of a young mother and older, freethinking father with grown children, Sigmund's promise was allegedly first noticed by the midwife who delivered him. She took his odd crest of black hair to signify that he would "seize fame by the forelock. He will be a great man!" Bright, willful, and imperious, Sigmund was given his own room by his adoring mother so that he could better study and read; the six younger children were crowded together in one bedroom. Jacob Freud, though proud, saw his son with a more critical eye. When Sigmund, at age eight, entered his parents' forbidden bedroom and urinated in front of them in his excitement, his father declared, "No good will ever come of that boy!"

The shameful memory of his father's comment goaded Freud to excel. He graduated from the University of Vienna in 1881 with a medical degree. Although he practiced medicine, he was more interested in research and "nervous diseases" whose etiology was unclear. Freud traveled to Paris in 1885 to study hypnosis under Jean Martin Charcot. Even before that an older colleague, Josef Breuer, introduced him to the case of "Anna O.," a young woman who developed a multitude of hysterical symptoms — paralysis, double vision, choking fits, and feelings of being tortured — which vanished when she was able to recall the buried feelings which had precipitated them. To bring about a complete cure, it was also necessary for her to confront her sexual feelings about Dr. Breuer and her father.

The work of Charcot and Breuer, combined with his own work with neurological patients, helped move Freud to a definition of the unconscious. He saw it as a maximum-security prison of the mind, a place where memories, dangerous impulses, and unacceptable feelings were incarcerated — inmates who caused havoc when they inappropriately broke out. By exploring them through dreams, free association, and slips of the tongue, it seemed possible to relieve stress and fulfill these desires in more constructive ways.

As Freud developed his theories and techniques of psychoanalysis, he encountered resistance — the self-protectiveness of the psyche to the uncovering of painful or unacceptable material — in his patients. He also began to encounter resistance on a larger scale from the European and American medical establishments, particularly over his theories of infant sexuality and family attachments. The idea of sexual love or passionate rivalry in the breast of an innocent child brought accusations of perversion, irresponsibility, and "mental masturbation." Freud did not turn back from what he saw to be the truth, continuing his explorations despite their unpopularity.

Freud lived quietly in Vienna with his wife Martha, sister-in-law Minna, and his six children, putting in long, precise days and evenings of seeing patients, writing books and academic papers, and editing psychoanalytic journals. The family sat down to dinner at 1:00 every afternoon, after which he took a walk before beginning more consultations. On Saturdays he lectured at the university from 5:00 to 7:00, then proceeded to a friend's home for their long-standing card game, tarock. Sunday mornings he visited his mother. Summers were reserved for long family vacations. The children were a joy. Martha ran an immaculate household, but dismissed the problems of her husband's patients: "If they kept busier, they wouldn't be nervous." Minna provided more intellectual companionship.

Freud's books were an agony and a necessity for him. He embarked on them eagerly, but was depressed before publication, certain that the writing was terrible and that the book would be a failure. From his first major work, *The Interpretation of Dreams* (1900) to *Totem and Taboo* (1913) and *The Ego and the Id* (1923), his books all generated controversy, but they were widely read. Disciples came to learn — Carl Gustav Jung, Wilhelm Stekel, Alfred Adler, Otto Rank — and left with their own interpretations.

Beginning in his forties Freud had feared the idea of getting old and its limitations. Old age brought him fame, painful cancer of the jaw (from the cigars he would never give up), and exile to London under the threat of Nazism. He had never hidden his Jewishness — indeed, he felt that being in a minority had given him more freedom to abandon mainstream positions — but it cost him dearly. Storm troopers confiscated his passport, and it took most of his savings and the intervention of the world to get him released from Austria. He left in June 1938.

Freud's expressed wish, "to see [us] all together and to die in freedom," was fulfilled. A year later at 83, his mind still lucid but the pain from his cancer intolerable, he requested a shot of morphine and died. His ashes were placed in a Grecian vase from his extensive collection of antiquities, one given by a close family friend, Princess Marie Bonaparte.

In the East Columbarium up on the third level and back against the wall, opposite the doorway and in the extreme right, is the light tan funeral urn of **Bram Stoker** (1847–1912).

Had he not written *Dracula* in 1897, Stoker would probably be unknown. His other work was described by one critic as "a noxious potpourri of plagiarism . . . racism, and semi-conscious sexual titillation, the entire tincture being then suspended in sadistic violence and pseudo magic." Yet Dracula lives. This myth of the vampire touched off deep primal memories in respectable English folk, a fascination kept alive by movies and, of late, Anne Rice and Stephen King. But somehow it all goes back to Transylvania.

Stoker, who had studied law, also acted as drama critic for the *Dublin Mail* and held other jobs before turning to writing in 1880. An attractive man whose wife was rumored to have locked her bedroom door shortly after their only son was born, Stoker died of tertiary syphilis.

Also in Golders Green

Sir **James Dewar** (1842–1943), inventor of the thermos; **Elinor Glyn** (1864–1943), who wrote a number of romantic novels including *The Career of Catherine Bush* and *Three Weeks*; Sir **Isaac Pitman** (1813–1897), the deviser of the method of shorthand that bears his name; and **Wilhelm Stekel** (1868–1940), one of the fathers of psychoanalysis, who developed the theory of dictators as father substitutes and established a jealousy clinic in Vienna. Stekel believed that jealousy "was more deadly than typhus or bullets, causing the death of a person somewhere every minute."

JEWISH CEMETERY

Across Hoop Road in the Jewish Cemetery is **Jacqueline du Pré**. Walk into the cemetery, take the path to the left, and you will come to a large, dark-gray marble slab. "Beloved wife of Daniel Barenboim. 26–1–45 to 19–10–87." Her name is in gold script on the back.

Du Pré was a supremely talented cellist noted for her

flawless technique, burnished tone, and innate musicality, whose career was cut short when she developed multiple sclerosis. As with all great musicians, du Pré showed early signs of extraordinary talent. She started lessons at the age of five, won her first competition at eleven, and won every prize offered to cellists by the Guildhall School of Music. Starting her studies with Herbert Walenn and William Pleeth, she moved on to study with some of the greatest cellists of her time: Paul Tortelier, Mstislav Rostropovich, and Pablo Casals. After hearing her play, Rostropovich declared that he had finally found someone who could carry on his work.

In 1961 du Pré received as an anonymous gift a 1672 Stradivarius. She played the instrument that same year to rave reviews at Wigmore Hall in London and her career was launched. In 1966 she met another wunderkind, the pianist and now conductor Daniel Barenboim. It seemed a perfect match. "Instead of saying good night we sat down and played Brahms," she said. A year later they were married. Their careers continued to expand and they performed the world over, both separately and together. Fortunately, because of her early fame, she recorded a fair amount of material, most notably Brahms, Delius, and Elgar. Her interpretation of the Elgar *Cello Concerto* is especially fine.

Du Pré was only 26 when the disease began to manifest itself, first in fatigue and then in the numbness of her fingers. Unable to feel the strings, she simply could not play. With the disease in some remission, she attempted a return a year later but it was short-lived. By the mid-1970s she was paralyzed, unable to dress herself or stand unaided. Still she continued to teach whenever she was physically able, and worked to help multiple sclerosis research. Benefit concerts were held to aid the Jacqueline du Pré Research Fund and the National Multiple Sclerosis Society, featuring such performers as Yo-Yo Ma, Pinchas Zuckerman, and Eugene Istomin. Tom Kempinski's play *Duet for One* (1981) is based on du Pré's career and illness. Though her body was paralyzed and bloated by drugs, she tried to be optimistic about a cure but died after a long period of suffering.

On the same path is a gray stone with an ivy design commemorating portrait painter **Julia Goodman** (1812–1906). It has the epitaph, "Thank God she is free from pain." A "granddaughter" of Sir Joshua Reynolds (she studied under one of his pupils), Goodman began by copying works of the old masters but moved on to successful portrait painting. She exhibited at Royal Academy shows for 51 years before dying at 94.

ST. MARYLEBONE

Founded in 1854, the cemetery covers 33 acres. It is the last resting place of conductor Leopold Stokowski and contains some wonderful pieces of sculpture, including Thomas Tate rearing up from his deathbed, and a bronze statue by William Reid Dick. When you enter from East End Road, bear to your left around the Gothic chapel. You will not be able to miss the monument to Sir **Peter Nicol Russell** (1816–1905), an engineer who endowed the Peter Nicol Russell School of Engineering at the University of Sydney, New South Wales. The monument shows a bare-chested engineer in work pants and boots, holding a sledgehammer which rests on an anvil. He is looking innocently ahead, but behind him hovers an angel ready to make off with his soul. At the top of the monument is a formal bronze bust of Sir Russell, whose fortune came from his foundry and shipbuilding works. His epitaph reads, "The memory of the just is blessed."

Continue past Russell and make another left at the very back corner. Here is a touching memorial, a marble sculpture of a woman with her head on her arm, mourning, "a perfect husband and devoted father, **Leonard John Hawkins** (1890–1934). Love Never Dies."

From here retrace your steps to Central Avenue. On your right you will see a white marble stele, "In Loving Memory of **Louis Alexander Mouflet**, age 42, his dear wife **Nancy**, age 32, and their two eldest children, **Alex Henry**, age 7, and **Annie Ethel**, age 4, also **Phyllis Sarah Flatman**, age 30, beloved sister of the above Nancy Mouflet, who were all drowned in the Thames through the collision between the Princess Anne and Biwell Castle, September, 1878. They were united in life, not parted in death."

Nearby is the large Celtic cross of **Rebecca Jane Hart** (d. 1890) with the following stirring inscription from the epilogue of Robert Browning's *Inapprehensiveness*: "Who never turned her back, but marched breast forward, never doubted clouds would break. Held, we fall to rise, are baffled to fight better, sleep to wake."

At the next intersection bear left around the small chapel. On your right you will see a squared-off rose granite monument, with a cameo, to Sir **Henry Bishop** (1786–

Peter Nicol Russell

1855). Bishop was the first musician to be knighted, by Queen Victoria in 1842.

Return to Central Avenue to the full-sized sculpture of a young woman with a 1920s look, her hair parted in the middle and flowing down her back. She is clinging to a block which says simply, "At Rest." It is in memory of **George Henry Thurston** (1869–1927).

Further down on your left is a white marble monument with a rectangle which reads, "In the world's garden of memories lives the beloved genius **Little Tich**, English comedian, dancer, musician, composer, linguist, artist, Né Harry Relph 21–7–1867, died 10–2–1928." Below it is the quote, "Le plus petit et le plus grand comique (the smallest and the largest comic) of the world." Tich lived up to at least part of that description. The four-foot-high comedian had his first success in the United States in blackface in 1888. Later on his specialty was dancing in thigh-high boots and doing wonderful comic pantomimes of Carmen, a juggler, and a ballet dancer.

Tich's actress wife **Ivey Latimer** (1892–1973) is also here with the epitaph "Unconquerable Love."

After seeing Little Tich, retrace your steps back to the circle and turn left into the center of the cemetery. At the crossroads you will find what appears to be a copy of Napoleon's tomb at Les Invalides, though on a much smaller scale. Unlike Napoleon's tomb, there are bronze angels at the corners and it houses **Thomas Scarratt Hall**, "for forty years an Australian colonist" who died in 1903.

To Hall's right is a nice sculpture of two angels carrying a young woman away. One is crowning her, the other one bearing her up. It is in memory of **Gaynor Roland**, a young woman who died aged 23 in 1906.

Thomas and Esther Tate

Notice the four rams' heads on the corners of the monument to **Henry James Boynton** who fell in the Battle of the Somme, September 14, 1916, at age 25. He was the only son of Sir Harry Boynton, M.P. for East Marylebone.

Further down on your left is a lovely bronze sculpture to **Dwight Ripley** (1864–1915) of New York, sculpted by Sir William Reid Dick. It shows a young woman, her hair pulled back in a knot, one hand reaching from below her draped robe to touch her lips. She looks modestly down at her sandals.

Across the way is a companion piece, a memorial to **Thomas Joseph Tate** (1832–1909) and **Esther Tate** (1837–1909). The bronze sculpture by F. Lynn Jenkins shows a man pushing up on an ornate couch, looking heavenward. One arm is dramatically raised, as if in assent. Two cherubs lurk behind his head.

Further down on your left is a modern sculpture, a surprising discovery in the midst of crosses and Victorian angels. It is "in loving memory of **Duncan Munro Mac-**

Donald (1889–1949), Fine Art Dealer." The piece of art is about three feet high, oval-shaped with two openings, and appears to be unsigned.

You may want to make a detour as you enter the circle, going up the road to your right, to a marker you would not find in America. Halfway up the road is a cross with a crossed cricket post, cricket bat, and ball. It is the memorial of **C.I. Thornton** (1850–1929). Thornton, an exuberant cricketer nicknamed "Buns" by his contemporaries, was the Babe Ruth of the wicket. He stayed forever at bat, on one occasion hitting the ball out of the stadium and over a four-story house into Trafalgar Square.

Make a last detour to East Avenue and walk all the way down to its junction with Rosemary. You will first see a hedge enclosing a private gravesite and then, two markers down, Leopold Stokowski, "Music is the voice of the All." His monument is a variegated gray and white granite. Across the way is a much older weathered cross, "In loving memory of my dear husband Kopernik Joseph Stokowski who was born in St. Marylebone, February 3, 1862, and passed away October 10, 1924."

LEOPOLD STOKOWSKI *b. April 18, 1882, London; d. September 12, 1977, Nether Wallop.* "There is no cow in my name. It is pronounced Sto-kov-ski." For once we have the truth about this enigmatic, infuriating, and inspiring figure. The date and place of his birth are also correct. After this, however, even the biographical bloodhounds have been unable to follow precisely the trail of his life because the foxy Stokowski deliberately obscured the scent. Not the least of the deceptions lay in his variable and indeterminate middle-European accent. He would speak of "mu-seec" and "no-ledge" or describe someone taking an "ahkteef" part or being a "mahvelous wooman." His English childhood was not merely ignored, it was hidden under the guise of glamor. Wanting to be identified as neither working-class nor rustic, Sto-kov-ski fit him to a tee.

The deception seemed to be born out of insecurity. Stokowski's musical background was marked by talent but not genius. At the Royal College of Music he specialized in the organ. At this he showed flair and several years after graduating made his way as organist to the prestigious St. Bartholomew's Church in New York City. From there he made the unlikely leap to conductor of the Cincinnati Orchestra — unlikely because he had never conducted an orchestra at the time his name was proposed. Of course, he claimed to have "studied" under the great Artur Nikisch — but "observed from a theater seat" would have been more accurate. His greatest assets were his showmanship and his behind-the-scenes support in the person of the famous pianist, Olga Samaroff, née Lucie Hickenlooper of San Antonio, Texas (American names did not have the requisite cachet in those days). Olga had become enraptured with Stokowski and was the first of his four wives.

Cincinnati was a city with a strong musical tradition, but Stokowski took it by storm. The public adored him, the leading critic was disparaging, and the board of directors suffered a mercurial change from love to hate. After three years he resigned (or was fired, depending on whose side you believe). More backstage machinations ensued and in 1912 Stokowski was leading the even more prestigious Philadelphia Orchestra. Here his fame blossomed into that of a major star. He rebuilt the orchestra, giving it the glorious "Philadelphia sound" for which it has been famous for so many decades.

Philadelphia experienced the best and the worst of Stokowski. While his Beethoven and Tchaikovsky were poor, he excelled with more modern scores like Debussy's *Afternoon of a Faun* and Stravinsky's *Firebird*. He programmed Schoenberg's *Kammersymphonie No. 1*, and when the audience wailed its disapproval he furiously left in midperformance only to return and play the piece over from the start. He later reenacted the same scene with a piece by Webern. If that were not enough, he also played Berg and Varese. Such modernism was to eventually undermine his standing, but in the meantime his fame and ego grew.

Stokowski's usual entrance to a concert saw him dash in from the wings, leap upon the podium, and stab at the orchestra, which responded immediately with the opening note. Such theatrics were not enough. After clumsily breaking his baton while conducting he petulantly gave it up and took to using just his hands. He quickly became enamored of his long, graceful fingers. Under the guise of eliminating the orchestra and conductor from view and emphasizing the mystery and eloquence of the music, Stokowski scheduled a concert where the house lights were extinguished, the orchestra's stand lights shining at their barest minimum. From under the podium a spotlight projected Stokowski's profile and arms onto the walls and ceiling, his ten fingers dancing like independent batons. His ego threatened to outstrip him; while feeding it he fed his critics.

By 1936 Stokowski was embroiled in another public donnybrook with the board of directors, and his future with the Philadelphia Orchestra was soon over. His glamorous life ran apace, however. He continued to conduct widely and to program and premiere modern music. He conducted youth concerts and the American Symphony Orchestra as well as many of the world's top orchestras. His eye for glamorous women was unfailing. He married three more times, the last to Gloria Vanderbilt in 1945 when he was 63 and "old enough to be her grandfather," and his private affair with Greta Garbo was front-page material. A leading sex symbol in the '20s and '30s, it is rumored that he could never fully satisfy himself or his partner.

Stokowski was a pioneer in recording orchestras and experimented endlessly with microphone and orchestral placements. This interest, coupled with his glamorous image, made him a logical choice to conduct the score for Walt Disney's *Fantasia*, where once again the Stokowski silhouette took prime billing. His orchestrations and arrangements sparked lively debates. The purists rebelled, the romantics applauded. Even now the mention or sound of Bach-Stokowski or Wagner-Stokowski can still the listener with admiration or dread.

Stokowski continued conducting until his death at the age of 95. Part poseur, part genius, part womanizer, and part child, he never stopped pushing his ego or his music. The results ranged from the sublime to the ridiculous but they were never dull. Several years before he died Stokowski reconciled with his brother, ending over 50 years of estrangement. He now lies buried under a small plain stone opposite his parents, as if in old age, realizing the futility of his escape, he hoped to reconcile with them as well.

DIRECTIONS TO GOLDERS GREEN: Take the Northern Line to the Golders Green stop and exit on Finchley Road. Turn right and walk several blocks, turning right on Hoop Road. The crematorium is on your right.

DIRECTIONS TO ST. MARYLEBONE: Continue on the Northern Line to Finchley Central stop, and take the bus that runs along East End Avenue. The cemetery is at the junction of East End and North Circular Roads.

Windsor Castle

SOUTHWEST
LONDON AND
WINDSOR

Putney Vale and St. Mary Magdalene

THOUGH ALEXANDER KERENSKY and Bruce Ismay of *Titanic* fame are interred at Putney Vale, they are not necessarily people you would make a long drive to visit — particularly for a one-sided conversation. You might make the trip to this suburban cemetery, however, to see a wonderful collection of Victorian angels and spend time in the Garden of Remembrance.

PUTNEY VALE

Putney Vale, which covers 45 acres, was founded in 1891; its most interesting monuments lie along the original sweep up the hill. As you come through the main entrance, the first monument you will see is a granite cross with a metal sword superimposed on the front. The cross is "one in design and intention for those which have been set up in France and Belgium and other places throughout the world where our dead of the Great War are laid to rest." On the front is the biblical epitaph, "Their name liveth forevermore," and on the back the names of those buried or cremated here who died in World Wars I and II.

Walk past the chapel, and go left onto the high road. There are many angels and beautiful young women in this area, but the young woman lying on the right on her back, "In ever loving memory of our darling **Winifred Parry**, only daughter," is particularly attractive. Having fallen from her base, she looks as if she has finally found rest. As if to secure that sleep the vines have begun to anchor her to the spot.

Winifred Parry

279

In the next aisle, if you circle around, is an unusual memorial to **Jessie Burroughs** (1846–1907). It has a bas-relief with a kneeling angel, but at the top there is an upside-down angel approaching earth with a floral wreath. It is a perspective not often seen.

In the second row, not far from the chapel, is the monument of **Percy Matthew Hart** (1825–1902), a dome with six black granite columns and his cameo below it with the inscription, "Thou shalt be missed for thy seat will be empty."

Behind Hart is an interesting life-sized bas-relief of a woman, head cast down and clasping her breast, noting, "Love, Service, and Sacrifice." Below the sculpture are the words "Laborare est orare" (Work is prayer) and above it the epitaph, "She gave her life to her family and her soul to God." It is the monument to Baronness **Frederica Louisa Renwick** (d. 1927).

In counterpoint to the Renwick monument, there is a similar statue to **Lilian Hughes** (d. 1938) further up the hill with the words, "Love, Life, Happiness." The young woman of that sculpture has attractive, exposed breasts and a pert beauty, suggesting that there is indeed more to life than sacrifice and service.

On your right up the path is the elaborate **Lyons** family vault. The memorial to **Caroline** (1869–1924) has three angels, and the words:

She is not dead, she lives where she did love
Her memory on earth, her soul above.

On another side it notes, "She vanquished in beauty all other women and surpassed in wisdom most of the men." Presumably the former was the greater achievement.

A little further along is the in-ground marker "Sacred to the memory of **Percival Wilson**, Royal Irish Constabulary who was assassinated at Gorey, County Wexford, Ireland, June 15, 1920, age 33. Father forgive them, for they know not what they do."

Slightly down the pathway to the right is what appears to be a statue of Jesus walking on water. His arms have been broken off but the waves on the water are impressive. It is the monument of the **Sidney George Brown** family, per-haps initially erected to their son **Sidney John Russell Brown**, "Goo Goo," who died at 15 in 1924.

Further along is a marker showing a lightly carved wom-an, modernistic in design, holding flowers and feeding several birds. It is "in tenderest memory of my darling wife Phylip [**Phyllis Falconer Watney**, d. 1946] deeply loved

Lilian Hughes

and admired for her kindness, gaiety and courage despite constant ill health. May her soul rest in peace."

On the periphery, halfway to the back, is an upbeat marble of **Roy Plomley** (1914–1985) "who created 'Desert Island Discs' BBC." At the top is a three-dimensional design of a shell with two fish swimming in opposite directions, and a heart below. The sculptor is F. Skinner. At the end of the bed of flowers are the words, "He was a joyous man."

Back across the road and up is a monument to Dr. **Oleg Alexander Kerensky** (1905–1984) and his more famous father, **Alexander Kerensky** (1881–1970) who is under a Russian cross. Kerensky (pronounced KAY-ren-ski) was the leader of the first portion of the Russian Revolution of

1917. Eleven years younger than Lenin, the two men were both born in the town of Simbirsk (now Ulyanovsk) on the middle Volga. Kerensky's father, the school superintendent, praised Lenin's academic record and made recommendations for his university education. Kerensky was also a good student who originally leaned toward the theater or music but who became drawn to history, law, and philosophy while at the university in St. Petersburg.

Kerensky's sympathies lay from the start with those oppressed by czarist rule. He offered free legal services to the urban poor in 1904, and participated in the Revolution of 1905. He was arrested the following year for possession of revolutionary materials. After his short imprisonment he continued his activist ways by defending revolutionaries, peasants, and strikers. His oratorical skills and fiery determination soon marked him as special. Re-entering politics with his election to the Fourth Duma in 1912, he was a vocal critic of the czar. In 1914 he was again imprisoned, this time for eight months, for attacking the judicial system.

In 1917 Russia was besieged by the war and in economic and social collapse. The czarist government crumbled and Kerensky emerged as a leader of the Petrograd Soviet, and initiated democratic reforms. But freedom of speech, assembly, religion, and press, and universal suffrage were not enough. The peasants wanted land reforms and the populace as a whole wanted an end to the war. Trouble began for Kerensky with the release of political prisoners such as Stalin but, more importantly, with the return of both Lenin and Trotsky. Concentrating on land reforms Lenin preached "all power to the Soviets" and the people listened. And as brilliant a speaker as Kerensky was, Trotsky was even better. Personally exhorting the army to fight, Kerensky launched a disastrous offensive in the summer of 1917. In the aftermath over two million soldiers deserted. This, coupled with Kerensky's inept handling of General Kornilov's attempted coup d'état, signalled the end of Kerensky's rule. On October 25 the Bolsheviks gained power.

Kerensky escaped Russia disguised as a Serbian officer and eventually settled in New York, blaming his defeat on many factors, all of which he felt to be stabs in the back. Engaging in research and lecturing he spent a good deal of time defending his actions against the negative views of historians. It is generally conceded that after three centuries of czarist rule Russia was simply not ready for democracy; not even in the best of times, and for the inexperienced

Kerensky World War I was not the best. For years he was a house guest of Mrs. Kenneth Simpson and could frequently be seen on one of his favorite walks which took him around the Central Park reservoir. He died of arteriosclerotic heart disease.

Beyond Kerensky is a marker to painter **Anthony Devas** (1911–1958). On it is a lightly carved contemporary angel and the words, "He was a rare man."

A proper British tomb belongs to the **Fraser** family. It has the family coat of arms and a Celtic cross above it. William Fraser (1888–1970), First Lord Strathalmond, and William Fraser (1916–1976), Second Lord Strathalmond, were both chairmen of British Petroleum.

As you approach the corner you will see the monument of **John Clayton Pugh** (1922–1976) with the paradox, "Only when you drink from the river of silence shall you indeed sing, and when you have reached the mountaintop, then shall you begin to climb. When the earth has claimed your limbs, then shall you truly dance."

At the top intersection is a large shiny black granite monument to **Karabet Torosyan** (1924–1986). The inscription on the open book reads, "Here lies only the body of a great man. Just as a great artist, the real value only appreciated after death. During life the suffering he endured for his family should be held as an example to all. His love and protection for his family are without parallel which death has not hindered. K.T. lives."

Just across the way is the hard-to-read stone of **Reginald Fraser** (d. 1966), scientist and inventor with the quote, "Génie, c'est la patience" (Genius is patience).

In the top back corner, enclosed by a single rail, is the complex of the Ismay family. Most of the inscriptions have nautical themes. On entering you will see the Bible verse James 3:4, "Behold also the ships, which though they be so great and are driven of fierce winds, yet are they turned about with a very small helm whithersoever the governor listeth." Behind is a squared-off sarcophagus whose sides are decorated with carvings of schooners in a stylized sea.

At the top on one side the inscription reads, "To the glory of God and in memory of **Bruce Ismay** who died October 7, 1937, his wife, **Julia Florence Smyth** died December 31, 1963." On the other side is Psalm 107:23–24, "They that go down to the sea in ships and occupy their business in great waters, these men see the works of the Lord and His wonders in the deep."

Ismay, an outstanding sportsman at six feet four inches, excelled at soccer, tennis, and shooting. But he suffered as

Bruce Ismay and Julia Smyth

the son of a famous father. He had inherited a steamship company and a large fortune from his father in 1899, though perhaps not the grit it had taken to parlay a Liverpool shipyard into an international concern. By 1902 he had been pressured to sell to the J.P. Morgan combine. Though Ismay retained his dignity and his White Star Line chairmanship, he was, in essence, a Morgan employee. Dark and taciturn, he preferred to keep out of the public eye.

It was ironic then that, after the events of April 14, 1912, Ismay was suddenly as famous as Captain Bligh and disliked even more. If the *Titanic*, replete with squash courts, bronze statuary, and "millionaires' suites," had made an ice-free maiden voyage to New York, J. Bruce Ismay might have lived out a pleasant tenure as chairman of the White Star Line. But on that night the floating palace which had been christened "unsinkable" hit an iceberg and quickly disappeared. Brought to New York along with the other survivors, the ship's owner was quickly dubbed "J. Brute Ismay" by a furious American press.

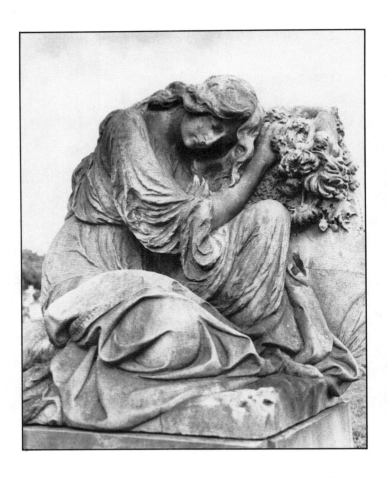

Commissions of inquiry in Washington, D.C., and then in London investigated the accident and concluded that Ismay had, in fact, helped board passengers into lifeboats until he could find no more women and children. Given the darkness, confusion, and panic on the tilting deck, this was believable. But the fact that he had survived at all, when 1,635 others—many of them in steerage—had perished, continued to rankle. There were other accusations as well, such as that of inadequate access to the top deck for third- and fourth-class passengers and too few lifeboats. In testimony, citing his ignorance of navigation principles and the significance of icebergs, Ismay sounded like a farmer who had wandered on board by mistake.

Forced to resign as chairman of the White Star Line, Ismay moved into a comfortable retirement. Yet the horror of that night had exacted its toll. When he attended concerts alone he purchased the seat beside him for his coat and hat, perhaps to keep humanity at bay.

Julia Schiefflin Ismay, American heiress to a pharmaceutical fortune, married Bruce Ismay in 1888. An imposing personality, Mrs. Ismay raised two boys and two girls and lived to be 90, playing bridge and lying about her age. According to a family member, she would never permit her husband to mention the *Titanic* disaster.

The Gardens of Remembrance at the front of Putney Vale are very beautiful to walk in during the spring when everything is in bloom. The only evidence that you are not in a country garden comes from the plaques set in the low brick wall surrounding various areas. These are compliant, with no raging against the dying of the light:

> Take my ashes where the sunshine plays,
> In quiet gardens splashed with golden light.
> And where the stars peep from dark pools at night,
> There let me rest.

ST. MARY MAGDALENE

A cemetery guide which did not include Richard Burton's stone tent would be like a dinner with no wine; bearable, even pleasant, but not complete. Yet Burton's memorial is surprisingly hard to find. First you must make your way to the western suburb of Mortlake, then be very clear that you want the Catholic church called St. Mary Magdalene, not Mortlake Roman Catholic Cemetery or the nearby Protestant church. St. Mary Magdalene is just off Mortlake High Street, and you enter the burial ground through an outside church alcove.

Once here, there is no problem locating the tent at the back of the tiny churchyard. The structure, 12 feet square and 18 feet high, has a frieze of Islamic crescents and stars. The front has been cemented shut, but in the back is an iron ladder with four rungs which leads to a glass plate that allows you to peer into the tomb's interior. Inside are two coffins—one a simple mummy shape, the other more ornate with lanterns—a painting of a crucifix, and some brass ornaments. The Muslim design was originally gilt, and the window in back had been stained glass with the Burton family crest, but, due to vandalism and natural causes, both have disappeared. In 1973 a small group of volunteers began working to restore the tent.

When Burton died his wife, the redoubtable Isabel, finally acceded to Burton's request that they be buried together in a Bedouin tent; she simply made it of English marble rather than canvas.

The marble tablets on the door include a tribute by Justin Huntly McCarthy:

Farewell, dear friend, dead hero! The great life
Is ended, the great perils, the great joys;
And he to whom adventures were as toys,
Who seemed to bear a charm 'gainst spear or knife
Or bullet, now lies silent from all strife
Out yonder where the Austrian eagles poise
On Istrian hills. But England at the noise
Of that dread fall, weeps with the hero's wife.
Oh, last and noblest of the errant knights,
The English soldier and the Arab shiek [sic]!
Oh singer of the East who loved so well
The deathless wonder of the "Arabian Nights,"
Who touched Camden's lute and still would seek
Ever new deeds until the end! Farewell!

A plaque states that Isabel Arundell (of Wardour) died March 22, 1896. "Jesus Mercy Mary Help Pray for Her."

RICHARD FRANCIS BURTON *b. March 19, 1821, Torquay, Devonshire; d. October 20, 1890, Trieste, Italy.* Traveler, discoverer, poet, translator, linguist, ethnographer, archeologist, soldier, swordsman, raconteur, and liar, Richard Burton lived many lives in one lifetime. For sidelines he pursued geology, botany, zoology, and medicine. He was above all an actor who assumed many roles and disguises, and one whose audience would have killed him on more than one occasion if his skills had unraveled. Like an actor though, he knew the limits of his role and could return to the self he seemed to be escaping.

Swinburne remarked that Burton "had the jaw of a devil and the brow of a god." Of this Burton was well aware. His prominent jaw, dark complexion, and piercing eyes all fed the Satanic image which he suitably emphasized with his sculpted moustache and beard. Later a nasty scar on his cheek completed the image. Intensity became ferocity and glower. "So Satan is the true hero of Paradise Lost . . . and Mephistopheles is much better society than Faust and Margaret," wrote Burton.

As a boy he was wild and uncontainable — fighting, stealing, and playing pranks with his brother, Edward. What Burton wrote of his parents was less than warm or flattering. His father was a drinker who hunted and dabbled in chemistry. When not supplying the discipline that Burton so greatly resented, his father was amiable, distant, and ineffectual. Mrs. Burton was more actively formative but equally unable to discipline him. Perpetually swinging from aloofness to seductiveness and back, Burton felt deprived of her maternal affection, despite living and studying at home until he was 19. The sexual and emotional confusion split him three ways: romantic seducer of women; staid, dutiful husband; explorer of foreign lands and erotic practices.

Burton's disguises began at age 15 when his family was living in Italy and he and Edward dressed as croquemorts and helped one night to bury the peasant victims of a cholera outbreak. Attending Oxford he sharpened his fencing skills (he would become one of the best swordsmen in Europe and write a book about bayonet use which the English ignored for many years to their own peril) and continued his pursuit of languages (he would eventually learn 25 plus 15 dialects). Rusticated from Oxford for auda-

Richard and Isabel Burton

cious behavior, Burton was bought a commission in the East India Company and sent to India.

His talent for language and his interest in ethnography made him an ideal candidate for gathering information and settling disputes. Burton took these researches even further by involving himself with an Indian woman and later studying the homosexual brothels of Karachi. Of the former he felt that Indian women with their knowledge of "Ismac" (delayed satisfaction) were far ahead of their English counterparts; of the latter it may be assumed that Burton, with his wide-ranging, untamed sexual interests, was a participant.

His report on the brothel, submitted to Sir Charles Napier in secret, was, as were all of Burton's reports, complete with graphic and clinical detail. When an enemy made them public two years later, Burton left India in disgrace. But he had had a taste of travel and of exotic places and found the flavor intoxicating. He wrote and published ethnographic studies based on his stay in India. He became a secret convert to Islam through his initiation into Sufism and later traveled to the Middle East where, disguised as an Arab, he entered the holy cities of Medina and Mecca, even penetrating the Kaaba and sketching its interior on his sleeve while feigning prayer. Discovery would have meant instant death. Burton similarly entered Harar, but during his return journey his entourage was attacked by bandits. He escaped wearing a javelin which had pierced his cheek and jaw and come out the other side.

Again Burton wrote, published, and then journeyed, this time in search of the source of the Nile. Traveling companionably with John Speke, as older brother to younger, the relationship quickly deteriorated to envy and animosity. They struggled mightily and suffered severely: malaria, mouth ulcers, paralysis, blindness, fever and delirium, tsetse flies, pismire ants, and mildew. Although he came remarkably close to discovering the Nile headwaters, Burton failed to find them, as did Speke on his second trip. On their return the dispute with Speke became public to the detriment of both men. Further journeys took Burton to South America, Iceland, Damascus, and Utah, where he visited with Brigham Young and touched, of course, on the subject of polygamy. Each place stirred Burton's sharp eye and engendered new ethnographic volumes. Some of his books were models of native study, others mere compilations of voluminous facts.

In England Burton renewed his acquaintance with Isabel

Arundell. She was everything he was not: romantic, religious, and scrupulously Victorian in her morals and sensibilities. She claimed to have twice encountered a gypsy woman named Burton who predicted that Isabel would marry her namesake. For Isabel, Burton was inexhaustably romantic; for Burton, Isabel was the uncompleted segment of his twin nature (not the whole twin, his ego was too large for that). Philosophically, sexually, and temperamentally ill-matched, she provided a maternal harbor for his wildness, but one from which he sailed for years at a time.

Burton's sexual interests were eclectic and lifelong. Translating erotica until his death, his unexpurgated editions of the *Kama Sutra*, *The Arabian Nights*, and *The Perfumed Garden* were banned in England. He displayed an ongoing interest in flagellation, castration, clitoridectomy, and other forms of mutilation. Surprisingly, he found de Sade repugnant. He befriended Monkton Milnes, who made Burton privy to his impressive pornographic library, and Fred Hankey, a knowledgeable homosexual sadist whose interests ran to the extreme of desiring a book cover made from the skin of a living woman. Burton was drawn to these men, deriving vicarious pleasure from their extremes. Such company and activities placed a substantial strain on the marriage.

Lady Burton tried to have the last word. Three hours after he died of a heart attack she deceived a priest into giving her now agnostic husband Extreme Unction. Then in an effort to recreate the man, she burned his notes and diaries, an inestimable loss, and wrote a biography of the man who never was: the good, faithful, Catholic husband. She tried to have him buried at Westminster Abbey, but the officials would not be fooled. Knowing Burton's feelings regarding Christianity, they refused Lady Burton. Finally acquiescing to his request, she left us this wonderful tent, a monument to adventure, foreign lands, and a life on the fringe, set in an oasis of civilized calm.

DIRECTIONS TO PUTNEY VALE: From London Bridge, follow A3 as it wends its way southwest. At Putney Heath, near Wimbledon, watch for the intersection of A3 with Roehampton Lane. Soon after, Putney Vale will be seen on the left.

DIRECTIONS TO ST. MARY MAGDALENE: From A3 take Roehampton Lane to Upper Richmond Road and go left. Bear right onto Sheen Lane and then right again onto Mortlake High Street. The church will be on your right.

St. Nicholas, Chiswick

ST. NICHOLAS CHURCHYARD, comfortably located on a curve of the Thames, is a pleasant place in which to wander, though many of the sentiments on the stones have been obliterated by age. Some monuments have the same coffin shape as ones described in Bunhill Fields, and others are upright slabs similar to those used in colonial America, but considerably larger. On that of **Richard Wright** (d. 1734), Bricklayer, you can make out a design of the heads of cherubs with a skull resting on palm fronds above them. One epitaph that is still decipherable commemorates two little boys in the **Thomas** family; one died at eight, the other at three months:

> The little tenants of this tomb were beautiful from birth.
> We fondly hoped to see them bloom as lovely flowers on earth.
> But they were born for better things, the high bequest was given
> And holy angels wafted their wings to lead their souls to heaven.

As you come into the churchyard, the tall monument you see first is to **William Hogarth**. On one end it has a mask that is more smiling than frowning and a paint palette with brushes supporting a wreath. The epitaph explains that "Here lyeth the body of William Hogarth, Esquire, who died October 26, 1764, age 67 years. Mrs. **Jane Hogarth**, wife of William Hogarth, Esquire, obit. the 13th of November, 1789, age 80 years."

Anyone curious about *real* eighteenth-century England need look no further than William Hogarth's prints. The jostling, teeming crowd scenes show women nursing infants in alleyways, boys torturing cats, and worshippers nodding off in church. Though considered satirical, works such as *Southwark Fair*, *Gin Lane*, and *A Rake's Progress*

St. Nicholas Churchyard

may have depicted manners and vices, but did not invent them. Indeed, people of his era looked affectionately on his engravings; it was only a century later that viewers became horrified.

William Hogarth, growing up in the belly of London, had a good opportunity to oberve crowds firsthand. His father ran a coffee house where he was always ready "to entertain gentlemen in the Latin tongue." When the coffee house failed for lack of interest, the elder Hogarth spent four years in debtor's prison while his wife peddled Gripe Ointment and other patent medicines. Young Hogarth began his career as an engraver, switching to painting at the school of Sir James Thornhill. At 32 he married Thornhill's daughter, Jane, and lived quietly in a house in Chiswick with no windows facing the front.

Hogarth was nothing if not uncouth. His favorite activities with friends were eating, drinking, and throwing dung at each other. Visiting France he made loud, coarse remarks about the women and the architecture, calling French houses "all gilt and beshit." For his efforts he was arrested in Calais on suspicion of spying. Released under humiliating but unspecified conditions, the satirist returned to England and began a lifelong practice of ferociously mocking foreign fashions and arts. *The French Lady in London, or the headdress for the year 1771* shows a woman charging into a drawing room with a 12-foot-high hair decoration, terrifying a gentleman and cats and knocking over furniture.

Once he began painting, Hogarth discovered the popularity of large topical pictures which could then be adapted and sold as engravings. This worked especially well with series pictures such as *A Harlot's Progress* (1732) and the work considered his masterpiece, *Marriage à la Mode* (1743–45).

There was much satire in Hogarth's art as well as affection for his subjects. He portrayed sturdy English virtues and love of freedom along with the vices by which his contemporaries were secretly fascinated. Believing that virtue could be acquired by eating beef, he helped found the Sublime Society of Beefsteaks. Whatever the effect on his personality, this daily fare probably helped contribute to the heart disease which killed him at 67.

Just before he died Hogarth completed his last engraving, *Finis*. In it the world is shown coming to an end as Time himself, a gaunt, winged figure, is dying. An hourglass has run out, and a cracked, discarded artist's palette lies in the foreground. A last will slips from Time's fingers. Yet mounting the sky is a small, brightly lit chariot of the kind said to have carried Elijah off to heaven.

As you come out of the churchyard and into the small cemetery, stay on the right-hand path. Halfway down is the sarcophagus of James Abbott McNeill Whistler and his wife Beatrix. The top of the monument is made of copper turned green, the base a shiny black-green granite. In each of the four corners were once decorative statues which have now been stolen. On either end is a wreath and a bow design. Whistler has the epitaph "The place where I also at last hoped to be hidden for in no other would I be."

JAMES ABBOTT (McNEILL) WHISTLER *b. July 11, 1834, Lowell, Massachusetts; d. July 17, 1903, London.*

> Sir John Holker: The labour of two days [to paint Nocturne in Black and Gold], then, is that for which you ask two hundred guineas?
> Whistler: No. I ask it for the knowledge of a lifetime.

Jimmy Whistler's response was typical of his acuity of mind and sharpness of tongue, and brought applause from the curiosity seekers who packed the courtroom to witness testimony in the libel suit he had brought against John Ruskin. The suit guaranteed him further notoriety, won him a legal victory, and earned him the handsome compensation of one farthing. In many ways it summed up his life: wit, soliloquist, brawler, artist, and pauper.

Poor though he almost always was, Whistler never showed it. He displayed a thatch of prematurely white hair as if he were wearing a feather and dressed in patent leather boots, white pants, jacket, monocle, and top hat. Sporting a slender three-and-a-half-foot walking stick he was the diminutive, strutting, bantam cock of London's artistic and social world. Though mired in debt and bankruptcy his dress never changed, and his celebrated Sunday buckwheat breakfasts continued with their accustomed pomp and pretense. It was a facade strung tight over a thin but enduring frame.

Asserting that "the time has gone by when a man shall be born without being consulted," he declared Baltimore to be his place of birth and claimed southern ancestry. In fact, he was born in Lowell, Massachusetts, to Major George Whistler and his pious second wife, Anna McNeill. When Jimmy was nine the family moved to St. Petersburg, Russia, where his father, now retired from the army, was doing engineering work for the czar. When the major died three years later of cholera and a rheumatic heart, Anna moved the family back to America.

While Jimmy had already displayed a precocious talent for art, such a career was considered unsuitable. The ministry was preferred, but West Point was chosen. It was a poor idea. His rebellious nature and sophomoric wit did not endear him to the officers. Mounting demerits caused no change in behavior and when, by the end of his third year, they reached two hundred he was invited to leave.

Military structure held no appeal, but its antithesis, bohemian life in Paris, certainly did. Whistler quickly settled in the Latin Quarter where he made friends and began attending art school. Among his friends was George Du Maurier who would later satirize Whistler in his popular novel, *Trilby*. In the cafés he fell in with Fantin-Latour and Legros and all came under the influence of Courbet. His new-found lifestyle consisted of a poverty which was to be repeated throughout his life. A wastrel for whom debt became a familiar companion, Whistler's money went for food, drink, and good times. His friendships were intense but short-lived and fist fights were not uncommon. As his wit matured and sharpened he began to dominate gatherings with his monologues.

Whistler's artistic style began emerging when he was in his late twenties. By then he was settling in the Chelsea district of London and painting the first of his *Symphonies*, *Harmonies*, *Nocturnes*, and *Arrangements*. The titles, chosen to emphasize the abstract qualities of his paintings, drew attention to his work, though not all of it was positive. Evening would often find Whistler on the Chelsea embankment or in a rowboat near Cremorne, obsequiously shadowed by his assistants, the Greaves brothers, memorizing a scene which he would later paint by day. His night scenes, such as the *Nocturne in Blue and Gold*, conveyed a murky impressionistic moodiness and drew much criticism. One critic declared Whistler to be "imperiled by original absurdity."

Portraits were also a forte and Whistler's most famous painting, *Arrangement in Grey and Black, No. 1: The Artist's Mother*, was painted in 1872. Its puritan starkness pleased both the artist and his mother, although Whistler preferred that it be viewed as an arrangement, while his friends and the critics saw it as a sensitive portrait. His equally fine second such arrangement, of Thomas Carlyle, was frequently lodged in pawnshops. Whistler signed his paintings with a trademark butterfly fashioned from his initials. Once, spearing a scorpion with his walking stick, he admiringly watched the tenacious creature repeatedly sting the stick, emitting poison with each strike. Feeling the kinship, he soon added a sting to his butterfly.

Perhaps the greatest wit and most caustic critic in England, Whistler could not take as he gave. He sued Ruskin and Du Maurier for their satire, and saw his friendship with Oscar Wilde decay when he accused Wilde, not without some justification, of stealing his witticisms. Nor could he forgive. Upon hearing that Wilde was working on a book during his incarceration for homosexual acts with a minor, Whistler remarked that the title "must be known as 'The Bugger's Opera.' " Whistler, no slouch with the pen, outlined and embellished his bon mots in *The Gentle Art of Making Enemies.* But his humor, intended to deflect his pain at the expense of another, revealed all too clearly his underlying agony and fragility.

Whistler's love life was strained as well. His two long, live-in relationships with models Jo Hiffernan and Maud Franklin suffered from his failure to legalize them. Both ended when each woman posed naked for other artists (Jo most famously for Courbet's erotic and lesbian *Le Sommeil*). In 1888 Whistler married Trixie Godwin and was devastated by her death from cancer in 1896.

Whatever his failings and affectations Whistler was a man who knew his worth. When asked by a wealthy American collector how much he wanted for a group of paintings Whistler replied, "Five million." He clarified the collector's astonishment. "My posthumous prices. Good Morning." Had he but known that, for once, he was being modest.

To the left of Whistler is a monument with a palette and paintbrushes, that of **Helena Piffard** who died in 1900 at age 29.

At the end of this section is a modernistic sculpture showing a large angel at the top with nude humans pressed together, their hands raised upward. Crosses are scattered upon it. It commemorates Sir **Percy Harris Bart** (1876–1952), a member of Parliament from Bethnal Green and onetime deputy leader of the Liberal Party.

The left side of the cemetery is unexpectedly long. In its center is the striking memorial of **Frederick Hitch** (1856–1913), with a Union Jack draped over a large granite stone and a giant-sized pith helmet on top. The memorial was erected to commemorate Hitch's heroism at Rorke's Drift on January 22, 1879. He was severely wounded when he and a comrade rescued six men from a hospital set on fire by the Zulus. After the war he became a taxi driver; at the funeral his cab, filled with flowers, was pulled by his colleagues.

Though Chiswick Cemetery is not well planted and has few trees, it is enlivened by angels. There is also a poignant feeling, created by the number of people here who died young.

Sir Percy Harris Bart

DIRECTIONS TO ST. NICHOLAS: St. Nicholas Churchyard is most easily reached by car, by taking the M-4 east through Chiswick to its intersection with Great Chertsey Road. Then take Church Street south two blocks to the churchyard.

YOU ARE ENTERING A
CONSECRATED BUILDING

THE BURIAL PLACE OF A
QUEEN AND HER CONSORT

PLEASE BE AS QUIET
AS POSSIBLE

Windsor Castle and Frogmore

THE TOWN OF Windsor is both enchanting and puzzling. As you exit from the Windsor and Eton Central Railway Station expecting history, you will see instead Madame Tussaud's permanent wax collection, "Royalty and Empire." The winding streets outside lead to colorful pubs, and china and wool outlets. Windsor Safari Park is only two miles away. Windsor Castle lies further up Castle Hill Road. It has dominated the countryside in various forms since William the Conqueror put up a wooden fortification in the eleventh century.

The fact that the throngs of tourists are queuing up for Queen Mary's dollhouse and the State Apartments helps make the wait for entry into St. George's Chapel short. It is a magnificent building in its own right, completed in 1528, with soaring Gothic arches which dwarf the chairs and people below. From the beginning there were burials here, complete with a schedule of fees; but those original monuments and inscriptions have been purloined by time. Memorial brasses have disappeared, inscriptions have worn away, and floor monuments have been moved or covered over in periodic repavings. In 1790 some stones were used to pave a cellar in the chapel; a guidebook from that era notes that "none but those that are most entire or that belong to the most eminent persons have been preserved."

Since the 1840s there has been a concerted effort at preservation; the chapel has a wealth of monuments.

ST. GEORGE'S CHAPEL

Touring St. George's Chapel is made easier by the way visitors are routed in and around the perimeter. The first monument of historic interest you pass is that of the Prince Imperial **Napoleon** (1856–1879), son of Napoleon III and

Frogmore

Empress Eugénie of France. Queen Victoria took a particular interest in young Napoleon, whom she had met as a boy of 14, and who was often in London. There were rumors that he and the Queen's youngest daughter, Beatrice, were romantically involved. Napoleon insisted on taking part in the Zulu Wars and, on a reconnaissance mission with several others, was ambushed and speared to death. Victoria wrote, "This is the end of all that was once so splendid and brilliant, and of one who promised to be a blessing not only to his country, but to the world."

The recumbent marble effigy of young Napoleon clasping his sword is five feet ten inches long and was sculpted by Joachim Boehm. His feet are lying against an upturned helmet, his spurs by his side.

In the surrounding area are plain in-ground dark slate burial slabs, some with coats of arms.

Inside the chantry to your left, the tomb of **Charles Somerset** (d. 1526), First Earl of Worcester, and his wife Lady **Elizabeth Herbert** (d. 1514) is interesting for its medieval look. Dwarfed by her husband, her hair frames her face in long natural waves and her clasped hands wear short gloves. Although he is dressed in the tunic and cape of his time, his expression is stylized and his pipestem legs in tight breeches seem abnormally long.

It is impossible to avert your eyes from the horrifying monument of Princess Charlotte, but for the sake of chronology look first at the long bronze tablet which reads, "Near this spot lies buried **Alamayu** (1861–1879), son of Theodore, King of Abyssinia, a young prince whom Queen Victoria befriended." The brass with its verse from Matthew 25:35, "I was a stranger and ye took me in," was placed here by Victoria. The design on top is that of a frowning lion with a crown; on the bottom is St. George slaying the dragon.

If **Charlotte Augusta** (1796–1817), Princess of Wales, had not died unexpectedly the reign of Queen Victoria might never have occurred. Heiress to the throne after her father, George IV, the newly married Charlotte was healthy and high-spirited. But after a labor of 50 hours in which she gave birth to a stillborn son, Princess Charlotte also succumbed. It is said that the attending physician, Sir Richard Croft, committed suicide.

Charlotte's monument, sculpted by Matthew Cotes Wyatt, is actually a double view. Below, her dead form lies prostrate under a sheet with only her fingers showing. Four totally draped figures are mourning around the steps. Above this her spirit—clad in a diaphanous gown which is pulled back to reveal one full breast — is ascending to heaven. She is attended by two angels, one of whom cradles her tiny newborn son.

Nearby is the statue of **Leopold** (1790–1865), husband of Princess Charlotte, who went on to remarry and become first king of the Belgians. The white marble statue shows him as an attractive man in his prime, clutching a scepter and displaying the Order of the Garter. Of all Queen Victoria's "evil uncles," Leopold was the one she trusted and to whom she turned for advice. The inscription indicates, "Erected by her majesty Queen Victoria in loving memory of Leopold, the first king of the Belgians, her maternal uncle who was as a father to her as she was to him a daughter." Leopold is buried not here but in Belgium.

Diagonal to Charlotte are two newer arrivals, **George V** (1865–1936) and his queen, **Mary** (1867–1953). Their marble portraits seem stiffly formal, hands clasped in prayer but not raised. The sculpture, done by Sir William Reid Dick, is slightly larger than life, with both figures well over six feet tall. There is no inscription other than their titles and dates in Roman numerals.

George V ascended to the throne when the unexpected death by pneumonia of his brother, Prince Eddy, Duke of Clarence, brought him into succession. Sometimes accused of being Jack the Ripper, Eddy was hyperactive and unable to read, but sweet-natured. By contrast George, though more given to outdoor pleasures than the joys of the intellect, was of normal intelligence. Not expecting to reign, he had trained in the navy, and maintained a spit-and-polish discipline among his children. He brought England through World War I, the development of the Irish Free State, and the demands of the suffragettes, drawing the country together toward the end of his reign through radio broadcasts.

Queen Mary of Teck, who had first been betrothed to the deficient Eddy, was no doubt relieved at this unexpected consolation prize. Cognizant of the importance of dynasty and succession, she produced six children then turned to an interest in needlework. Mary also became an authority on art and antiques, refurbishing the palaces and royal apartments and establishing the dollhouse collection which bears her name.

The dogs on the **Rutland** monument (ca. 1513) in the next chantry are particularly charming, their necks ringed with bells.

As you go up the steps stay to your left. You will come to the black slate floor slab of **George VI** (1895–1952); his cameo is lit up and on the ledge above. The inscription on his marker is from his Christmas broadcast of 1939 and is from the work of Minnie Louise Haskins: "I said to the man who stood in the gate of the year, Give me a light that I may tread safely into the unknown and he replied, Go out into the darkness and put your hand in the hand of God, that shall be to you better than a light and safer than a known way."

In many ways his accession to the throne resembles that of his father, George V. Another second son who was trained in the navy, Albert, who took the name George VI, was not expecting the abdication of his older brother. But when Edward VIII chose to be demoted to the Duke of Windsor, George had three weeks to learn how to be King of England. Suffering from his father's naval discipline, he had gastric trouble and a stammer that may have come about when his father gave orders to make him right-handed. With little actual political power left to him, George VI did a creditable job of supporting his country throughout World War II. Suffering from arteriosclerosis, he died in his sleep after a day of shooting rabbits.

Just beyond where you will turn right is the monument of **Edward IV** (1442–1483), the builder of this chapel, and his wife, **Elizabeth** of Woodville. Little of this monument remains compared to what once was. The banner and coat of mail which hung above it were stolen in 1642, and the brass head of the king disappeared at the time of the Civil Wars. What is left is a black marble slab with the letters set in brass.

Caught in the Wars of the Roses, the feud between the Yorks and the Lancasters, Edward was on and off the throne several times. There were the requisite number of battles and murders, and when the handsome Edward was on the throne he lived with extravagant pleasure. As the Lorenz Hart song declared of another ladykiller, "He wouldn't look at a lady under ten." Although he was often compared, in retrospect, with his grandson Henry VIII, Edward is best known as the father of the Princes in the Tower. Rumored to have drowned his traitorous brother George in a vat of Madeira wine, his judgment failed him when he appointed his other brother, Richard III, to look after his sons.

From here walk through the center aisle of the choir, noting the elaborate stalls carved between 1478 and 1485. They were given to Knights of the Garter who displayed their own banners above them. As you enter here you will pass the in-ground vault, approximately three feet square, of several kings.

Here rests the monarch whose history was bound up with that troublesome colony, America, and who had the second-longest reign of any British ruler, bettered only by his Hanoverian descendant, Victoria.

GEORGE III b. *June 4, 1738, London; d. January 29, 1820, Windsor.* Frederick, the son of George II and Queen Caroline, was thoroughly detested by both his parents. The King ignored him as if he were a "void in space." The Queen's dislike was more active: "My dear first-born is the greatest ass and the greatest liar and the greatest canaille and the greatest beast in the whole world and I heartily wish he were out of it." Yet royal blood was thicker than royal venom; it was Frederick who sired his father's successor.

Little is known of George's childhood. Frederick proved a better father than son, but left the job uncompleted when he died in 1751. George's possessive mother, Augusta, was eagerly at hand and throughout her life remained a profound influence on her son. The future Lord North, a childhood friend, was carefully taught how to treat his royal playmate. "If you play a game with him he must win . . . if you play your part well, you may get a sinecure post."

George III was the first royal Hanoverian to be born and raised in England, and the first to speak English without a foreign accent. He was a pious man of high principles and sought to infuse government with a higher standard of ethics. Reluctantly he succumbed to the same loathsome tactics as his opponents and forebears, sighing with regret and lost naiveté, "We must call in bad men to govern bad men." In love he submitted to the will of his mother and his chief political advisor, Lord Bute, foregoing his love of the beautiful but non-royal Lady Sarah Lennox for Charlotte of Mecklenburg, to whose singular ugliness he remained constant—their 15 children representing a drunkenness with duty rather than love.

George was only 22 when he assumed the throne. Intelligent, earnest, hard-working, and unassuming, he was also a trifle dull. While he gathered back authority lost by his predecessors, and limited the power of the well-established Whigs, the first years of his rule were marked by political instability. Lord Bute, the first prime minister, resigned after establishing peace with France, but remained the power behind the throne much to the dismay of his successors. Prime minister followed prime minister before

George settled on his former playmate, Lord North, who had polished up his sovereign so carefully that he became the leader of the whole country.

North held sway for ten years, a not inconsiderable feat, but it was a time marked by the loss of the American colonies. Both men have suffered, perhaps unjustifiably, by historical reputation, for neither was incompetent. Contemporary criticism was equally severe. Fellow monarch Catherine the Great declared that rather than granting the colonies independence she would have "fired a pistol at my own head."

In England the loss of the colonies signaled the downfall of North and trouble for George. With faith lost in his judgment his power to appoint his own ministers was threatened. Here, much to everyone's surprise, the mild-mannered George exerted his power by dismissing the opposition in 1783, and appointing the 24-year-old William Pitt the Younger as prime minister. It was a wise choice, for Pitt remained in power for 21 years, overseeing a renaissance in English power and the extension of British colonialism in India and Australia. George matured in these years, becoming less prudish, developing his knowledge of botany, and writing pseudonymous pamphlets on agriculture.

In the 1760s George suffered his first bouts of porphyria, a rare metabolic disorder which derives its name from the port-colored urine which characterizes it. It was his misfortune that the disease, now treatable, was unknown at that time. His first symptoms consisted of fever, hoarseness, chest pains, and coughing fits. The disease did not manifest itself again until October 1788 when George had his first attack of madness. It was during this time that he allegedly leapt from his carriage to address an oak tree, imagining it to be the King of Prussia.

As his condition deteriorated he attacked the Prince of Wales and spoke gibberish while foaming at the mouth. The treatments were less than enlightened. The straitjacket was used with frequency as were poultices of mustard and Spanish Fly. A degraded George was sometimes strapped to a specially made iron chair which he grimly referred to as his "coronation chair."

George recovered, witnessed with some pleasure the French Revolution, and reigned for another 20 years with only two brief interruptions by his disease in 1801 and 1804, the latter rendering him almost totally blind. In 1810 he was permanently struck insane by porphyria. In the unhappy years that followed the treatments of the past were brought back into use. Confined to his own quarters in Windsor Castle he alternated between reality and delusion, but the ratio inexorably shifted for the worse. Frequently he conjured up the dead as conversation partners.

On February 6, 1811, the Prince Regent assumed power. Also living at Windsor, estranged but nonetheless saddened by his condition, his wife last visited him in 1812. While Napoleon roamed Europe in victory and defeat George alternated periods of torpor with those of bizarre ceremony and music making. To the end, even though having gone deaf, the bearded, Lear-like King would sit at the harpsichord playing Handel and singing with a strong voice.

Also in the vault are **George IV** (1762–1830) and his successor, **William IV** (1765–1837). Because of his father's marathon reign, George IV did not technically become King until he was 58, although he exerted his influence for ten years before that. In the interim he married a commoner named Mrs. Fitzherbert and, when that marriage was declared void, wept drunkenly through the legal ceremony to his cousin Caroline. From that union came only Princess Charlotte, whose haunting monument stands in the back of the chapel.

Spendthrift, obese, debt-ridden, and probably alcoholic, at his accession there was a move to put his equally obese, unwashed, and estranged wife on the throne instead, with cries of, "The Queen forever! The King in the river!" George forced a bill to deprive her of any rights as Queen. Though a weak ruler, when sober he was a fascinating conversationalist and a decorator with a sense of style.

William IV, younger brother of George IV, was 64 when he moved onto the throne for the next seven years. Nicknamed "Silly Billy" early in life, he had been trained in the navy, for which he showed no aptitude, and had had ten illegitimate children by his mistress, Mrs. Jordan. It is a rather appealing image of William that, on the first day of his reign, he raced, grinning wildly, through London in an open carriage, offering kisses and rides to anyone who would accept them. Politically he was inoffensive, making sure that he lived until his niece, Victoria, was 18, so that her hated mother would not be the power behind the throne.

Further down in the aisle is the vault of Henry VIII, his sometime wife Jane Seymour, Charles I, and one of the 16 babies of Queen Anne. They are memorialized by a large black marble slab with brass inset letters and the basic information.

HENRY VIII *b. June 28, 1491, London; d. January 28, 1547, London.* Henry the Eighth! Scourge of clerics and wives, the square-faced, bejeweled monarch portrayed so graphically in the Hans Holbein portrait was the King who planted his sturdy legs across English history and challenged anyone to equal him. Few did, either in appetite, intellect, or insensitivity.

Henry was not born a killer. As the second son of Henry VII, the boisterous ten-year-old danced happily at his brother Arthur's wedding, with little thought that in five months he would be next in line for the throne. The country mourned the loss of sensitive, gifted Arthur at 15, but rejoiced when Henry was crowned King in 1509 after the death of their father. More robust than Arthur, there seemed little that the golden youth could not accomplish. He was skilled in jousting, riding, and tennis, fluent in Spanish, French, and Latin, and composed music and poetry in his spare time. As Lord Mountjoy wrote to Erasmus, "When you know what a hero he now shows himself, how wisely he behaves, what a lover he is of justice and goodness, what affection he bears to the learned, I will venture to swear that you will need no wings to make you fly."

To differentiate his reign from his father's, Henry had two of his father's staff, Richard Empson and Edmund Dudley, tried and executed for financial mismanagement. Though it did not dim his popularity, it was the first indication of a certain callousness toward human life — a trait that was recognized early by his good friend, Thomas More. When it was commented on how the two young men discussed astronomy, geometry, and theology for hours, walking arm in arm in the royal garden, More agreed, but added, "If my head would win him a castle in France, it would not fail to go."

More's head would not leave his shoulders at Henry's behest for another 25 years. In the meantime Henry waged war with France, though in 1519, in a temporary cessation of hostility, he met with Francis I in an extravaganza known as the Field of the Cloth of Gold. But the more mundane aspects of daily government business bored him, and were left up to Cardinal Thomas Wolsey. Henry used the time to hunt and sport. In 1521 he had himself declared Defender of the Faith in England by Pope Clement VII. To woo the Pope he had written an attack on Martin Luther called *The Defence of the Seven Sacraments*.

But the King was most preoccupied by his lack of a male heir. To create a dynasty, he had chosen his dead brother's bride, Katharine of Aragon. She had been constantly pregnant since their marriage in 1509, but only her fifth child, Mary, born in 1516, survived. Henry was genuinely attached to Katharine but, as the pregnancies ceased, he grew restive. In 1525 his conscience, as described in Anne Boleyn's story, began to plague him. He informed Katharine sorrowfully that they had been living in sin and that Mary was illegitimate, citing Leviticus 18:16 which prohibits a man's "taking his brother's wife." Katharine fought back. She avowed that due to Arthur's ill health she had remained a virgin until her marriage to Henry, and that, in any case, the Bible verse applied to adultery among the living.

Thus developed the King's Great Matter, which was to rip the English church from Rome's fragrant garden and transplant her in the cold North as Anglicanism. The uprooting was agonizing. For eight years the legality of Henry's marriage was debated by scholars and theologians, and considered by the pope. Defenders of Katharine in England were given rooms in the Tower. When it appeared that the Matter would not be resolved in Henry's favor, Anne Boleyn allowed Henry to have his way with her, and gambled on becoming pregnant. They were secretly married in 1533, and Henry's marriage to Katharine declared annulled. The presumed-to-be-male heir, Elizabeth I, was born later that year.

To justify his actions, Henry ordered sweeping new legislation passed: a series of acts to cover all contingencies. The Act of Dispensations cut off Rome's authority to grant special licenses; the Act in Absolute Restraint of Annates ordered monies normally paid to Rome to go to the Crown instead; the Treason Act stopped anyone from declaring the King a heretic; and the Act of Supremacy made Henry the head of the Church in England instead of the pope. Henry demanded that his clerics swear an oath agreeing to these changes. It was then that Bishop John Fisher and Thomas More, Henry's Lord Chancellor, who would not do so, were arrested and executed in 1535.

Anne Boleyn, of course, was blamed for the carnage. The King ranted that it was her fault that his dearest friend was dead, and sent her to the block the following year on trumped-up charges of adultery. Her place was immediately filled by another lady-in-waiting, Jane Seymour, who gave Henry the son, Edward VI, for whom he had so long yearned. Two weeks later, before she could fall out of favor, Jane died. The sagas of Henry's other wives — Catherine Howard and Anne of Cleves — are told in Chapters 5 and 3 on the Tower and Westminster Abbey. The sixth and last wife, Catherine Parr, was a staunch Protestant who had been widowed twice.

By his last marriage in 1543, the golden youth had been lost to obesity and was suffering from fevers and a painfully ulcerous leg. Despite his bright intellect, he had never developed any contemplative life of the mind. His need to appear powerful was, finally, reduced to petty games. He allowed his advisers to draw up charges against Catherine Parr for attempting to convert him to Protestantism and even signed an order for her arrest. But then he leaked the news to Catherine, which brought her to him quickly, asserting she only wanted to be instructed by him. "And is it even so, sweetheart?" the King beamed. When the delegation came to arrest her, Henry savagely attacked them.

Although he had brought England to bankruptcy and murdered anyone who opposed him, Henry was still popular when he died in 1547. While most historians acknowledge that he strengthened the power of the monarchy by his stand against Rome, empowered Parliament as a result, and gave England a national identity, they would also agree with Charles Dickens who suggested that "he was a most intolerable ruffian, a disgrace to human nature, and a blot of blood and grease upon the History of England."

Charles I (1600–1649) was a small, dapper monarch with good taste in the arts. He was also a staunch Christian, and believed that God had given him supreme power over England. He dissolved Parliament whenever he chose, once for 11 years. Under his absolutism Charles also billeted soldiers without paying their expenses, forced wealthy subjects to lend him money, collected taxes on a whim, and tried to impose the Anglican prayerbook on Scotland to make religious observances more uniform.

After antagonizing most of the British Isles, there was nowhere left for him to go but down, with Oliver Cromwell there to make sure he didn't enjoy his trip. King Charles I was publicly beheaded on January 30, 1649, his body secretly brought to Windsor for burial. The year 1648 is inscribed on his coffin because England retained the Julian calendar, which began the new year on March 25, until 1752.

In Bray Chapel, now the bookshop, there is a wonderful effigy of Bishop **Giles Tomson** (1553–1612). Set against the backdrop of a half-shell, the bishop is a beefy man with a wavy beard halfway down his chest. He is clutching a small prayerbook or testament and looking sober. Although carved in alabaster, here is one of the earliest instances of coloration after the fact. A bill from 1789 from a Sarah Crook itemizes "Cleaning the monuments in the Bray Chapel and putting Bishop Thompson [*sic*] in Colours." In this instance it is a good addition. Giles Tomson was one of eight scholars who worked on the King James Version of the Bible.

On your way out of the chapel, notice the image of the hemp-bray, an instrument used for pulverizing, reproduced ten times along the top of the screen. It was the symbol of Sir **Reginald Bray** (d. 1503).

Slightly down the corridor on your left is the monument of **Mary** (d. 1857), Duchess of Gloucester, daughter of King George III and Queen Victoria's aunt. There are many Gloucesters here in this brown and white marble sarcophagus. The four scenes of Good Works above — feeding the hungry, clothing the naked, visiting the sick, and providing hospitality to the weary traveler — were designed by the Queen herself. They were executed by William Theed.

Just beyond, notice the chantry of Canon **Oxenbridge** (d. ca. 1520) which has a charming rebus overhead — an ox, an N, and a bridge.

Henry VI (1422–1471) lies beneath a huge black slab near the altar. He was moved here from Cheltsey Abbey by Richard III in 1484 to make money, as miracles were being attributed to his body. A hat was kept on top of the stone that people could place on their heads in the hope of being cured.

Crowned when he was one year old, rumored to be feebleminded until 30 when he alternated clearheadedness with bouts of insanity, Henry never seemed interested in the job he was supposed to be doing. He was pious, generous to his subjects, and prudish, though he finally conceived a son with Margaret of Anjou. Meanwhile, the Wars of the Roses were raging around him, with his own wife raising an army against the Yorks to try to protect the throne for their son, Prince Edward. The intrigues were many — Henry was off the throne for nine years — and when he was restored he was "mute as a crowned calf." His 17-year-old son died in battle; Henry himself was imprisoned in the Tower by the Yorks, and to prevent further rebellion in his name, murdered in Wakefield Tower while at prayer.

Nearby are the marble effigies of **Edward VII** (1841–1910) and his queen, **Alexandra** (1844–1925), wonderful green-gold figures on a white marble base. The dog at the foot is a sculpture of the King's favorite, Caesar. The monument, by Bertram Mackennal, shows two women mourning at the base of the tomb.

"Bertie," the eldest son of Queen Victoria, is, unfortunately, remembered by many as one of the trials of her life. An unforgettable caricature by Max Beerbohm entitled, "The Rare, the Rather Awful Visits of Albert Edward, Prince of Wales, to Windsor Castle," shows him wide but somehow diminutive standing in the corner, his bald conehead bowed. In the foreground sits Victoria, massive in righteousness in her widow's weeds, eyes shut against what she considers his debauched life. At the time the future Edward VII was nearing 60.

He upset his mother by his constant indiscretions, the gambling scandals he became embroiled in, and the liaisons which led him to be named in matrimonial disputes in court. It is said that Victoria blamed him for Albert's death. Just before the Prince Consort died he faced the additional stress of extricating Bertie from an affair with an actress some fellow officers had smuggled into his tent for him on maneuvers.

Perhaps because Victoria kept him ignorant of government affairs and would not allow him to see the papers she received from Parliament, Edward ruled by personality during his nine-year tenure. He traveled all over Europe spreading cordiality and earning the nickname, "Edward the Peacemaker." Charming, happiest when he was involved in public occasions, his era was one of intellectual brilliance and social change which introduced national insurance, old-age pensions, and the rise of trade unions. He, however, had little sympathy for any of it, considering the clamor of women for the vote "a damn'd nuisance," and opposing natives of India having any say in home rule. White-bearded and massive by the time he died, given to four or five ten-course meals and twelve cigars a day, Bertie expired at 68.

Queen Alexandra, procured from Denmark for the Prince of Wales when she was a teenager, was his better half in every meaning of the word. Beautiful, gracious, faithful, generous, she was adored by her children and the Court circle around her. She tolerated Bertie's mistresses and scrapes, although during one gambling scandal she prolonged her visit to the Continent until a son's illness forced her to come home. Deafness isolated her in middle age, forcing her to seek her greatest pleasures in the company of her youngest daughters.

Further along is the Lincoln Chapel, showing the effigies of **Edward Clinton** (d. 1584), First Earl of Lincoln, and his wife, **Elizabeth Fitzgerald** (d. 1589). The pair, hands raised in prayer, wear the high neck ruffs popular during the Elizabethan age, and he is dressed in armour. Both have their family animals at their feet. His is a delicate greyhound. The Fitzgerald ape is small and gamboling on all fours. There are many kneeling female weepers carved into the base of the monument, but figures of their two sons are now missing.

The outer courtyard has memorial plaques on its walls and is interesting to wander through on your way out.

THE ROYAL MAUSOLEUM

Frogmore, one of the most fascinating places in England, opens its gates for three days in May, then locks them again for another year. Behind those gates is a strange mixture of history, art, and mortality. The Royal Mausoleum at Frogmore, Queen Victoria's shrine to Prince Albert and her own burial place, is only open to the public on a designated Wednesday and Thursday in early May and on the Wednesday closest to May 24, the Queen's birthday.

Lush deep-pink and purple rhododendrons some 20 feet high line the path to the Royal Mausoleum, and a stream runs across the way. The mausoleum, designed by Ludwig Gruner and completed in 1868, is of thirteenth-century Italian design with arched doorways and an octagonal copper dome. The tile work on the inner porte-cochère is beautiful, with figures of angels against a field of blue. Flanking the door are two stern bronze angels, one holding a trumpet and a quill, the other the Book of Life and a sword. A terra cotta cameo of Christ, a gift from Victoria's daughter, Crown Princess Vicky, is set above the doorway.

Yet the Chapel itself is not mournful. The 70-foot dome, painted blue, is peopled with angels, clouds, and bright gold stars. The religious murals and trompe l'oeil images of geese, griffins, and cupids with feathers for bodies are done in the style of Raphael, who was much admired by Albert. The interior has four tiny chapels off the center room, with sculpture in the passageways between them.

The main attraction of the mausoleum, directly under the dome, is the double monument of Victoria and Albert. Executed by Carlo Marochetti in 1868, it is raised five feet from the floor; a set of wooden stairs and a platform have been provided for a better look. Because the marble has never been exposed to the elements, it seems unnaturally white. The couple lie side by side, their heads slightly inclined toward one another. Albert's hands are folded, his chest covered with medals. Victoria is holding a scepter. At the corners of the monument are four dark angels whose oversized wings nearly touch. Because the effigies were made at Albert's death, Victoria looks unexpectedly young.

ALEXANDRINA VICTORIA *b. May 24, 1819, London; d. January 22, 1901, Osborne.* In St. George's Chapel is the touching and terrifying white marble memorial of Queen Victoria's cousin, Princess **Charlotte** (1796–1817), which shows her motionless body lying under a shroud while her spirit rises to heaven; an accompanying angel carries the infant she has just delivered. Charlotte was expected to inherit the English throne. Her shocking death at 21 set off a zany race among the 11 younger siblings of her father, George IV. Though some had longstanding mistresses, none of the brothers were properly married with families. Weddings with suitable brides were hastily contracted, and royal heirs soon erupted like growths.

Edward, Duke of Kent, made his contribution in the form of Alexandrina Victoria. Dying of pneumonia the next year, he did not live to see his daughter's hopes progressively fall and then rise again as baby cousins higher in the succession were born, then expired. Her watchful mother, Princess Victoire of Saxe-Coburg, safeguarded Victoria's health, and monitored her education. She also displayed her to the public at strategic points but kept Victoria away from the jealous uncles whose positions the child had usurped in the line of succession.

Victoria was 18 when her uncle, William IV, died in 1837. As soon as she was on the throne, she benched her overbearing mother and developed a crush on Lord Melbourne, her 58-year-old prime minister. More suitable marital prospects were quickly put forward, and Victoria finally settled on her cousin, young Albert of Saxe-Coburg. But she was in no hurry. She enjoyed opening the red dispatch boxes from Parliament and making decisions on the contents.

Victoria took her own importance with great seriousness, though after her marriage she learned that certain situations demanded more equality. A royal attendant overheard her at Albert's bedroom door one night. It seemed to be a variation of the old joke: *Knock knock.* "Who's there?" "It is the Queen." No response. *Knock knock.* "Who's there?" "It is your sovereign, Albert!" Still no response. *Knock knock.* "Who's there?" "It's your wife." With this humility she gained entrance to the conjugal bed.

That settled, the marriage developed into a love match. It took the Queen nine children, however, to understand the implications of their affection. When her obstetrician

Angel marking tomb of Prince Christian Victor

finally gave her the unhappy news she is alleged to have exclaimed, "Oh Doctor, can I have no more fun in bed?" Her other pleasures were solidly middle-class, her tastes running to wax museums, sentimental novels, and paintings of animals. She was enthralled by the circus and P.T. Barnum's Tom Thumb, and invited the midget to perform privately at Buckingham Palace.

Albert, more intellectual, attempted to interest her in classical music and the joys of the mind. Raised in the small German state of Saxe-Coburg-Gotha, his education was excellent but his family disastrous. His father was notorious for his affairs, yet charged his wife with adultery when Albert was seven, and divorced her. Banished to Switzerland, she was never allowed to see her children again.

From the time he set foot on English soil, Albert was a target of the British press. They railed against this "pauper prince" who, instead of being sent to the workhouse with other beggars, had won England's greatest prize. Despite Victoria's protestations, Parliament resisted making him her Consort and voting him his own allowance. He was German, speaking German to his wife and children in private. At the time of the Crimean War, newspapers hysterically reported that he was a Prussian spy who dictated the

Queen's memoranda, conversed secretly with other foreign princes, and twisted England's policies to suit his own devious needs. In January 1854 a rumor spread that Albert had been dragged off to the Tower and the Queen herself had been arrested. Thousands of Londoners actually believed the story, and thronged Tower Green to watch.

It is true that Albert had great political influence. His intellect and personality would not allow him to vegetate, and he had gradually taken over the reading of political memoranda which Victoria now found tedious. It was Albert who promoted the literary and scientific achievements credited to the Victorian age, creating the Great International Exhibition of 1851, and developing a favorable atmosphere for such thinkers as Charles Darwin and Thomas Huxley. He was interested in the plight of the poor and in domestic issues, but pushed hard for Victoria to have a greater say in foreign affairs. With his help she altered the dispatches of Foreign Secretary Lord Palmerston, leading to great conflict between them.

By the end of the Crimean War hostility against Albert had begun to fade. But the years of harassment and the nature of life at the palace seemed to sap some of his will to live. Though he loved Victoria, he was the frequent target of the accusations she made when upset; because of her family history of mental instability, he dared not provoke her further. Instead he kept his peace, but suffered excruciating stomach pain. When Crown Prince Bertie became involved in an escapade with an actress in 1861, the morally outraged Albert was reminded of his own unhappy family. He died shortly afterward of diphtheria.

Victoria was inconsolable. In an attempt to assuage her grief, she tried to subdue the country into mourning as well. When Frogmore was completed Victoria visited constantly, bringing their children and prospective spouses to the bier to get Albert's "blessing." She erected so many statues of her beloved husband in public places that Charles Dickens joked about finding "an inaccessible cave anywhere to which a hermit could retire from the memory of Prince Albert and testimonials to same."

There were more serious consequences, however. Victoria withdrew from even minimal participation in royal functions. She did not appear to formally open Parliament or entertain visiting dignitaries at the palace. Calling her "the royal malingerer," newspapers ran cartoons of an empty throne and mournful English lion. Slowly she returned to some aspects of public life. She responded to Disraeli's flattery and his making it possible for her to become Empress of India. She remained always at odds with William Gladstone, however. When he became prime minister it was he who tried to keep her from as much knowledge of current affairs as he could. It was his suggestion that she celebrate her Diamond Jubilee by abdicating.

But Victoria had no intention of passing the throne on to Crown Prince Bertie. The future Edward VII flouted the strict moral code that was synonymous with his mother's name, enjoying himself enormously with mistresses such as actress Lillie Langtry, and in illegal gambling. While unsuccessful with Bertie, the Queen engineered the lives of her other children and grandchildren. There were marriages to be arranged, living allowances to be begged for them from Parliament, decisions to be made about a grandchild's schooling. Victoria took more pleasure from her children as adults than when they were growing up.

As the symbol of her age Victoria became wildly popular; in her last years her plump, disdainful face was seen everywhere. Her childlike, unequivocal view of life was accepted as stability. Like an indulgent grandmother, in 1899 she sent all the soldiers in the Boer War tin boxes of chocolates with her picture embossed on the lid. The candy became a talisman rather than a snack. The tin boxes were claimed to have stopped bullets, and more than one soldier refused the offer of two months' salary in exchange for his gift from the Queen.

When Victoria died a little more than a year later, however, it was an American, Henry James, who summed up the peculiar hold she had on her country's sensibilities: "I mourn the safe and motherly old middle-class Queen, who held the nation warm under the folds of her big, hideous Scotch-plaid shawl and whose duration had been so extraordinarily convenient and beneficent. I felt her death much more than I should have expected; she was a sustaining symbol."

If you visit on Queen Victoria's birthday, there will be fresh flowers around the monument, and such tributes as:

> How we miss that welcome voice,
> How we mark that vacant chair.
> For the loved one taken from us
> Seems the one we least can spare.

To the left of Victoria and Albert is the most touching sculpture in the mausoleum, the white marble likeness of Princess **Alice** (1843–1878) lying on her deathbed, cradling her four-year-old daughter, **Mary** (1874–1878); she was nursing the child back from diphtheria in 1878 when they both succumbed to the disease. In true Victorian fashion, sculptor Joseph Boehm has recreated every detail, down to strands of the child's hair on the pillow. Alice, Victoria's third child, had been living in Germany with her husband, the Prince of Hesse, when she died. It was a grievous loss to Victoria, although when she spoke of Alice she always identified her in the Albertine context of "the dear child who nursed her father in his last illness." Like her father, Alice died on December 14.

Continuing to your right you will see a sculpture, done by William Theed in 1867, which shows Albert in a kilt and Victoria in a crown with a medieval headdress. Albert has his right hand raised and pointing upward, his sword cast on the ground beneath him. Victoria is clinging to him longingly, looking into his eyes, as if she already knows the end. The inscription below reads, "Allur'd to brighter worlds and led the way," a line from *The Deserted Village* by Oliver Goldsmith.

On the opposite side is a monument to Queen Victoria's grandson, Prince **Christian Victor** (1867-1900), which is typical of the age. Sculpted by Emil Fuchs, it shows an angel wearing a war helmet and a willful expression. On the hilt of her sword is a miniature woman resembling the angel herself. At the top of the monument is his coat of arms. Christian Victor, nicknamed "Christle," was preparing to return home from South Africa when he contracted malaria and died at 33. Victoria wrote in her diary that "Lenchen [Princess Helena] so worshipped this son. . . . Again and again the terrible thought of this fresh blow and irreparable loss brought tears to my eyes."

On Victoria's birthday the mood at Frogmore is festive, presided over by vergers, a group of elderly gentlemen wearing matching ties. Well-dressed dowagers who look like the descendants of Victoria's ladies-in-waiting, and boys in school caps alike come to pay their respects. With the passage of time, the mood at the Royal Mausoleum has become pleasantly nostalgic.

DIRECTIONS TO WINDSOR AND FROGMORE: Windsor is about 25 miles west of Central London and can be reached by car on M4. By train, take the Northern or Bakerloo Line to Waterloo Station and connect with Windsor and Eton Central Railway which leaves twice hourly. Windsor is the last stop. Walk past Madame Tussaud's Waxworks to High Street. You will see Windsor Castle, on Castle Hill Road. To reach Frogmore, walk down High Street to your right to Park Street. Go right, and make another left through the big gates onto the Long Walk which takes you to the mausoleum.

Isambard Kingdom Brunel, Waterloo Station

Sources

Alexander Fleming, The Man and the Myth. Gwyn Macfarlane. Cambridge: Harvard University Press, 1984.

Anne Boleyn. Norah Lofts. New York: Coward, McCann and Geoghegan, 1979.

Apes, Angels, and Victorians. William Irvine. New York: McGraw-Hill, 1955.

The Ascent of Man. Jacob Bronowski. Boston: Little, Brown, 1973.

Atlantic Brief Lives. Louis Kronenberger, ed. Boston: Little, Brown, 1971.

Ben Jonson. David Riggs. Cambridge: Harvard University Press, 1989.

Captain Bligh and Mr. Christian. Richard Hough. New York: E.P. Dutton, 1973.

Captain Sir Richard Francis Burton: Edward Rice. New York: Scribners, 1990.

Chaucer. Donald Howard. New York: E.P. Dutton, 1987.

Christina Rossetti, A Divided Life. Georgina Battiscombe. New York: Holt, Rinehart and Winston, 1981.

Coming of Age in the Milky Way. Timothy Ferris. New York: William Morrow, 1988.

Constable. John Walker. New York: Harry N. Abrams, 1978.

The Devil Drives. Fawn M. Brodie. New York: W.W. Norton, 1967.

Daniel Defoe. Paula Backscheider. Baltimore: Johns Hopkins University Press, 1989.

Dickens. Fred Kaplan. New York: William Morrow, 1988.

The Duke of Wellington. James Harding. London: Morgan-Grampian Books, 1969.

The Edge of Objectivity. Charles Coulston Gillispie. Princeton: Princeton University Press, 1960.

Elizabeth I. Susan Bassnett. Oxford: Berg, 1988.

Elizabeth the Great. Elizabeth Jenkins. New York: Coward-McCann, 1959.

England in the Age of Hogarth. Derek Jarrett. New York: Viking, 1974.

The English Notebooks. Nathaniel Hawthorne. New York: Russell and Russell, 1969.

The Enigma of Mary Stuart. Ian B. Cowan. New York: St. Martin's, 1971.

Essays in Biography. Bonamy Dobree. Freeport: Books for Libraries Press, 1967.

Freud: A Life for Our Time. Peter Gay. New York: Doubleday, 1988.

George III. J.C. Long. Boston: Little, Brown, 1960.

George Eliot. Gordon S. Haight. New York: Penguin Books, 1985.

George Eliot. Jennifer Uglow. New York: Pantheon, 1987.

Ghosts of the Tower of London. G. Abbott. London: Nelson, 1980.

Henry VIII. Frank Dwyer. New York: Chelsea House, 1988.

Historical Memorials of Westminster Abbey. Arthur Penrhyn Stanley. New York: Anson D.F. Randolph, 1882.

In the Presence of the Creator. Gale E. Christianson. New York: Free Press, 1984.

John Bunyan. Ola Elizabeth Winslow. New York: Macmillan, 1961.

John Donne and His World. Derek Parker. London: Thames and Hudson, 1975.

Karl Marx, His Life and Thought. David McLellan. New York: Harper and Row, 1973.

The Kings and Queens of England. Jane Murray. New York: Scribners, 1974.

Lady Jane Grey and the House of Suffolk. Alison Plowden. New York: Franklin Watts, 1986.

Leopold Stokowski. Abram Chasins. New York: Da Capo Press, 1979.

The Life and Times of Henry VIII. Robert Lacey. New York: Praeger, 1972.

The Life of Charles James Fox. Edward Lascelles. London: Oxford University Press, 1936.

The Life of John Milton. A.N. Wilson. London: Oxford University Press, 1983.

Livingstone. Tim Jeal. New York: G.P. Putnam, 1973.

London Cemeteries. Hugh Meller. Amersham, England: Avebury, 1981.

The Major Achievements of Science. A.E.E. McKenzie. Ames, Iowa: Iowa State University Press, 1988

Makers of Modern Thought. New York: American Heritage, 1972.

The Man Who Wrote Dracula. Daniel Farson. New York: St. Martin's, 1976.

Mary Queen of Scots. Jean Plaidy. New York: G.P. Putnam, 1975.

Milton and His England. Don Wolfe. Princeton: Princeton University Press, 1971.

The Monuments of St. George's Chapel. Shelagh M. Bond. Windsor: Oxley and Son, 1958.

The Norton Anthology of English Literature. M.H. Abrams, ed. New York: W.W. Norton, 1962.

Novelists and Prose Writers. James Vinson, ed. New York: St. Martin's, 1979.

The Oak and the Ivy. Joyce Marlow. Garden City, NY: Doubleday, 1977.

Operetta. Richard Traubner. Garden City, NY: Doubleday, 1983.

Our Three Selves: The Life of Radclyffe Hall. Michael Baker. New York: William Morrow, 1985.

P.S. I Love You. Michael Sellers. New York: E.P. Dutton, 1982.

The Personal History of Samuel Johnson. Christopher Hibbert. New York: Harper and Row, 1971.

Peter Sellers. Alexander Walker. New York: Macmillan, 1981.

Peter Sellers. Derek Sylvester. New York: Proteus, 1981.

The Pre-Raphaelites. Christopher Wood. New York: Viking, 1981.

Pre-Raphaelites in Love. Gay Daly. New York: Ticknor and Fields, 1989.

The Prime Ministers. Herbert Van Thal, ed. New York: Stein and Day, 1975.

Prominent Edwardians. Dudley Barker. New York: Atheneum, 1969.

Radclyffe Hall at the Well of Loneliness. Lovat Dickson. New York: Scribners, 1975.

Reconstructing Aphra. Angeline Goreau. New York: Dial, 1980.

Reynolds. Ellis Waterhouse. London: Phaidon, 1973.

Robert Browning. Donald Thomas. New York: Viking, 1983.

Rudyard Kipling. Martin Fido. New York: Viking, 1974.

Samuel Taylor Coleridge. E.K. Chambers. Westport, CT: Greenwood Press, 1938

A Short History of Scientific Ideas to 1900. Charles Singer. London: Oxford University Press, 1959.

Sir Christopher Wren. John Summerson. Hamden, CT: Archon Books, 1965.

Sir Isaac Newton. Colin A. Ronan. London: International Textbook, 1969.

Sir Larry: The Life of Laurence Olivier. Thomas Kiernan. 1981.

The Story of Emmeline Pankhurst. Josephine Kamm. New York: Meredith Press, 1961.

The Story of Philosophy. Will Durant. New York: Simon and Schuster, 1926.

The Survival of Charles Darwin. Ronald W. Clark. New York: Random House, 1984.

Tennyson. Christopher Ricks. New York: Collier Books, 1972.

Thomas Hardy. Michael Millgate. New York: Random House, 1982.

Thomas Hardy. Timothy O'Sullivan. New York: St. Martin's, 1975.

Three Eighteenth Century Figures. Bonamy Dobree. London: Oxford University Press, 1962.

Titanic, The Death and Life of a Legend. Michael Davie. New York: Knopf, 1987.

To Be in England. Richard D. Altick. New York: Norton, 1969.

Trollope, His Life and Art. C.P. Snow. New York: Scribners, 1975.

An Uneasy Victorian, Thackeray the Man. Ann Monsarrat. New York: Dodd, Mead, 1980.

Vaughn Williams. James Day. London: J.M. Dent and Sons, 1961.

Victoria. Stanley Weintraub. New York: E.P. Dutton, 1987.

Westminster Abbey Official Guide.

Westminster Abbey. Walter Annenberg, Ed. Philadelphia: Annenberg School Press, 1972.

Whistler, A Biography. Stanley Weintraub. New York: Weybright and Talley, 1974.

Who's Buried Where in England. Douglas Greenwood. London: Constable, 1982.

Wilberforce. John Pollock. New York: St. Martin's, 1977.

William Blake. Michael Davis. Berkeley: University of California Press, 1977.

Index

Addison, Joseph, 47-49, 70, 74, 76, 87
Aksarova-Sturtz, Valentina, 239
Alamayu, 302
Albert, Prince, 313-17, 318
Alexandra, Queen, 311-12
Alice, Princess, 317
Allingham, Alexandrina, 194
André, John, 24-25
Anne of Bohemia, 68
Anne of Cleves, 68-69, 309
Anne, Queen, 62-63, 75, 307
Archer, Fred, 255
Arnold family, 251
Arnold, Matthew, 94
Atcheler, John, 202
Attlee, Clement, 11
Aubin, Jonathan St. John, 193

Baden-Powell, Olave, 9
Baden-Powell, Robert, 9
Baillie, Joanna, 233-34
Balfe, Michael, 28, 187
Bancroft, Squire, 163, 165
Banting, William, 176
Barritt, Charles, 252, 253
Barry, "James," 194
Bart, Percy, 298, 299
Batten, Mabel, 197, 202-3
Baylis, Peter, 239
Bayne, William, 35
Beatty, William, 195
Beaufort, Margaret, 61
Beer, Julius, 197, 206
Beerbohm, Max, 146-47
Behn, Aphra, 102-3
Bell, George, 188
Bianchi family, 252, 254
Birla, Ghanshyamdas, 262-63
Bishop, Henry, 270
Blair, William, 35
Blake, William, 100, 117, 124-27, 145
Bligh, William, 114-15, 285
Blondin, Emile, 188-89
Blow, John, 32
Bolan, Marc, 262
Boleyn, Anne, 45, 51, 108-10, 309
Boult, Adrian Cedric, 32-33
Boulter, Hugh, 35
Boynton, Henry, 273

Brain, Dennis, 243, 253-55
Brass, Horace, 172
Bray, Reginald, 311
Britten, Benjamin, 29, 261
Brocas, Bernard, 64
Bromley, Thomas, 46
Bronowski, Jacob, 209-10
Brown family, 280
Browne, Samuel James, 156
Browning, Elizabeth Barrett, 99-100
Browning, Robert, 98-100, 137
Brunel, Isambard Kingdom, 184, 319
Brunel, Marc Isambard, 183-84
Bulwer-Lytton, Edward, 65
Bulwer-Lytton, Edward Robert, 148
Bunyan, John, 117, 118-21, 169
Burroughs, Jessie, 280
Burton, Isabel, 287-91
Burton, Richard, 24, 287-91
Butler, Samuel, 93

Caldecott, Randolph, 144
Carey, Henry, 45-46
Carlyle, Thomas, 139-40, 297
Carmichael-Smyth, Anne, 181-83
Caroline, Queen, 53-54, 305
Casement, William, 184
Catherine de Valois, 68
Cavendish, William, 37
Cecil, William and Mildred Cooke, 63-64
Chapman, Elizabeth and Peter, 230
Charles I, 37, 114, 144, 307, 310
Charles II , 27, 53, 61-2, 101, 102, 106, 119, 132, 143
Charlotte Augusta, Princess of Wales, 302-3
Charlotte, Princess, 314
Chaucer, Geoffrey, 68, 71, 94-98, 102
Christian, Fletcher, 114-15
Christian Victor, Prince, 315, 318
Churchill, Winston, 7
Clementson, Georgina, 187-88
Clinton, Edward, 312-13
Clossop, Augustus Henry, 162, 172
Coleridge, Samuel Taylor, 137, 225-27
Collins, Charles, 176
Collins, Wilkie, 65, 189

Congreve, William, 9,10
Constable, John, 148, 229, 231-33
Cooke family, 186
Coombs, Robert, 175
Cooper, Gladys, 243, 249-50
Coote, Eyer, 35
Costa, Michael, 195
Crewe, Jane and Clipesby, 46
Cripps, Stafford, 153-54
Crisp, Ann, 221-22
Croft, William, 32
Cromwell, Oliver, 61, 62, 101, 118, 132, 310
Cunard, Samuel, 176

Dacre, Gertrude, 192
Dadoo, Yusef, 219
Darwin, Charles, 20, 22-24, 220, 316
Davies, Michael, 238
Deacon, Henry, 188
de Ferranti, Sebastian, 243, 246-47
de la Mare, Walter, 147
Defoe, Daniel, 117, 121-24
Devas, Anthony, 284
Dewar, James, 268
Dickens, Catherine, 78-79, 206
Dickens, Charles, 71, 77-79, 179, 189, 193, 206, 310, 316
Disraeli, Benjamin, 41, 43, 316
Donne, John, 135-37, 138
Douglas, Margaret, 58
Drayton, Michael, 94
Druce, Thomas, 201
Dryden, John, 49, 100-2, 210
Du Maurier, George, 229, 237-8, 296-97
Du Maurier, Gerald, 238
du Pré, Jacqueline, 268-69
Duckworth, Robinson, 27
Ducrow, Andrew, 184-85

Edgar, Elinor, 245
Edward I, 67, 69
Edward II, 67
Edward III, 67-68, 96
Edward IV, 53, 304
Edward V, 45, 47, 53, 55, 106
Edward VI, 54, 309
Edward VII, 42, 311-12, 316-17
Edward VIII, 304
Edward the Black Prince, 45, 68
Edward the Confessor, 5, 45, 65-66
Eleanor of Castile, 67
Elgar, Edward, 28, 33
Eliot, George, 212-15, 220
Eliot, T. S., 71, 98, 137
Elizabeth I, 34, 45, 46, 49-53, 59-61, 63-64, 106, 109, 112, 309
Elizabeth II, 9
Elizabeth of Woodville, 304

Elizabeth of York, 55, 61
Ellis, Havelock and Edith, 205, 257-58
Erne, Ronald, 165, 166-67

Fairley, Gordon Hamilton, 150-51
Fane, George and Elizabeth, 64
Faraday, Michael, 21, 206-9
Fauntleroy, Henry, 128
Ferrier, Kathleen, 261-62
Fischer, Harry, 252
Fisher, John, 106, 309
Fitzgerald, Elizabeth, 312-13
Fleming, Alexander, 148-50
Fleming, James, 25
Fletcher, Bannister, 249, 250
Fox, Charles James, 9-11, 37, 88
Foxe, John, 131
Frampton, George, 145
Frankau, Arthur, 243
Frankau, Pamela, 243, 255
Frankau, Ursula, 255
Fraser family, 284
Fraser, Reginald, 284
Frederick Louis, Prince of Wales, 54, 305
Freud, Sigmund, 41, 82, 265-68
Frobisher, Martin, 131

Gaitskell, Hugh, 229, 234, 235-36
Garrick, David, 71-72, 86
George I, 24, 75-76
George II, 36, 53-54, 305
George III, 11, 25, 36, 37, 187, 305-07, 311
George IV, 192, 307, 314
George V, 303-4
George VI, 303-4
George of Denmark, 62
George, David Lloyd, 12, 158
Gibson, Mary Austen, 178, 184
Gladstone, William Ewart, 40-42, 317
Glyn, Elinor, 268
Godfrey family, 262
Godwin, George, 170-71
Goldsmith, Oliver, 85, 87, 141, 318
Goodman, Julia, 269-70
Grahame, William, 186
Grant, Mary, 235
Gray, Thomas, 91
Green, Charles, 223
Green, William Friese, 224
Greenaway, Kate, 243, 249
Grey, Jane, 50, 51, 112-3

Hall, Radclyffe, 197, 202-5
Hall, Thomas, 272
Halley, Edmund, 17
Hammersley, Eve Marie, 229, 235

Handel, George Frideric, 32, 54, 74-77
Hanway, Jonas, 35
Hardcastle, Joseph, 127-28
Hardy, Thomas, 79-81
Hargrave, William, 25
Harrison, John, 230
Harrison, Reginald, 223
Hart, Joseph, 128
Hart, Percy, 280
Hart, Rebecca, 270
Hart-Carey family, 231
Hawkins, Leonard, 270
Hawksmoor, Nicholas, 7
Hengler, Frederick, 245
Henry III, 66-67
Henry IV, 68
Henry V, 66, 67, 68
Henry VI, 47, 67, 68, 106, 311
Henry VII, 47, 55, 61, 68, 308
Henry VIII, 45, 46, 50, 51, 52, 54, 69, 106, 108-112, 304, 307-10
Herbert, Lady Elizabeth, 302
Herbert, Frederick, 172
Hesketh, Thomas, 34
Hitch, Frederick, 298
Hobart, Frederick, 198
Hodgson, John and Carolyn, 231
Hogarth, William, 293-95
Holland, John, 108
Holyoake, George, 214, 215
Hood, Thomas, 186-87
Horrocks, Jeremiah, 8
Howard, Catherine, 51, 111-12, 309
Hughes, Lilian, 280, 281
Hunt, James Henry Leigh, 192-3
Hunt, William Holman, 139, 140-41
Hutchison, Leslie, 224
Huxley, Thomas, 23-24, 220, 316

Ismay, Bruce, 279, 284-87

Jackson, Frederick, 156, 157
Jackson, John, 175-6
Jackson, Sara, 239
James I, 55, 58, 137
James II, 56, 62, 101, 106, 122
James V, 58
James, John, 7
Jellicoe, John Rushworth, 156-58
John of Eltham, 65
John, Marthe, 242, 245-46
John, William Goscombe, 243, 246
Johnson, Samuel, 85-87, 141
Jones, Claudia Vera, 219
Jonson, Ben, 91-93

Katharine of Aragon, 50, 108-9, 308-9
Kendall, Kay, 229, 234, 236-37

Kennedy, William, 221
Kensit, John, 243
Kerensky, Alexander, 279, 281-84
Kipling, Joseph Rudyard, 81-84, 221
Kneller, Godfrey, 28
Knox, E. V., 148, 241

Lambert, Percy, 175
Landseer, Edwin, 145, 148
Latimer, Ivy, 272
Laye, Gilbert, 175
Leibniz, Gottfried, 18, 54
Leopold, 303
Lettsom, John, 128
Lewes, Goerge, 213-15
Leyland, Frederick, 171-72
Lister, Joseph, 29, 243, 247, 248
Little Tich, 271-72
Livingstone, David, 12-14
Lloyd, Marie, 251-52
Long, John St. John, 185
Lucas, Margaret, 37
Lutyens, Edwin Landseer, 145-46
Lyons family, 280

Macaulay, Thomas, 74
MacDonald, Duncan, 273
MacDonald, James Ramsey, 12
MacIntosh, James, 231
McNaughton-Jones, H., 247
Mallard, Richard, 230
Manners, Robert, 35
Marx, Karl, 216-19
Mary II, 62, 63, 101
Mary, Duchess of Gloucester, 311
Mary, Princess, 53
Mary, Queen, 301, 303
Mary Queen of Scots, 45, 46, 47, 51, 52, 55, 58-61, 106
Mary Tudor, 49-50, 51, 106, 112-13, 309
Masefield, John, 98
Mason, Guglielmo, 91
Matthews, Bert and Rebecca, 241
Maxwell, Herbert, 245
Mayer, Carl, 224
Mellitus, 5
Mellon, Albert, 170
Meyerstein, Edward, 238
Michaelovitch, Michael and Sophie, 245
Millais, John Everett, 139-40
Milton, John, 91, 131-33
Monck, Christopher, 61
Monck, George, 61
Monckton, John, 174-75
Monk, William, 221
Montagu, Edward, 49
Montague, Charles, 49
Moore, Henry, 148

More, Thomas, 107, 169, 308-9
Moss, Sarah Jane, 33
Mouflet, Louis, 270
Mountbatten, Edwina, Countess, 9
Mountbatten, Louis, First Earl, 9
Mulready, William, 184, 185

Napoleon, Prince Imperial, 301
Necom, Teresa, 240
Neilson, Julia, 250
Nelson, Horatio, 158-61
Newman Robert, 249
Newton, Isaac, 14-18, 23, 54, 143, 210
Nightingale, Elizabeth, 37-38, 39
Nightingale, Florence, 156
Nighy, Thomas, 222
Novello, Ivor, 148, 258

O'Connor, Feargus, 179, 181
Olivier, Laurence, 72-74
Orage, Alfred, 240
Owen, Thomas, 27, 29
Oxenbridge, Canon, 311

Page, Mary, 127
Pankhurst, Emmeline, 163, 166-69
Parr, Catherine, 112, 310
Parry, Winifred, 278, 279
Parsons, John, 32
Pavlova, Anna, 263-65
Peacock, Jane Ruth, 34
Peel, Robert, 42-43
Pettigrew, Thomas, 163
Pettit, Henry, 165
Philippa, 68, 96
Phillips, Jane, 113
Piffard, Helena, 298
Pitman, Isaac, 268
Pitt, William, 8, 36, 54
Pitt, William, "the Younger", 8, 9, 26, 36-37, 38, 306
Plomley, Roy, 281
Pole, Margaret, 106
Pope, Alexander, 28, 48, 71
Priddell, Alfred, 176
Prince, Arthur, 243, 255
Prinsep, Florence and Valentine, 172
Prosser, Albert, 200
Puckering, John, 46-47
Pugh, John, 284
Purcell, Henry, 32

Railton, David, 7
Rayner, Hewitt, 221
Reed, Langford, 235
Reynolds, Joshua, 87, 141-42, 269
Rhodes, Cecil, 58
Richard II, 64, 66, 68

Richard III, 47, 53, 304, 311
Richard, Duke of York, 45, 47, 53, 55, 106
Richards, Henry, 176
Richardson, Joseph, 195
Richardson, Ralph, 223-24
Ripley, Dwight, 273
Ritson, Joseph, 128
Roland, Gaynor, 272
Roosevelt, Blanche, 174
Roosevelt, Franklin D., 5, 8
Rossetti, Christina, 200
Rossetti, Dante Gabriel, 139, 140, 200
Rossetti, Elizabeth Siddal, 139, 200
Rossetti, Gabriel, 200
Roubillac, Louis François, 25, 35-36, 37
Ruskin, John, 139, 249, 295, 297
Russell, Elizabeth, 44, 64-65
Russell, Henry, 194, 195
Russell, John, 65
Russell, Peter Nicol, 270, 271
Ruthall, Thomas, 46
Rutherford, Ernest, 19-21
Rutland family, 303
Rysbrack, John Michael, 14, 24, 35

Saville, George, 49
Sayers, Thomas, 202
Schwabe, Randolph, 240, 241
Scot, James, 106
Sebert, 5, 69
Selby, James, 198
Sellers, Peter, 258-61
Seymour, Jane (1509–1537), 51, 69, 307, 309
Seymour, Jane (1541–1560), 65
Shakespeare, William, 5, 71, 88, 91, 92, 131
Sharpe, Daniel, 231
Shaw family, 193
Sheffield, John and Catherine, 56-57
Sheridan, Richard Brinsley, 88-89
Short, Albert, 246
Short, Horace, 243, 246
Shovell, Clowdisley, 28
Shrubsole, William, 128
Sibthorp, Abraham, 231
Sidney, Frances, 46
Sievier, Robert, 185, 188
Smith, Richard, 212
Smith, Victoria Modupe, 251
Smyth, Julia, 284
Snow, John, 163
Soddy, Frederick, 20
Somerset, Charles, 302
Sophia (Princess), 53, 187
Sotheby, S. Leigh, 175

Southey, Robert, 85, 225-27
Speed, John, 131
Spencer, Charles, 198, 200
Spencer, Herbert, 11-12, 213, 219-21
Spenser, Edmund, 63-64, 93-94
Stanhope, Anne, 64
Stanhope, James, 24
Stanley, Arthur Penrhyn, 57-58
Steele, Richard, 48
Stekel, Wilhelm, 268
Stevens, Henry, 247-48
Stoker, Bram, 268
Stokowski, Leopold, 274-76
Storey, George, 245, 246
Strudwick, John, 118, 121
Stuart, Ludovic, 58
Sullivan, Arthur, 151-52
Sydney, Morgan, 176
Sylvester, Victor, 262

Tate, Thomas and Esther, 273
Tauber, Richard, 163, 169-70
Taylor, William, 229-30
Tennyson, Alfred Lord, 73, 89-91, 98
Terry, Fred, 250
Thackeray, William Makepeace, 77, 181-83
Thomas family, 293
Thomas, Alexander, 238
Thomas, Brandon, 163, 174
Thomas, Stephen, 239
Thomson, Joseph John, 19, 21
Thomson, William (Lord Kelvin), 18-19, 21
Thornton, C. I., 274
Thornton, Harry, 222, 223
Thurston, George, 271
Thynne, Thomas, 27
Thynne, William, 56-7
Tilling, Robert, 128
Tomson Giles, 310
Torosyan, Karabet, 284
Tradescant, John (Elder and Younger), 113-14, 115
Tree, Herbert Beerbohm, 229, 237

Tregaskis, James, 234
Trollope, Anthony, 189-92
Tyndale, William, 28

Van Dyck, Anthony, 144
Vaughn Williams, Ralph, 29-31, 33
Victoria, Queen, 41, 42, 45, 108, 145, 156, 163, 193, 209, 302, 303, 305, 307, 311, 312, 313-17, 318
Villiers, George, 55-56

Wallace, Alfred Russell, 23
Walpole, Catherine, 61
Walton, William, 29
Warneford, Reginald, 172, 173
Watney, Phyllis, 280
Watt, James, 29
Watts, Isaac, 28, 117
Waugh, Andrew, 176
Webb, Beatrice Potter, 11-12
Webb, Sidney James, 11-12
Wellington, First Duke of, 154-56
Wesley, John, 28, 116, 128-30
Wesley, Susannah, 128
Westmacott, Richard, 8, 10
Wheatley, Sara, 127
Whistler, James, 295-98
Wilberforce, William, 33, 34, 38-40, 128
William III, 62, 63, 101
William IV, 307, 314
Wilson, James, 245
Wilton, Marie, 165
Wingfield, Walter, 195
Wolseley, Garnet, 158
Wombwell, George, 201
Wood, Mrs. Henry, 205-6
Wood, William and Hannah, 113
Woodcroft, Bennet, 176
Wordsworth, William, 225-27
Wren, Christopher, 7, 135, 142-44, 210
Wright, Richard, 293
Wyclif, John, 152-53
Wymark, Patrick, 210

Permanent Londoners
was designed by Julia Rowe and Ann Aspell.
It was typeset by Dartmouth Printing Company
in ITC Garamond Light and printed on
Finch Opaque, an acid-free paper,
by Princeton University Press.

Detail from Tate memorial